D0338461

Finding an Ending

Finding an Ending

Reflections on Wagner's *Ring*

Philip Kitcher
Richard Schacht

2004

OXFORD
UNIVERSITY PRESS

Oxford New York
Auckland Bangkok Buenos Aires Cape Town Chennai
Dar es Salaam Delhi Hong Kong Istanbul Karachi Kolkata
Kuala Lumpur Madrid Melbourne Mexico City Mumbai Nairobi
São Paulo Shanghai Taipei Tokyo Toronto

Published by Oxford University Press, Inc.
198 Madison Avenue, New York, New York 10016

www.oup.com

Library of Congress Cataloging-in-Publication Data
is available.

ISBN 0-19-517359-7

1 3 5 7 9 8 6 4 2

Printed in the United States of America
on acid-free paper

To Carol Plantamura and Nicholas DiVirgilio,
and to the memory of William Miller
and Carl ("Doc") Weinrich

Since Singing is so good a thing,
I wish all men would learn to sing

Contents

Acknowledgments

This book began with a conversation between Lydia Goehr and one of us (PK), and with an invitation to write an essay on Wagner's *Ring*. Since both of us (PK and RS) had been exchanging ideas about opera in general and about the *Ring* in particular over many years, it seemed natural that this should be a collaboration. Drafts were exchanged, revised, expanded, and exchanged again, until our original essay had grown beyond all reasonable bounds. Lydia advised us that she needed something shorter, but encouraged us to keep going and to think about the possibility of a book. We are grateful to her for that suggestion and for her constructive comments.

We have been extremely lucky to have the support and encouragement of Robert Miller at Oxford University Press. His deep knowledge of the *Ring* and his acute critical intelligence has helped us enormously. Indeed, it has become clear to us that he is one of those great editors who once upon a time existed but are supposed now to be extinct. We would like to express our profound gratitude to him.

Robert arranged for a draft of our book to be reviewed by five outstanding referees. Four of them allowed their names to be disclosed to us, so we would like to thank Paul Boghossian, Charles Larmore, Michael Tanner, and Bernard Williams, as well as one anonymous music scholar. Each of the referees made valuable general points, as well as offering suggestions about matters of detail. Our task in revising was made much easier by their unanimity about the weaknesses (and the strengths) of the version they saw. They have enabled us to produce what is, we believe, a much better book than the one that was sent to them for review.

We hesitate to single out one among our eminent readers for individual thanks, but we would like to express a special debt of gratitude to Bernard Williams. When we received his detailed comments, based on a careful, deeply insightful, critical and yet sympathetic reading of our draft, we were honored and delighted. A large part of our delight stemmed from the thought that this valuable report must indicate that Bernard was continuing to win his battle with the cancer that he had fought for several years. To our sorrow, we learned a few weeks later of his death. It is fortunate that we had been able to thank him in the interval; but there is no way we can adequately express our appreciation of the interest taken and attention given by that brilliant creative philosopher, outstanding and wide-ranging public intellectual, and warm and humane person.

We have also been helped by conversations with and comments from a number of other people. We are especially grateful to Charles Kitcher, Patricia Kitcher and Judy Rowan in this regard (and for much else as well).

Finally, we want to thank four musicians who have guided our aspirations as (relatively serious) amateur singers. They have taught us much, not only about singing, but also about listening—and about what they both have to do with living. We dedicate this book to the teachers—Carol Plantamura and Carl Weinrich (PK), and William Miller and Nicholas DiVirgilio (RS)—who have helped make vocal music such a central and rewarding part of our lives.

Preface

We intend this book not only for readers who already know and love Wagner's *Ring*, but also for those who have doubts about the work, or who have encountered parts of it but find them bewildering, or who even do not know it at all and are simply curious. To help those who are relatively unfamiliar with the drama in whole or in part, we have included a relatively detailed synopsis of what transpires in the four operas of which it consists. This synopsis may also be helpful to readers who wish to refresh their memories with respect to some of the scenes we discuss. We have placed it at the end of the volume, but it might usefully be read first.

There is a large literature about Wagner and about the *Ring*. We aim to do something rather different from most of it: to probe its philosophical and psychological themes with some precision and to relate them in some detail to the action of the four-part cycle. For our purposes, and for what we hope readers will gain from our discussion, we have not felt it necessary to provide an extensive scholarly apparatus. We have drawn on a number of excellent sources, to which we would refer anyone who wishes to grapple seriously with Wagner's music drama. We list some of them in the Bibliography and also mention some large-scale approaches to the *Ring* that contrast with our own. We hope this will be helpful to those who want to reflect further on the ideas we present and the aspects of the *Ring* we discuss.

Finding an Ending

Introduction

What is to be made of Wagner and his *Ring of the Nibelungs?* Some, among whom we count ourselves, treasure performances of his vast four-part music drama as high points in our cultural lives, and are prepared to go to considerable effort and expense to be able to sit in an opera house for four evenings in fairly close succession and immerse themselves in it. For others, such esteem and devotion are mysterious (at best). Many regular opera goers fail to see the point of Wagner's expansive efforts, and some are even repelled by them. Lovers of classical music who prefer different genres often regard Wagner as emblematic of everything that went wrong with music in general—and with opera in particular—in the nineteenth century. For many, it is all sound and fury, signifying nothing. From the broader standpoint of popular culture, his music dramas make no sense and (apart from "The Ride of the Valkyries," perhaps) have no appeal; the fuss made about the *Ring* is paradigmatic of the ludicrous reverence often lavished on so-called High Art.

Ardent Wagnerians are usually (and reasonably) unmoved by such complaints. Yet here as elsewhere, confronting the more serious forms of skepticism can be useful. For, on the face of it, the

Ring's power to fascinate is surprising. Why should people, many of whom profess a thoroughly demystified view of the world, ruminate—and even argue passionately—about the exploits of gods, dwarves, giants, and dragons, or about the magic powers of gold, potions, and headgear? What justifies the claim that Wagner was a great dramatist, and that his elaborate myth, concocted from a variety of sources, deserves the serious attention of mature and thoughtful adults?

These are reasonable questions. We pose them because we think that while scathing or belittling responses can certainly be given to them, they also can be answered in ways that are both positive and revealing; that the better answers have to do with the human possibilities the *Ring* illuminates; and that it can be rewarding—personally, philosophically, and even operatically—to articulate and explore them. Our goal in the following pages is to offer some ideas with respect to the *Ring* for the consideration of other sympathetic listeners. To some (and, we hope, no few) these ideas may ring true, articulating things about it that they have sensed themselves and justifying their sense that those who scoff or sneer at it are missing something important. To others, who have genuine doubts about the significance of the *Ring*, our suggestions may at least offer useful provocation; to at least some of those who have not yet felt the *Ring*'s power but are open enough to it to be reading these words, we hope that our efforts may afford an entrance to its world.

Before we start in earnest, it will be worth reflecting briefly on some alternative ways of addressing the skeptical questions we have raised, to set the stage for our own preferred answers. We begin from the sense that the dedication of audiences to the *Ring* is not simply a matter of the work's musical richness. We think there is more to it than meets the ear, even though there is a great deal of that. Even when simply heard without words, its music is extraordinary and often truly glorious. But we disagree with a common view that there is no mystery about why ardent fans flock to productions of the *Ring*, despite what anti-Wagnerians conceive as its legendary myth-mongering silliness: "It's the music, stupid!" We think it would be impoverishing (to say the least) to experience the *Ring* without giving any thought to what is being said, done, and shown.

Wagner's libretto, ponderous and mannered though it may sometimes seem (and be), is charged with life and significance. To be sure, he himself confessed in a letter of 1854 to his friend August Röckel that once he had set *Rheingold*, he could no longer bear to look at his text without music; and we find that sentiment eminently understandable. Yet it must be admitted that at the very least, the text heightens the power of the music; and it is difficult if not impossible to separate the force of some of the greatest moments from the anxieties, threats, or exultations that the characters are expressing. Following Wagner's words while listening to an excellent recording is better than treating the *Ring* as if it were a symphony in which exceptional voices figure as unusual instruments; but, like reading Shakespeare at home, even with the best of intentions and focus and imagination, that is only a distant second to the real thing.

Concert performances without staging (or even without words altogether) can be and have been presented at far less expense than that of a fully staged version; but we seriously doubt whether a sequence on roughly the usual schedule for the complete *Ring* would arouse anything approaching the same level of enthusiasm. This means that Wagner's text and drama must somehow add significantly to the music, *expanding* it and filling it out rather than simply accompanying it. They cannot be merely a deadweight on the score, or even an embarrassment in the experience of everyone drawn to the work again and again. Words and music are in the service of the drama, to be seen and heard with attention to text, voices, orchestra, movement, gesture, and spectacle. That is why the *Ring*'s devotees clamor for tickets and, after a great production, inform their private listening with the memories of their experiences in the opera house. If the *Ring* turns on a mere childish plot about a cast of mythical figures nobody can or should ever take seriously, then fascination with it is genuinely peculiar, its musical glories notwithstanding.

Negative judgments about Wagner and the *Ring* are, as we have noted, quite common. Some are obviously grounded in reactions to the man (rather than being based directly on a response to his work). Scholars as well as many others have written at length about Wagner's anti-Semitism and chauvinistic German nationalism—and there is no doubt that his views about Jews were thoroughly vile. Whether the anti-Semitism pervades his music dramas in general and the *Ring* in particular, however, is a much more difficult question. Although some Wagnerian characters are often taken to present Jews as conniving, base, contemptible, or detestable—the favorite candidates being Beckmesser in *Meistersinger* and Alberich and Mime in the *Ring*—our view is that the identification of these characters as portraying Jews already presupposes prejudicial stereotypes. If someone firmly in the grip of hideous biases attends a production, then that person may respond to Mime or Alberich or Beckmesser in the suggested fashion, so that the drama can be seen as resonating to antecedent prejudice. We are inclined to think, however, that an operagoer of sound sensibility—free not only of such biases but also of "political" hypersensitivity—would respond differently. Someone who knew nothing of the debates about Wagner's anti-Semitism and its relation to what we see and hear on stage (assuming that the characters are not being played in deliberately caricatured ways) would likely think that anyone who identified Beckmesser, Alberich, and Mime as stereotypically Jewish was making a wild interpretive conjecture. Our imaginary audience member might more probably (and properly) experience greater discomfort from the expression of nationalism that closes *Meistersinger*.

Despite the amount of ink devoted to the criticisms just considered, we take the principal negative reaction to Wagner to be quite different. For many, the music dramas, and in particular the *Ring*, are simply not to be taken seriously. Popular culture expresses the theme by finding fun: stout ladies in martial gear figure in advertisements, and the "Ride of the Valkyries" turns up everywhere, from Bugs Bunny cartoons to *Apocalypse Now*. A more literary version of the idea that the music dramas are overblown bombast occurs in a poem by Rupert Brooke, simply entitled "Wagner." The first stanza runs:

> Creeps in half wanton, half asleep,
> One with a fat, wide, hairless face.
> He likes love music that is cheap,
> Likes women in a crowded place,
> And likes to hear the noise they're making.

So it goes for two more verses, culminating in

> And all the while, in perfect time,
> His pendulous stomach hangs a-shaking.

Brooke leaves it ambiguous whether the unimposing character described is supposed to be Wagner or his devoted listener, but the complaint is very clear: Wagnerian opera is emotionally shallow, a grandiose surrogate for genuine feeling, fundamentally coarse in conception, and invested with undue importance by people who find in it a disguise for base urges. Confused thoughts and cheap emotions can be satisfied by hearing sweeping themes played by a large orchestra in the context of a second-rate myth that any rational spectator should regard as silly.

One way of responding to this kind of complaint is to mount an argument in defense of the power of myth and against a narrow rationalism that would ridicule it. We agree with a celebrated Oxford professor of Anglo-Saxon who inverted the standard opinion of *Beowulf* by suggesting that the critics were focusing, wrongly, on the poem's historical episodes while ignoring the monsters at its heart. That professor, J.R.R. Tolkien, went on to defend his claims about the power of myth by creating one of his own—indeed an elaborate narrative with a cast of dwarves and monsters, with plenty of magic, and even with a Ring of Power at its center. Yet we do not want to suggest that the dramatic power of the *Ring* rests on the force of myth *in general*; and we hold no brief for the idea that Wagner's tetralogy works because, like other ventures in myth, it taps into universal (Jungian or other) archetypes, or anything of that sort. There are myths and myths. Some of them, like Tolkien's own, are immensely absorbing and entertaining, even rich in linguistic invention, yet they do not deserve the serious attention and reflection lavished on the *Ring*. Our response to the common complaint about Wagner will be much more specific.

The *Ring*, we suggest, is a work of philosophical substance and depth, far surpassing that of Wagner's overt theorizing. Wagner's relations to philosophy were complicated: he was, for example, and most notably, greatly influenced by his reading first of Feuerbach and then of Schopenhauer (about whom we shall have more to say shortly); and he was, for a period, on close terms with the young Nietzsche. Yet it would be quite wrong, we think, to see any of Wagner's music dramas as "applied Schopenhauer" (or "applied" anybody else), as if he simply picked up preexisting philosophical ideas and gave them concrete expression. Nor do we think that his operas are mere stagings of the "philosophical" ideas he himself attempted to articulate in his own voluminous (and virtually unreadable) theoretical writings. His letters—especially those to Röckel and to Franz Liszt—make it apparent that he took the *Ring* to embody philosophical themes, and even to connect with "what we read in works on philosophy"; but he insisted that he thought of himself as "little of a philosopher," adding that he could "speak only in works of art." Wagner was often self-deceived; but we take these judgments to be quite apt.

The *Ring*—like other great literary, musical, and artistic works, but more so than most—revolves around and grapples with large philosophical questions and expresses ideas that respond to them; and Wagner recognized that he could not formulate these ideas in a fully precise and explicit way. But we think that he was on to a number of things that are interesting and perhaps even truly important. We suspect that this is no small part of the reason so many reasonably sane and quite intelligent people are fascinated with the *Ring*. And we ourselves have found it very rewarding both philosophically and personally to try to come to grips with it not only immediately but also reflectively. Others have as well;

and it is our hope that this book will help to increase the numbers of those who will—not only in print, but also in conversation with one another, and with themselves.

Philosophers coming to the *Ring* can strive for an *interpretation* of it, endeavoring to capture in discursive prose what Wagner somehow managed to suggest and convey in his music drama. Or, more modestly, they can try to bring into focus some key concepts and relate them to aspects of the tetralogy. We think of our efforts here in the latter way; and we offer our reflections in the spirit of would-be-helpful bystanders, who venture tentatively to offer advice on how one might look at an intriguing but puzzling picture. What follows is not a full-blown philosophical interpretation of the *Ring*, but rather a philosophical excursion through it—guided by certain questions we believe to be at issue in it and which we find interesting. We have learned that thinking about these questions before and after—and even during—performances, broadcasts and recordings not only does not detract from our experience of the *Ring*, but actually enhances that experience and its rewards for us. If we did not suspect that doing so might affect others similarly, we would not have written this book. And by "others" we mean not simply "other philosophers," but rather anyone who feels drawn to try to think things through—things that matter in life but are not easily settled.

There are, of course, celebrated classic and recent attempts to interpret the *Ring*, some more philosophical than others. One familiar approach notes that it was the young, socialistically minded and politically involved Wagner who conceived and wrote the text pretty much as we have it, and proposes that the *Ring* resounds to the politics. So from George Bernard Shaw on, commentators have taken Wagner's mythical figures to represent social classes engulfed in conflict. In another construal the crucial message is that social and political contracts are inefficacious and that only the power of love can redeem the human condition. Yet another contends that Wagner's intensive study of Schopenhauer, undertaken while he was in exile and after he had given up on politics, deeply influenced the last Act of *Siegfried* and the whole of *Götterdämmerung*, thus reshaping the entire tetralogy. From this perspective, the central message is metaphysical, couched in terms of the renunciation of world and will.

We have learned from a good many such efforts at large-scale interpretation. And there is certainly something to be said for many of them—even though there are often reasons to question them as well. With some strain, the depiction of the gods at the beginning of Scene 2 of *Rheingold* might be seen, for example, as an exposé of an effete and degenerate capitalism. Anyone who wanted to present that message, however, could have done so more directly and incisively. Similarly, the suggestion that the *Ring* shows the redeeming power of love would seem better suited to a rather different story. The most complete and appealing expression of human love in the entire work—the magnificently intense devotion between Siegmund and Sieglinde—ends, almost as soon as it begins, with Siegmund's death. *Amor vincit omnia* (Love conquers all) was already a cliché when Chaucer's Prioress had it engraved on a trinket; and Wagner is unlikely to have devoted so much musical and dramatic effort to articulate so banal a theme. (Moreover, love is not exactly all-conquering here. Indeed, a more appropriate tag for the *Ring* would seem to be *amor vincit nihil* [Love conquers nothing].) Nor does the idea that the work proclaims the need to abnegate one's will make sense of what is supposed to be its principal source of evidence—the passing of the gods at the end of *Götterdämmerung*—either in the version Wagner actually set or in various alternatives to it that he contemplated. Brünnhilde *acts*. She does not just "see the world end"; she acts to end it—with something other than a bang, to be sure, but not exactly with a whimper.

The extent to which we do and do not agree with various interpretations will become clear as we proceed. Our approach will be somewhat different from those usually encountered in discussions of the *Ring*. Our principal reason for approaching it differently stems from a conviction that broad-brush treatments illuminate very little of the substance, complexity, and subtlety of some of the most interesting issues dealt with in the course of its 15 or so hours (not counting intermissions, and depending on *tempi*). While our title is intended to suggest a broad problem, we are not concerned with identifying and establishing any single overriding theme as the *Ring*'s guiding idea or bottom line. Instead of staking out a general claim about the overarching meaning of the work, we shall try to focus on some of its most puzzling facets, using these as clues to finding a path through it.

One of our strategies will be to consider and interpret particular episodes that intrigue us, drawing attention to features of them that are perplexing, and then trying to come to terms with the perplexities we have articulated. We do not suppose that the puzzles we use as *foci* are the only appropriate starting points for an approach like ours; there are surely many ways to enter the world Wagner constructs for us. Indeed, we appreciate the possibility that rival routes could generate divergent broad perspectives. There is no end to possible perspectives that may shed further light on what goes on in the world, Nietzsche maintained; and there may even be no end to those that may prove to be differently and importantly illuminating. It is our experience that he was right—at least with respect to this point as it applies to the *Ring*.

There is a rich musicological literature about the *Ring* that we admire, but to which we do not purport or even aspire to contribute. Scholars from many disciplines have pursued Wagner's sources, mined his theoretical writings, and offered detailed analyses of the relations among passages in the score, and we have gained from their discoveries. What we see less of than we would like in the literature, and attempt here to provide (and to prompt by example and provocation), is extended consideration of some of the major concepts that suggest themselves to us with respect to the events of the drama. So we shall pose questions about such things as Wotan's purposes, Brünnhilde's loves, and Siegfried's lacks, and we shall venture some reflections with respect to them.

We write primarily as philosophers who are intrigued by this extraordinary work. But that does not mean that we see it as grist for our professional-philosophical mills. Throughout, we shall be doing the things philosophers become used to doing—drawing distinctions, identifying alternatives, and elaborating on various interpretative possibilities to see what they might look like when fully developed. We think this can be useful for anyone who not only enjoys seeing and hearing the *Ring* but also senses that it is rich in food for thought, and that it may be rewarding in its implications for this life in this world. As we bring our philosophical tendencies and sensibilities to bear on Wagner's drama, however, we shall try to integrate them with other modes of response to the *Ring* that we share with a good many others whom it continues to fascinate.

An obvious danger of an approach like ours is that it will give priority to the words—or the drama—over the music. As noted, we are not musicologists, but that does not prevent us from learning from the musicological research of others and being guided to hear connections in the score that attention to the words and gestures alone would have overlooked. Moreover, although we write primarily as philosophers, we write with the sensibility of those who know music as something to be sung and played as well as heard; for we are also singers (and in one of our cases, a French horn player as well)—even if not artists who would be up to any serious Wagnerian role, either on the stage or in the pit. Listening to the *Ring* prompts us not only to think philosophically but also to imagine ourselves doing what we are hearing, and even (in suitable circumstances, we hasten to add) to give it a try, exploring the possibilities of expression of the vocal and instrumental lines. This may add nothing musically to the world, but it often does add to our sense of what we are talking about.

So although we shall often seem to be interpreting Wagner's *text*, our responses are typically to the words *as they are set*, paying attention not only to the vocal line but also to the rich orchestration, the complexity of which increases as the tetralogy unfolds. Specific passages in the libretto serve as useful markers to identify places in the score that seem to us especially important; but we are concerned with *everything that is occurring at the moments our markers identify* and what it all works together to express. Often it is the suggestions of the music, rather than the words, that carry most weight. We shall sometimes point to specific features—intervals, rhythms, changes of key or of tempo—

that underlie the moods, ideas, and themes we discover; but even when we do not, we take our claims to rest not on a mere reading of words but on careful *listening* to Wagner's extraordinary melding of text and music. Those claims should be evaluated by their fit with the *combined textual, musical, and dramatic* resonances of the passages to which we point.

Our goal in the following pages is to make sense of some aspects of the *Ring* as a philosophically rich work, and in doing so to suggest and reflect upon what we take to be some of the things about it to which its devotees may be responding. We shall start by considering the notions of *authority* and *judgment*, asking about the kinds of judgment that are made by the protagonists of the music drama, about the characters who have authority to make those judgments, and about the sources of that authority. This will lead us to consider a pivotal moment in a scene that Wagner regarded (as he indicated in a letter of 1855 to Liszt) as the center of the whole *Ring* ("the most important scene for the development of the whole of the great four-part drama"): Scene 2 of the second Act of *Walküre*, featuring Wotan and Brünnhilde alone. The analysis of authority and judgment we bring to that scene will lead us to a perspective that we will then develop with respect to large parts of the action of the tetralogy. As that perspective becomes clear, we hope that it will constitute a satisfying response to the skeptical questions with which we began—a response that shows the depth and interest of the *Ring's* central characters and their world and thereby reveals how this work illuminates enduring features of our human condition and important human possibilities.

Before embarking upon our *Ring* journey, however, we will engage in a bit of stage-setting. First we will say something about several philosophers who were of great importance to Wagner at different points in his intellectual development and whose influences on his thinking and its operatic expression were as different as they were profound. Then, in a second and quite different preparatory chapter, we will take a brief look at one of the *Ring*'s greatest—and, for our purposes, most interesting and important—predecessors, Mozart's *Don Giovanni*, with the concepts of authority and judgment in mind.

Why the apparent detour not only through "Wagner's philosophers" but also through *Don Giovanni* before we get down to business with the *Ring*? We admire Mozart's masterpiece almost as much as we do the *Ring*, but that alone would not be reason enough. One way to consider the philosophical import of great works of literature, drama, or music drama is to think of them as presenting us with a world whose structure embodies relations among ideals and values. Readers and audiences are invited to reflect on those ideals and values and the ways the world of the work structures them, and then to pose and answer questions about themselves and about their own world, the one that they inhabit. In thinking about operas, or about other kinds of dramatic works, we can try to make those questions precise by considering the kinds of judgments offered by the characters who inhabit the world of the drama. (We do not mean to suggest that this is the *only* sound and fruitful approach, but this is one such approach which we believe has much to offer.) If the composer (or dramatist) has something to say that deserves to be taken seriously, it can often be heard best by examining how certain individuals in the drama are endowed with authority, and what kinds of things they say and do.

Wagner's *Ring* offers us an extremely complex and alien world—one that requires extensive exploration before we can settle issues about authority and judgment. Yet there are other dramatic and operatic works whose worlds are closer to ours, in which the relations and conflicts of values and ideals are more readily apparent and in which the attributions of authority and the pertinent judgments seem (at first sight, at least) more obvious. Mozart's *Don Giovanni* is a case in point. Moreover, it raises in a more familiar setting some of the kinds of questions that are, we believe, central to the *Ring*. A brief look at *Don Giovanni* will provide a valuable introduction both to our general strategy and to the particular use of that strategy in the chapters that follow. This also enables us to introduce and develop some of the concepts and distinctions that will prove useful. Readers impatient to get into discussion of the *Ring* itself can turn immediately to Chapter 3, returning to these first two chapters as the spirit moves them.

1

Wagner's Philosophers

Wagner was no philosopher, but as he tells us in his autobiography *Mein Leben [My Life]*, philosophy interested him enough that he made efforts to inform himself about it. His encounters with philosophy left their mark in various respects on at least some of his music dramas as well, the *Ring* operas among them. Three philosophers loomed especially large in his life. The best known of them today, and the only one with whom he became personally acquainted and associated, was Friedrich Nietzsche; but his decade-long relationship with Nietzsche occurred relatively late in Wagner's life. At that time Nietzsche was still quite young, in his student years and early career as a classical philologist; it was long before Nietzsche developed into the thinker we now recognize as one of the major figures in the history of modern philosophy. Their relationship was indeed a remarkable one; but Nietzsche can hardly be said to have been a formative influence on Wagner in any respect, even if he did provide Wagner with encouragement in his completion of the *Ring*, and—for a time, at any rate—with welcome publicity and praise in several early adulatory works (*The Birth of Tragedy* and *Richard Wagner in Bayreuth*, the fourth of his *Untimely Meditations*).

The other two philosophers in question, however, influenced Wagner significantly, even if only through their work rather than in person. The first was Ludwig Feuerbach, who flashed across the Central European intellectual firmament in the 1840s, attracting and exciting a great many bright young minds ready for something post-Christian, post-Hegelian, and vigorously liberal and uplifting. Wagner was among his enthusiasts, as was the young Marx. Both were attracted by the values Feuerbach espoused, which seemed to cry out for radical social and cultural change, as well as by his critique of traditional religious and philosophical ways of thinking and his naturalistic reinterpretation of human life. Wagner and Marx both wanted more from philosophy than had been offered by Kant and Hegel, the two great prior eminences of German philosophical thought. For a brief moment it seemed to them, and to many others of their generation, that Feuerbach had surpassed both Kant and Hegel, not only in intelligibility but also in human significance.

Wagner's second philosophical discovery, made in the early 1850s, was Arthur Schopenhauer, whom Wagner embraced with fervor as his philosophical mentor for the rest of his life. Two more different philosophers can hardly be imagined—Feuerbach the breathlessly optimistic apostle of secular humanism, on the one hand, and Schopenhauer the searingly cynical proponent of pessimism, on the other. In the aftermath of his disillusionment with Feuerbach, Wagner became an ardent admirer of Schopenhauer. Yet he retained residues of Feuerbach's influence to the end, his celebration of Schopenhauer notwithstanding, even after he had become convinced that Feuerbach's hopes for a future in which humanity would live happily ever after were impossibly naïve and unattainable.

Feuerbach was one of the pioneers of the "naturalistic" turn in German philosophy after Hegel. His name literally means "stream of fire"; for a time, that was just what he seemed to be—a firebrand in the intellectual tinderbox of post-Hegelian central Europe. A passionate early proponent of what later came to be called "secular humanism," he sought to base a new value theory and moral philosophy on philosophical-anthropological foundations. His best-known book, *The Essence of Christianity*, published in 1841, attracted considerable attention, not only in Germany but also in Britain (where it was translated by George Eliot [Mary Ann Evans]).

Feuerbach's critique of religion made him the champion of Enlightenment to some and a dangerous threat to others. Religion for Feuerbach involves a kind of confusion, resulting in the projection of features of our own nature and of genuinely human life into an imaginary realm beyond this life and this world. He called for a "philosophy of the future" in which both theology and metaphysics would give way to a scientifically informed philosophy centering upon the naturalistic reinterpretation of human life, human knowledge, and human value. The key to understanding our humanity, however, is taken not merely to be the recognition that we are a part of living nature, but also that a developmental process has occurred, in the course of which human beings have come to be qualitatively different from other animals, through the transformation of our nature under the social conditions of human existence. Our humanity emerges out of the ways in which community has affected our emotional, sensuous, and intellectual capacities.

As Wagner tells us in his autobiography, he began his attempt to educate himself philosophically by reading Hegel, who had succeeded Kant as the reigning philosopher of the day. While finding Hegel impressive and edifying, however, he soon realized that he really grasped very little of what he was reading. Feuerbach was recommended to him as a much more down-to-earth and comprehensible writer, and also as the great new thing among the young Hegelians who were coming into their own in the decades following the master's death in 1831. Wagner took a look and was converted. His introduction to Feuerbach was an early critique of Christianity, in which Feuerbach attacked and rejected the idea of personal immortality. Wagner then went on to his *The Essence of Christianity*, which he found to be heavier going but of which he clearly read enough to appreciate its basic thesis: all of the main concepts of Christianity—"God" included—are mythical and confused versions of important points about human nature, human life, and human possibility. They are not mere fictions; but they are not to be taken literally either, and need to be reinterpreted in naturalistic and humanistic terms to be properly understood. Wagner found this position quite congenial, and his treatment of the gods in the *Ring* is in complete accord with it. (The opening chapter of *The Essence of Christianity*, entitled "The Essential Nature of Man," is particularly pertinent.)

Wagner undoubtedly also read Feuerbach's next book, *Principles of the Philosophy of the Future* (1843), his philosophical manifesto in which he announces that "the new philosophy rests on the truth of love and feeling." Its title is echoed in Wagner's own manifesto *The Artwork of the Future*. Just as Feuerbach concluded his *Principles* with a call for "a really new philosophy, that is, an independent philosophy corresponding to the needs of mankind and of the future," Wagner conceived a desire to create a musical-dramatic art that would answer the same needs, in the even more powerful way that he believed his art would be able to do. The *Ring* was meant to show the way.

Feuerbach maintained that when we speak of the nature and existence of God, we are confusedly trying to imagine certain admirable qualities in substantial form. So, for example, to say that "God is loving" or "God is love" is really just an indirect (and muddled) way of saying that "love is God"—which in turn simply is to say that love is *divine*, or of transcendent worth and importance. For Feuerbach, as a child of Romanticism, there is nothing of greater worth than "feeling" or emotion; and among the feelings or emotions of which we are capable, love surpasses all others. Wagner may already have thought so; but if he did, he found his conviction confirmed by Feuerbach.

Wagner also would seem to have embraced Feuerbach's thesis that no such phenomena are of supernatural origin, any more than is anything else in this world; rather, they are outcomes of the transformation of capacities that are part of our natural endowment as living creatures—and it is in human social and interpersonal relationships that the magic of such transformation occurs. Our highest and most truly human qualities are the results of sublimations of our vital functions, which human community and interaction make possible—but only if our relationships are of the appropriate sort. If they are not, human beings can and do turn out poorly, or even very badly—hence the need for the transformation of social life in a manner that will be conducive to the development of admirable rather than base or vicious human qualities.

Another of Feuerbach's ideas that undoubtedly appealed to Wagner is that the expression of feelings transforms what begins as merely subjective into something objective. Loving action is one such expression of feeling; another is music. Music, Feuerbach maintains, is objectified feeling, and so it is a medium in which a new and higher form of objective reality comes into the world; we can enter and attain this higher reality when we make and experience music. In expressing our vital nature in its most exquisitely sublimated forms, as in the case of music or love, we achieve the highest of kinds of self-realization—and a higher sort of human reality than those to whom such things are alien will ever know.

Schopenhauer certainly read Feuerbach and undoubtedly found all of this quite naïve. He is notorious for his profoundly pessimistic outlook, to which he gave relentless and powerful expression throughout his long life, and for his seemingly curious interpretation not only of human nature but of all of reality in terms of what he calls "will." Schopenhauer's vision of humankind was bleak; he saw it as both product and victim of blindly operating forces beyond our control in a godless and heedless world, ceaselessly striving and suffering to no purpose, with death our inevitable fate and oblivion our only salvation. His views either appalled or amused most of his contemporaries while fascinating and gripping others, Wagner and the young Nietzsche among them. That vision is presented in Schopenhauer's most important work, *The World as Will and Representation* (WWR), originally published in 1818 and later substantially revised and expanded in 1844.

Schopenhauer's WWR sets forth his philosophical thinking in comprehensive and systematic fashion, at times turgidly, but often elegantly and powerfully. Accepting the Kantian distinction between the world as it is perceived ("the world as representation") and the world as it is in itself, Schopenhauer argues that the latter is to be conceived along the lines of our own inner nature, which is discernable as "will." The world's fundamental nature must be akin to ours, writ large, and operating in a similar way but without many of the complexities that have come to characterize our form of existence. Schopenhauer thus greatly extends and generalizes the notion of "will" in this wider and indeed ubiquitous employment of it, taking it at bottom to be a kind of nonrational dynamic principle, without form or content or purpose, but driven by its own inner nature ever to express and manifest itself.

While Schopenhauer takes all particular existing things to share the same fundamental nature, they also are held to be in constant competition and conflict, blindly struggling against each other in an attempt to maintain themselves in their ultimately pointless existence. This ceaseless strife moreover results in equally pointless suffering, wherever there is sufficient consciousness to register its consequences in this manner. Thus, for Schopenhauer, wherever there is "will" there is suffering, in one form or another (of which physical pain is only one instance). This theme, which reflects Buddhistic influences he readily acknowledges, underlies his pessimism. He considers suffering to be an ineradicable feature of life; and his abhorrence of suffering, taken together with its ubiquity and the contention that it can neither be justified nor outweighed by any attainable positive goods life may afford (either singly or collectively), yields his pessimistic conclusion, and with it his counsel of "denying" the will in every way possible. If the struggle for existence is worse than senseless (owing to the suffering it generates), then oblivion is preferable to life, and the extinction of the will in any and all of its forms—and thus of the entire world, as both will and "representation"—would be the best of outcomes.

Schopenhauer's ethics is an ethics of compassion, revolving around the abhorrence of suffering, not only in one's own case but wherever it may occur. He does not think that *nothing* matters—for *suffering* matters, and matters greatly, but in a purely negative way. All seemingly positive values pale in relation to the magnitude of the reality of this negative one. The alleviation of suffering, wherever it is occurring, is thus the highest imperative. The only way truly to alleviate it, however, is to attack the root of the problem, which is "will" itself. Beyond seeking to mitigate the sufferings of others, therefore, Schopenhauer commends a variety of strategies serving to liberate one to a greater or lesser degree from the grip of "willing." Contemplation and aesthetic experience have their places here, on his analysis, as ways of loosening its grip upon one at least temporarily and partially. Ultimately, however, only a strategy of systematic radical asceticism can enable one to attain true deliverance. Schopenhauer rejects suicide as paradoxically self-assertive and therefore far from truly subverting the will, and he commends instead an ascetic existence that amounts to a radical negation of all aspects and manifestations of will-driven life.

Like Feuerbach, Schopenhauer considers music to be an expression of our affective nature, and indeed takes music to stand in a special relationship to the world's fundamental nature as well as to our own, affording a kind of deep knowledge of both that nothing else can. And like Feuerbach, he too holds that our emotional nature consists of sublimations of our vital nature. This includes our ability to love, which he considers to be very different from our capacity for compassion. Love, for Schopenhauer, is first and foremost *sexual* love and is fundamentally sexual in all its forms. "All love," he writes, "however ethereally it may bear itself, is rooted in the sexual impulse alone, nay, it absolutely is only a more definitely determined, specialised, and indeed in the strictest sense individualised sexual impulse."

This categorical statement occurs in one of the supplements to the Fourth Book of WWR entitled "The Metaphysics of the Love of the Sexes." Wagner surely was familiar with it, for he claims in his autobiography to have read WWR in its entirety numerous times, and can hardly have missed it. When one reads the essay, however, one has to wonder about the depth of Wagner's adherence to (or understanding of) Schopenhauer's philosophy, in view of the continuing importance Wagner so clearly attaches to love that is of a fundamentally (if by no means simply) sexual nature. For it is difficult to imagine a treatment of love that would be less sympathetic to it than is Schopenhauer's in this essay—just as it is difficult to imagine an interpretation of human life and its possible meaningfulness and worth that could be more negative than is his in WWR. All love, for Schopenhauer, whether more or less sublimated, is an expression of the sexual impulse. But the sexual impulse, in turn, is itself only an expression of what he calls "the will to live," manifesting the procreative requirement of life; and this "will to live," which he takes to be part and parcel of all life, is conceived in turn as expressing the irrational dynamic principle driving the whole of reality that he calls "will." It *is* "simply the will to live" in one particular mode of expression, and so is just as noxious and absurd as is that pointless, mindless, heartless "will to live" itself. This "will" might even be called "demonic" were it not for the fact that that would do it too much credit—for that would impute at least a modicum of intelligence and purposefulness to it, whereas in fact it is utterly devoid of anything of the kind.

Within the game of life, of course, the sexual impulse certainly does have a point: it works to keep life going, and more specifically to keep members of species reproducing themselves and their kind. Schopenhauer has a good deal to say about how cleverly it operates in the service of this outcome—very often, he observes, at great cost to the individual creatures involved and invariably increasing the amount of suffering in the world. What makes it so objectionable to him is that this striving is so absurd. There is no point to the game itself, and therefore there is no point to keeping it going; but there is much to be said *against* the perpetuation of a pointless affair whose only meaningful feature is the very considerable amount of suffering it creates.

The course of wisdom, for Schopenhauer, is therefore to repudiate *all* the forms of willing and striving, including this one, and so seek to extinguish the very will that is the root of all the world's suffering. Love is not the answer to the world's ills, for Schopenhauer; it is a very salient part of what ails it. The only cure (or palliative) for life lies in the attainment of utter oblivion, with complete asceticism, self-denial, and inaction being the next best thing.

There clearly was something about this idea and general way of thinking that appealed to a part of Wagner, for whatever reason or combination of reasons. And it is arguable—as Nietzsche argued—that in the end, in *Parsifal*, that part of him prevailed. *Tristan* is a more complicated case, because it would seem to pull strongly in contradictory directions, one at least quasi-Schopenhauerian and the other decidedly not. But it is very difficult indeed to see the *Ring* as a showcase for Schopenhauer's philosophy. It is easy, on the other hand, to see traces of Feuerbach in it—even though they have become transformed quite fundamentally. This is a topic to which we shall return, better equipped, in Chapter 20.

Before concluding this brief discussion, it is instructive in a number of respects to consider one particularly striking passage in the Fourth Book of WWR. This may or may not be what Wagner had in mind when he wrote in his autobiography that it was only when he read this work that he understood his Wotan. After having laid out the harsh truth about the human condition at great length, Schopenhauer writes:

> A man who had assimilated firmly into his way of thinking the truths so far advanced, but at the same time had not come to know, through his own experience or through a deeper insight, that constant suffering is essential to all life; who found satisfaction in life and took perfect delight in it; who desired, in spite of calm deliberation, that the course of his life as he had hitherto experienced should be of endless duration or of constant recurrence; and whose courage to face life was so great that, in return for life's pleasures, he would willingly and gladly put up with all the hardships and miseries to which it is subject; such a man would stand "with firm, strong bones on the well-grounded, enduring earth" [from Goethe's *Gränzen der Menschheit*], and would have nothing to fear. . . . This is for knowledge the viewpoint of the complete *affirmation of the will-to-live*. . . . The opposite of this, the *denial of the will-to-live*, shows itself when willing ends with that knowledge [that constant suffering is essential to all life], since the particular phenomena known then no longer act as *motives* of willing, but the whole knowledge of the inner

> nature of the world . . . becomes the *quieter* of the will, and thus the will freely abolishes itself. (WWR §54)

To anticipate our future discussions, one can readily see the Wotan whom we first meet as the type of being Schopenhauer is describing at the outset of this passage. Unlike Siegfried, whose exuberant youthful vitality might be considered to manifest an unqualified "affirmation of the will-to-live" but who is utterly naïve and oblivious to life's hard truths, that Wotan is no stranger to hardship and pain—but he is undeterred by them. For Schopenhauer, a person of this sort still has a long way to go before achieving true wisdom; for that requires taking deeply seriously the ineradicable and ubiquitous reality of "constant suffering" in one form or another. Once one has done so, the "affirmation of the will-to-live" will no longer be possible and will be replaced by its opposite. One *might* see that as Wotan's trajectory in the course of the *Ring*. We do not; but we do grant that there is something to the idea. One could also see it as Wagner's own trajectory. We do not dispute that view, if the trajectory is allowed to run beyond the *Ring* to *Parsifal*; but we do not take such a trajectory to be that of the *Ring* itself.

Although we reject that line of interpretation, it suggests an important question that should be kept in mind in the course of what follows. If Wotan's career does *not* consist in the attainment of Schopenhauer's kind of outlook—or, somewhat differently, if a main theme of the *Ring* is not the identification of true wisdom with pessimism—then what are we to make of Wotan's course and of the course of the drama in which he is embedded? (Nietzsche's parting with Schopenhauer, and with Wagner as well, after his early infatuation with them, can be charted very nicely by means of this passage; for his heart lay with the type of person first described, and his aim came to be that of finding a way to remain that type of person *even after* coming to terms with the full force of the case Schopenhauer makes.)

Wagner finished the entire *Ring* poem in December of 1852, nearly two years before he discovered Schopenhauer (in the fall of

1854); and he did not change it. It is therefore a product of the Wagner whose dominant philosophical influence was Feuerbach—even if also a product of the Wagner whose revolutionary hopes for a political transformation of Europe that would make Feuerbach's humanistic dreams come true had been dashed by the defeat of the revolutionaries of 1848–49. Wagner may have been ready for Schopenhauer, but he had not yet made the acquaintance. By that time the first *Ring* opera score had been completed, as had the composition of much of the music for the second. Neither they nor the first two acts of *Siegfried* (finished in July 1857) show any traces of Schopenhauerian influence, either musically or textually.

Then came the famous 12-year hiatus in the composition of the *Ring*, before Wagner returned to it (and began working on the third Act of *Siegfried*) in March of 1869—shortly after meeting Nietzsche (in November of 1868). During that hiatus, of course, he had hardly been idle; both *Die Meistersinger* and *Tristan and Isolde* were written and composed during those years. *Tristan* is sometimes said to be the quintessential Schopenhauerian opera, although to our way of thinking that distinction may more aptly be bestowed upon *Parsifal*. But there is nothing Schopenhauerian about *Meistersinger*—or, it seems to us, about the third Act of *Siegfried* either.

Götterdämmerung is a more difficult case. Wagner did at one point consider having Brünnhilde express Schopenhauerian sentiments at its conclusion. But (fortunately, in our view) he decided against this, and retained the original pre-Schopenhauer wording of her last lines along with the rest of the entire text. And to our ears the music with which it ends, while perhaps paradigmatically exemplifying Schopenhauer's conception of music's expressive power, is as far from delivering a Schopenhauerian negative judgment upon life and the world as Wagner could have written. Wagner seems to us to have been unable to be true to his Schopenhauerian convictions there, as his musical genius combined with the spirit with which he had earlier imbued the *Ring*'s text to sweep him and us toward a conclusion that we regard as resonating with something deeper and more profoundly insightful in his artistic soul than any such ways of thinking to which he may have been attracted and disposed to proclaim. It bespeaks a fundamental affirmation rather than negation of life—and of life rather than nirvana, notwithstanding life's tragic character even at its very best, and the suffering and destruction that are inseparable from it despite our best efforts and intentions. Small wonder, then, that Nietzsche responded so strongly to it; for, as he (unlike Wagner) came to understand, a response of this sort to which one is impelled trumps any intellectual attraction Schopenhauer's pessimistic indictment of life might have, even if it also has nothing to do with any countervailing optimism with respect to human prospects. And, as he observed, the fact that Wagner followed the *Ring* with *Parsifal* speaks volumes about Wagner, but says nothing to the contrary about the truth of the matter.

As we proceed with our exploration of the philosophical themes in the *Ring*, there will often be resonances with the ideas we have outlined here. Yet we are not going to start from those ideas, seeking places in the operas where we can find traces of Feuerbach or Schopenhauer, or anticipations of Nietzsche. Our strategy, instead, will be to explore the ways in which philosophical questions and ideas arise and are addressed in what we find in the *Ring* itself. Because this strategy may need clarification, and because its development in application to the *Ring* will take several chapters to unfold, we shall apply it to another opera in which it may readily be seen to be useful, and which serves to bring into focus some of the issues with which we will be concerned.

2

Authority and Judgment in *Don Giovanni*

Lear:	Dost thou know me fellow?
Kent:	No sir; but you have that in your countenance which I would fain call master.
Lear:	What's that?
Kent:	Authority.

From the moment the curtain goes up after the overture to *Don Giovanni*, Leporello seems to be trying to leave his master. His opening ruminations express a wish at least to change places (eventually granted in Act II, but with unfortunate consequences). In the recitative that begins Act I, Scene 4 he offers a frank judgment: ". . . *caro Signor padrone, la vita che menate è da briccone* [my dear master, you are living the life of a scoundrel]"; but his candor neither perturbs the Don nor heralds any effort on his own part to end his service. Later, after coping with the arrival of Zerlina and Donna Elvira, he announces his resolve to go his own way: "*Io deggio ad ogni patto per sempre abbandonar questo bel matto* [I must find some way to leave this elegant madman, once and for all]." Nevertheless, even after serving as scapegoat in the assault on Zerlina, Leporello is still dragged off (not unwillingly) by his master in the wonderful confusion that ends Act I.

He is no more successful in Act II. Once more he declares his intent to leave; but, a few minutes later, having been bought off, he has fallen in with the latest skirt-chasing scheme, and pursues his role of diverting Elvira with some gusto. Unmasked, he protests that the Don has stolen his innocence ("*l'innocenza mi rubò*"); but, failing to take advantage of the opportunity to fall in with the enemy, he steals back to his master. Even the terrifying encounter with the Statue is not enough to make him quit; he is still in place at the start of the Finale, sneaking pheasant and serving as his master's foil. His last solo declaration, made after the forcible removal of the Don, is to find a new and better master. But will he? Could he find another master who would be better *for him*? Indeed, does Leporello even really *want* to leave? Probably not. (Anyone who has ever sung the Catalogue Aria knows how the writing provides enormous opportunities for expressing satisfaction, delight, and even obsession.) And even if he wanted to leave, he could not. For the Don has, in his confident music as well as in his countenance, that which Leporello can only serve. The Don has authority.

More strictly, the Don has a *certain type* of authority, and one that Leporello lacks (along with most—but not all—of his fellow judges of the Don): namely, the ability to *make things happen*—the power (of one sort or another) to impose his vision of things and his designs upon others, and indeed to enlist them in the service of realizing his ends, even when their inclinations and interests are more or less strongly to the contrary. We shall call this power-based type of authority "*directive* authority." To recognize authority of this type, as Leporello does, is not necessarily to express approval or suppose that the authority is legitimate, but rather is simply to acknowledge, however grudgingly, the sway someone may have over others (oneself perhaps included). Directive authority can result from nothing more admirable than power or even sheer brute strength, although in the case of the Don, charisma and charm plainly play important roles, along with evident vitality and forcefulness.

Leporello is hardly alone in lacking directive authority; his deficiency in this respect is shared by almost all his fellow judges of the Don. Throughout the entire opera, Don Giovanni is judged; and the judgment—whenever made by someone not under his spell—is always negative (even if many of those who deliver it are hard put to be resolute when he sets out to beguile them): he is a moral monster, a murderer, a betrayer, a man with a heart of bronze, and so forth. But although the castigations rain down on him, they have absolutely no impact; he continues to do the sorts of things for which he is condemned, even enlisting those who judge him (most obviously Leporello) in his ventures. Even with the crowd of peasants chastising him and the avenging furies (the three maskers, Zerlina and Masetto) all cataloguing his sins, he is unaffected. Nor is this because he is either subhuman or inhuman, for he very clearly is neither (even if he is also no conventional hero). Because those who render the judgments have no directive authority, their condemnations amount to little more than poignant, sometimes dramatic and even moving musical phrases, remarkable chiefly for their ineffectuality.

So Donna Anna delivers her angular line against an impassioned accompaniment (*Or sai chi l'onore*), but nothing will come of it. Masetto grinds his teeth (*Ho capito, Signor si*), but he has no power to do more. Donna Elvira's arias are torn between pain and compassion, and she will never come to an unqualified vengefulness. And with Don Ottavio, a male of the Don's own social class, Mozart produces a character sketch of extraordinary effect. The ardent phrases of his beautiful arias (*Dalla sua pace*, *Il mio tesoro*) capture the weakness that is likely to leave him pining for Donna Anna into the indefinite future. Ottavio is a wonderful wimp, and Shaw took the measure of the character when he gave his counterpart in *Man and Superman* the nickname "Ricki-Ticki-Tavy."

There is another type of authority, however, that the Don's detractors claim and at least seem to have, and that he himself lacks. They purport to speak with the authority of those who know what the moral order allows and what it forbids. Even if they are not effective in making their judgments stick and getting results, Donna Anna and her supporters seem to be making the *right* judgments (or so one might propose). In other words, they may lack *directive* authority, but they suppose themselves to have a form of *epistemic* or *cognitive* authority: that is, they claim the sort of authority that is associated with having *knowledge* that entitles one to pass judgments—even if it is only knowledge of what prevailing conventional norms prescribe and proscribe. In the end, the two forms of authority seem to come together, the "correct" moral verdict is enforced, and the Don receives his supposedly just deserts in the hereafter. The implementation of judgment is deferred earlier on because most of those who try to make it have no directive authority; the drama is moved forward by their successive failures, until the final reckoning.

With the obvious exception of the Don, everyone who appears on stage would endorse the moral verdicts that are so frequently (and so ineffectually) issued: Donna Anna, Donna Elvira, Zerlina, Masetto, and the rest would recognize each of the others as having a clear vision of the moral order. Moreover, it is easy to embed this group of characters in a broader society within which their moral authority would be almost universally conceded. We, the audience, are invited to imagine ourselves participating in this broader society, joining the consensus, and taking the Don's judges to be cognitive authorities about the moral qualities of his conduct. To accept that invitation would be to suppose that the cognitive authority is not only ceded to them by almost everyone on stage, but that it is ceded *rightly*, that the judges are not just *taken* to know that the actions they denounce are morally wrong, but that they have reliable insights about genuine moral turpitude.

So, we might suppose, the cognitive authority of the Don's accusers is finally vindicated, and their triumph is celebrated on stage in a closing sextet. Yet that sextet not only sounds but surely is meant to be heard as feeble. This, we believe, is not only because there is little point in listening to the ratification of an assessment that these characters have been trying to make since the beginning of the opera and that has now been made for them. It is also because the very idea that these people have the right to the last word on the Don is suspect—indeed, almost a joke—and Mozart wants to raise qualms about our accepting the invitation to join the conventional moral consensus. The pallid jubilation of the finale, set in the context of the celebrants' lack of directive authority, raises questions about their cognitive authority as well, calling into question the simple interpretation that Moral Rectitude has ultimately triumphed. What is it, we are provoked to ask, that these people actually know, and what is their knowledge of it really worth?

The closing sextet undermines the simple idea that the drama has been moved by a clash between directive authority and cognitive authority, a disharmony that has ultimately been resolved. The Don's directive authority proved to be a spell that has now been broken; but the cognitive authority of his rejoicing detractors is little more substantial. If any resolution has come, that is because there is one character who does have the directive authority to judge the Don: the Commendatore. Mozart provides him with dramatic lines, full of confident fifths and octaves, lines that match the Don's own authoritative music. The combat of the first scene is balanced by the vocal duet of the final one, in a double confrontation of authoritative figures. In the second and decisive episode, in a struggle over keys, the Commendatore eventually forces capitulation into D minor, defining the musical space in which the Don sings his last lines.

Why (or how) does the Commendatore succeed where others who share his moral perspective fail? The simple interpretation we have been considering (based on the invitation to the audience to join the moral consensus on stage) would view him as an especially privileged cognitive authority: the Commendatore knows the moral order, and his station in society gives him the ability to enforce it. He is, after all, an injured father (his daughter has been abused, and the claims of patriarchy must be satisfied); besides that, he is a soldier, whose military prowess has probably contributed to the security of the state. Society and tradition are concentrated in him—whereas, by contrast, Anna, Elvira, and Zerlina are mere females, Masetto and Leporello are too low-class to count, and Ottavio is just a suitor, a lightweight, and a poor representative of the military virtues.

Yet the Commendatore only prevails posthumously, when he has been transformed into a superhuman figure—a preposterous phantasm who can redirect the action with his frigid clasp. Why should this massive marmoreal presence count even as a cognitive (much less directive) authority? Listening to the final sextet, it is easy to construct convincing explanations of why the Don's Lilliputian antagonists advance the moral judgments they do, explanations which are as unflattering to them as they are deflating to their cognitive authority. They issue their verdicts because they have been conditioned in particular ways by the surrounding society; and if they are taken to have cognitive authority, it is not because of their daring in probing matters for themselves but rather because they have acceded to convention, and the conventional wisdom has turned out to have the upper hand. The concurrence of their judgments is no touchstone of truth but rather is only an expression of their shared antipathy to any serious evaluation of the ethical ideas with which their society has supplied them.

But are matters so very different with the Commendatore? Or are the things he stands for and "knows" also the result of parental teaching, clerical guidance, the discipline of the military academy, acquiescence in the customs of the state? He returns, as a frozen monument, to reinforce all that, and perhaps we are meant to understand that return not as the triumph of a cognitive authority deserving acceptance and obedience but as the savage crushing of an individual who has asked, in an admittedly problematic way, whether what is commonly taken to be authoritative about moral matters really is so. In any event, if the very possibility of a viable alternative to the Don on the one hand, and to his Lilliputian antagonists on the other, hinges upon the plausibility of taking literally and seriously the figure of the Commendatore and the mythology he evokes, that would be a slender reed indeed upon which to stake everything.

In short, *Don Giovanni* presents and illuminates two kinds of authority: one epistemic or *cognitive* (knowledge-based, deriving from or relating to significant knowledge of some sort, but by itself impotent), and the other *directive* (power-based and action-related, having to do with the ability to get things done oneself or by others). They can and often do diverge, and even conflict. The opera's secondary characters make judgments, claiming authority of the first sort; and their judgments have both a *focus* and a *content*.

The focus of their judgment is the Don and his behavior; and the content of the judgment corresponds to conventional moral appraisals—various specific ways of expressing the thought that what the Don does is reprehensible. On a simple interpretation of the work, most of those who make such judgments not only take themselves to have epistemic authority, but actually do have it, in that they are *right* to think that the Don is morally awful; but they lack directive authority (they cannot make their judgments stick). The Commendatore, however, is an exception to the rule. He combines epistemic and directive authority; and so he is able to see to it that the Don receives his comeuppance.

We have suggested that the final sextet undermines this simple interpretation—and indeed that the opera as a whole actually subverts it, even though superficially seeming to lend it support. Throughout the opera, Mozart makes clear that even if the Don's judges are right, their judgment does not take his measure. For their being right is as problematic as it is contingently correct, and their judgments are frozen relics of cultural correctness. (Even if there are real moral insights in the cultural tradition, those who mouth the conventional pieties do not recognize those insights at all clearly.) The Don is no revolutionary epistemic authority; Mozart clearly does not offer him as a moral visionary and reformer, whose insights with respect to the moral order and its contingency are tragically rejected and defeated. He does, however, present him as sensing the shallowness and inadequacy of a sheepish acquiescence in tradition, and so as embodying the necessity of a "revaluation of values" (in Nietzsche's phrase). The conclusions he draws are premature and morally abysmal; he is, after all, a cheat, bully, thug, seducer, and (as the opening scene would appear to indicate) when seduction fails, a rapist. Yet to stop at that does not do justice to what is at once splendid and appalling about this problematic but fascinating prototype of a kind of *Übermensch*, who not only fancies himself "beyond good and evil" but actually is so.

Writing over a century after Mozart, in the shadow of Nietzsche and Wagner, Shaw made issues of authority and judgment easier by sanitizing his counterpart of the Don. Jack Tanner, the central figure of *Man and Superman*, talks a good game, raising respectable hackles by his spoken challenges to convention, but his actions reveal a kindness and concern for others that is antithetical to the Don's utter disregard for anyone other than himself, and for anything other than self-gratification. Mozart was more subtle and searching, drawing characters on none of whom a clear and unambiguous positive or negative verdict can be rightly given—his title character least of all.

In this most profound of his operas, Mozart already seems to be moving onto Nietzschean ground, offering a preliminary salvo in the contest of reinterpretation and revaluation that was to come a century later. His fundamentally optimistic secular humanism would not have convinced either Wagner or Nietzsche, who would surely have wanted to glorify the convention-shattering, self-defining protagonist, seeing in the Don's demise the stuff of tragedy. Mozart, by contrast, appears to have been animated by a Shakespearean conviction that, the death of the gods notwithstanding, the affirmation afforded by the attainment of a tragic sensibility, grand as it is, is not the best post-traditional stance we can aspire to. He would not have conceded the last word to Wagner—or to Nietzsche.

Much more could be said about *Don Giovanni*, in elaboration, critique and defense of the approaches we have sketched. Our interest here, however, has been to prepare the way for an exploration of the *Ring*; and we have used our discussion of *Don Giovanni* to provide an introduction to some concepts and questions that concern us, in a context in which they can be more readily discerned. More specifically, we think the notions of authority and judgment we have outlined prove useful in entering the world of Wagner's complex drama.

At many stages of the tetralogy, different characters offer judgments; and we shall begin by considering the kinds of questions with respect to the *Ring* that we have been exploring in *Don Giovanni*. Just as we have considered the foci of the judgments made in Mozart's opera—the Don and his conduct, on the one hand, and also the norms and values he was disregarding, on the other—so we shall want to ask "What are the foci of the judgments made in the *Ring*?" Our attention to the content of the judgments—that the Don's conduct was reprehensible, and conversely that the norms and values in question were mere conventions rightly disregarded—will find a parallel in a search for the content of the judgments made by Wagner's characters. We shall ask who has authority to make such judgments and what sort of authority it is. (In *Don Giovanni* the Commendatore, unlike Donna Anna and Leporello, has directive authority, as does the Don; what cognitive authority there is, however, is narrowly but opposingly perspectival and problematic—other than that of Mozart himself, perhaps, and of the entire opera.) And we shall ask about the sources of the forms of authority we encounter. (Plainly, all the characters in *Don Giovanni* know some things, but there are serious questions about whether any cognitive authority they may have transcends their own concerns. The Commendatore has directive authority because he represents the conventions and institutions of the society in a particularly powerful way. The Don has it owing to the force and vitality of his personality. In both cases, however, it is problematic, in different ways.)

As we shall discover, the answers to such questions about the *Ring* are far from obvious. Mozart's *Don Giovanni* introduces us in a relatively direct way to questions about the moral structure of a world—a world not too far distant from our own. Similar questions will be found to loom even larger in the world of the *Ring*. Because Wagner's mythical world seems so much more alien, we face a heightened challenge of identifying and addressing these kinds of questions in it; and the answers to them suggested in this extraordinary work will prove to be far from obvious. But their interest amply rewards the effort of attempting to discern them. We shall start with issues relating to judgment.

3

Alberich and Fricka

The most obviously judgmental characters in the *Ring* are Alberich and Fricka, both of whom spend a significant proportion of their vocal interventions evaluating the actions and attitudes of others. At first sight, the judgments offered by Alberich are so self-interested, pathological, and corrosive that it seems unprofitable to probe them further. His splenetic outbursts about the loss of the Ring, like his earlier boasts concerning what the power of the Ring will win for him, are important in unfolding the action and understandable as expressions of his situation, but are evidently quite lacking in any kind of authority.

Alberich is a sorry figure when we first meet him. If he is basically innocent at that juncture (a matter we shall explore further in Chapter 7), he is also innocently base. His crude fumblings toward the Rhinemaidens are met with lighthearted but deserved derision. In his wounded vanity, however, he makes a devil's bargain, renouncing love for power, symbolized by and magically concentrated in the golden Ring he fashions from the Rhinemaidens' treasure, and around which the action of the *Ring* proceeds to revolve. He is then apparently cheated out of what he made the bargain to get—the Ring—and by none other than Wotan, Mr.

Law-and-Order himself, whose commitment to the rule of law is not only his hallmark but the very basis of his power and preeminence among the gods (and concerning which we shall have much to say in due course).

Alberich has good reasons for becoming bitter, resentful, and eventually hateful. One can imagine him played with at least a measure of sympathy as a kind of Merchant of Nibelheim ("Hath not a dwarf eyes? Senses? Affections? Passions?"). He has no directive authority. His judgments do not prompt others—with the one (large and fateful) exception of his son Hagen—to try to pursue his cause. (Even in this case, Wagner leaves it ambiguous whether Hagen, were he to obtain the Ring, would give Alberich part of the action. The exchange between them is marked by no confidence on Alberich's part, and his own wheedling is accompanied throughout by orchestral reminders of his humiliation and pain.) But does Alberich have epistemic authority? That is a much harder question, and one to which we shall return when we juxtapose Alberich and Wotan.

Fricka is a different and simpler case. She fatefully compels Wotan to change course in the second act of *Walküre*. This requires some stage-setting. Before the gods enter Valhalla at the end of *Rheingold*, Wotan has first been obliged to relinquish the Ring in fulfillment of his contract with the giants Fafner and Fasolt for their construction of the new stronghold and has then been "seized by a great idea" relating to the recovery of the Ring—an idea that we see unfolding at the beginning of *Walküre*. Between these first two parts of the drama he has visited Erda, by whom he has had nine daughters (the Valkyries, Brünnhilde first and foremost among them), whose primary role is to procure dead heroes for the defense of Valhalla. He has also sired a son and a daughter by a mortal woman. These children, the twins Siegmund and Sieglinde, were separated in early childhood; and the first act of *Walküre* relates their reunion and burgeoning love for one another. Sieglinde has been married— against her will and lovelessly—to the brutish Hunding; and, on her wedding day, the disguised Wotan thrust a mighty sword into the ash tree at the center of Hunding's dwelling. Where many before him have failed, Siegmund wrests the sword from the tree. He and Sieglinde, now rapturously in love both despite and (in part) owing to their discovery of their kinship, flee together in the hope of escaping Hunding and finding bliss—which they manage to do just long enough to conceive Siegfried, after which they proceed to their separate fates.

Wotan rules by laws and contracts. Having been compelled to give the giants the Ring along with the rest of the Rhinegold in payment for their construction work on Valhalla (as the only alternative they will accept to the goddess Freia, whom Wotan had promised them in his contract with them), he cannot himself simply seize it from Fafner (who, having killed Fasolt to acquire it and the rest of the treasure, has turned himself into a dragon, the better to guard the hoard). Without the Ring, however, Wotan's rule is unstable, for it is the key to ultimate worldly power; and even if the Valkyries were to fill Valhalla with mighty post-mortem warriors, that would be insufficient protection from someone (Alberich, for example) who might use the Ring against Wotan, and thereby defeat him.

Wotan's "great idea" is to come up with a hero who would seize the Ring in his stead, thereby solving his problem of obtaining it without undermining the basis of his rule by flouting his own law (in the form of his contract). The hero-to-be in question, of course, is Siegmund, whom Wotan (in disguise) grooms for the job and for whose mission he carefully sets the stage. The next phase of the plan is for Siegmund—with the help of Brünnhilde, the Valkyrie most dear to Wotan, and using the mighty sword Wotan has so thoughtfully provided—to dispose of the threat posed by Hunding and his kin. That will clear the way for Siegmund to wield his sword yet again to kill the dragon Fafner and obtain the Ring. Wotan seems to be assuming that Siegmund, as a good and noble son, would then return the Ring to his father, thereby rendering Wotan's rule secure at last. (Or so he would like to think.) It does not appear to have been part of his plan for Siegmund and Sieglinde to become instant lovers (even though he is initially rather charmed by that turn of events) and expectant parents (a fact that he does not learn until very late in *Walküre*). Sieglinde's assigned role, if there was one, was simply to provide Siegmund with the occasion to launch his heroic career and to galvanize him into heroic action. And galvanize she does, in ways that are as momentous and fateful to Wotan's designs as are Brünnhilde's subsequently, for related reasons (of which more later).

Enter Fricka. A natural first reaction to her is that she has wandered into the wrong opera. Were she playing an aggrieved Elvira to Wotan's Don, she would attract more sympathy, and we might even conclude that her moral compass was accurate (in that world, at any rate). Her charges are thoroughly in line with the conventional moralizing of those who judge the Don. Already (in *Rheingold*) we have heard her chafe at Wotan's roving: "*Um des Gatten Treue besorgt /muss traurig ich wohl sinnen/ wie an mich er zu fesseln/ zieht's in die Ferne ihn fort* [Heedful of my husband's fidelity, I'm bound in my sadness to brood on ways of binding him fast whenever he feels drawn away]" (Scene 2). Now (in *Walküre*) she accuses him of profaning the laws of marriage by setting up the abduction of Sieglinde and of encouraging not only adultery but incest (the guilty pair are, of course, twins). And she links this toleration of vice to his own bad behavior: "*Trauernden Sinnes/ musst' ich's ertragen/ zog'st du zur Schlacht/ mit den schlimmen Mädchen/ die wilder* Minne/ *Bund dir gebar* [In sadness of spirit I had to stand by, while you fared to the fray with those ill-mannered girls, who were born of the bond of a dissolute love]" (Act II, Scene 1).

The opening of their exchange makes it plain that Fricka misses what Wotan sees as the important points. She is obsessed with what he regards as minor matters—in particular, who can have sexual relations with whom—without thinking either about emotional bonds or about the broader purposes of Siegmund's heroic career. Wotan's first four responses to her complaints are calm and confident. His music here recalls the untroubled majesty of his opening declamations of the splendor of Valhalla in Scene 2 of *Rheingold*. He is unworried, very much in control, even patronizing. Apropos of the incestuous relationship, Fricka asks primly,

"*Wann ward es erlebt,/ dass leiblich Geschwister sich liebten?* [Whoever heard of a brother and sister being lovers?]." To which question Wotan responds (accompanied by the warm theme that brought the Springtime into Hunding's hut in Act I): "*Heut' hast du's erlebt*" [Well, you have now!]" (*Walküre*, Act II, Scene 1). Whatever dignity Fricka could muster on her entrance is quickly shattered, as the orchestral themes pit the motifs associated with the love of Siegmund and Sieglinde against the more plodding accompaniments to her insistence on rigid rules. Her agitation increases, but it is shrill and impotent, unable to match Wotan's apparent control.

We are already prepared for the idea that Fricka's perspective will be myopic. In *Rheingold*, Loge's rhetorically brilliant introduction of the theft of the gold immediately disturbs Wotan with the dark implications of what has occurred. Fricka, by contrast, with her fixed idea of reviving Wotan's flagging interest in her and keeping him from wandering, fails completely to see the threat produced by forging the gold into the Ring. The only thing that occurs to her with respect to it is the astoundingly trivial question: "*Taugte wohl/ des gold'nen Tandes/ gleissend Geschmeid/ auch Frauen zu schönem Schmuck?* [Might the golden trinket's glittering gem be worn by women and serve as fair adornment?]." Wotan's musical lines, and the rising sequences in cellos and horns that follow, are full of power and menace—but they give way to the vapid lyricism and irrelevant ornamentation of Fricka's phrases. Similarly, at the close of the final scene of *Rheingold*, after Wotan has hidden the doubts that afflict him at this stage, squared his shoulders, and presented his "official view" of the might of Valhalla ("*So grüss' ich die Burg . . . Folge mir Frau:/ in Walhall wohne mit mir!* [Thus I greet the stronghold . . . Follow me wife! In Valhalla dwell with me!]"), Fricka responds with the equally shallow and uncomprehending question: "*Was deutet der Name? Nie, dunkt mich hört' ich ihn nennen* [What does that name mean? I don't think I've ever heard it called that before]." Again, the contrast is reinforced in the music. Wotan's sweeping lines aim at the confident majesty of the opening of Scene 2 (albeit against orchestral tremolandos that suggest the somber thoughts behind the bravado); Fricka sings a simple light phrase—one that might have occurred, in passing, in an eighteenth-century opera.

In *Rheingold* and in the early phases of the debate in Act II of *Walküre*, Fricka's limitations are made very clear. Her conventional moral judgments lack authority, since she has no sense of the dangers to the social order in which they are set; and she appears completely clueless about the broader perspective informing Wotan's plans. She never achieves that sense or that perspective. Indeed, once she has made her decisive intervention, she is no longer necessary, and disappears. But as an attentive listener to *Rheingold* may notice, she recognizes something that Wotan, for all his brain-wracking and understanding, has missed. In the first part of the drama, even before Wotan loses his confidence, she grasps that the contract with the giants is problematic. She worries about the cost of Valhalla, while he airily supposes that some way of fobbing off the giants will be found (Loge will find something that Fasolt and Fafner will accept in place of Freia). By the end of *Rheingold* the roles are reversed, and while Fricka now prattles about the attractiveness of their new home, Wotan realizes that he has paid for it with an "evil wage." Once he has seen the problem, Wotan recognizes its depth. Fricka is too easily satisfied that all will now be well; but she had seen signs of trouble before Wotan did.

In the second phase of the exchange in Act II of *Walküre*, Fricka achieves a more important insight. Wotan has responded to her earlier moralizing by telling her that she has learned nothing and is stuck in antiquated customs despite the fact that the gods' predicament calls for unprecedented action. With an air of superiority that borders on disdain for her obtuseness, he points out that he needs a hero who can do things that are forbidden to the gods. The moral structure of Wotan's reasoning seems very clear: the precepts on which Fricka harps presuppose a stable social order, grounded on laws and contracts. That social order is endangered by the existence of the Ring (and more specifically by the possibility that Alberich will regain the Ring and employ it in the way he threatened in *Rheingold*, exceeding Fricka's worst nightmares). As guardians of laws and contracts, the gods are unable to retrieve the Ring. Hence the need for Project Siegmund—the creation of a free hero who will be able to obtain the Ring and remove the threat. Fricka's scolding (as Wotan protests) appreciates none of this complexity. But at this point the tables turn. She attains epistemic authority, comprehending things he has missed; and in consequence, at least for the moment, and even if only negatively, she attains directive authority. She does so by giving Wotan a hard lesson in the meaning of freedom.

Suddenly, the musical lines set them on terms of complete equality, as Fricka responds in phrases that are strikingly similar to those in which Wotan has delivered his little lesson. From this point on, he will sing with increasing agitation, and ultimately despair, while she grows into a grandeur that we have not heard from her before. Project Siegmund, as Fricka makes painfully clear, is flawed to the point of incoherence. It is motivated, of course, by the principle that Wotan obtains his power through his establishment and enforcement of laws—a status manifested on stage by the spear he wields and reiterated by the descending octave motif that recurs when the rule of law is an issue. For Project Siegmund to succeed, then, there must be a genuine difference between Siegmund's disposing of Fafner and regaining the Ring, and Wotan's doing so. Wotan has convinced himself, by a variety of forms of wishful thinking, that his provision of the conditions under which Siegmund obtains a special weapon leaves the crucial choices to the hero. Fricka's insight is to see that Siegmund is simply a proxy for the god. Wotan hopes to resolve his predicament (and the crisis facing the gods) by engendering supposedly free agents, able to do what he can neither do himself nor command; but this ploy must fail because Siegmund's success is entirely dependent on his—Wotan's—actions. *He* has trained Siegmund, *he* has engineered the encounter in Hunding's hut, *he* has planted the sword and endowed it with magic powers. Even the dodge of allowing Brünnhilde to protect Siegmund is denied him; for Fricka is right to insist that, at this stage of the drama at any rate, Brünnhilde's will is an extension of his own. (Her quick response to his assertion that "The Valkyrie is free to choose," an emphatic "*Nicht doch!* [But no!]," displays an astuteness we would not have expected from her.)

Wotan has no alternative but to cede Fricka epistemic authority; and in bringing it to bear with undeniable force upon his central plan, she gains directive authority to terminate Project Siegmund. Her diagnosis of Siegmund's dependence on his father ("*in ihm treff ich nur dich* [in him I find only you]") is echoed in Wotan's bitter lament to Brünnhilde in the scene that follows Fricka's departure: "*Zum Ekel find' ich nur mich in Allem was ich erwirke!* [To my disgust I always find only myself in all that I bring about!]." Her accusatory rising major sixth (on "*nur dich*") prefigures his anguished rising major seventh (on "*nur mich*"). She departs in triumph, after an extraordinary expression of her sense of the importance of the honor of the gods ("*Deiner ew'gen Gattin heilige Ehre . . .* ")—music with a sweep and majesty that only Wotan (and that only occasionally) has previously achieved, serving as a brief but clear reminder of her own divinity and of her special place as the wife for whom he was once prepared to hazard his remaining eye (*Rheingold*, Scene 2: "*Um dich zum Weib zu gewinnen,/ mein eines Auge/ setzt' ich werbend daran: . . .* [In order to win you as wife, I staked my one remaining eye to woo you]").

Wotan takes her point, and takes it hard; as Wagner's stage directions make plain, the god is shaken and defeated. Is this an over-reaction? We think not. As we shall suggest in the next chapter, Fricka's directive authority threatens not only the current venture of using Siegmund, and the broader project of regaining the Ring, but an even more fundamental goal—one that Wotan has been pursuing from the beginning of the drama and even before in its prehistory. His great aspiration, seemingly on the verge of realization, is now beginning to look like an impossible dream.

Yet Fricka fails to grasp the purposes at which Wotan aims. The decisive judgment she expresses has only negative significance. Even in presenting it, although she is astute about the issues of freedom on which Wotan has lapsed into self-deception, she muddies the crucial point with subsidiary issues, which include not only conventional standards of sexual conduct but also her own dishonor if Wotan holds to his course. Fricka is anxious that she not be shamed by her husband's actions and that the gods not become a laughing stock. (Here she prefigures Gunther's shallow concern with the fame of the Gibichungs — a trivial vanity that will set in motion the final phase of the tragedy.) Wotan does not respond to Fricka's irrelevant additions; for what is devastating to him is not that Project Siegmund would dishonor her, but rather that it rests on a presupposition — of Siegmund's free agency — that he has now come to recognize as false.

Fricka is a foil and an accessory, someone who helps Wotan to a new judgment. Her crucial insight is embedded in a narrow and myopic moral perspective, the inadequacies of which are made clear in her exchange with Wotan. To take the conventional moral status of the relationship between Siegmund and Sieglinde as an appropriate focus for a disapproving judgment would be to misinterpret the *Ring* in a grotesque fashion. There are more encompassing perspectives from which other characters — including, most obviously, Wotan — evaluate various options for themselves and future possibilities for the world, perspectives that strive to go beyond good and evil as Fricka understands those notions. These more perceptive characters arrive at judgments that are more worthy of human allegiance. We can start to follow their efforts by considering where Wotan goes next.

4

Wotan's Challenge

Fricka extracts an oath from Wotan and leaves just as Brünnhilde returns, pointedly telling the Valkyrie that Wotan will explain the course of action he has chosen. Wotan laments his lack of freedom, portraying himself as caught in his own toils; and when Brünnhilde questions him further, he breaks out in passionate grief. But his daughter's devoted concern (beautifully expressed in the simple phrase, "*sieh, Brünnhilde bittet*! [see, Brünnhilde begs you!]"—a phrase that prefigures an even more poignant moment near the close of *Götterdämmerung*) prompts him to an extraordinary and lengthy revelation. Taking stock of his situation, Wotan passes from "the most terrible anguish" to "desperation" (Wagner's stage directions), culminating in a startling expression of his will. Just before we hear a fragment of the motif we associate with the Sword, he declaims: "*nur Eines will ich noch: das Ende—das Ende!* [One thing alone do I still want: the end—the end!]."

We regard this line, sung with utter despondency, wrenched from the god's heart in recognition of his own immediate betrayal of the hero whom he loves, as crucial to the understanding of the entire *Ring*. The most natural way to hear it, and correct enough as far as it goes, is to suppose that it involves a *change* of attitude: prior to the disturbing exchange with Fricka, Wotan was after something different; now all he wants to do is to end it all—including everything he has achieved. That interpretation receives support from the line before the passage we have quoted, in which Wotan announces that he is abandoning his work. It also appears to accord with what immediately follows—his profession of readiness to abdicate in favor of Alberich who, with his son (whose birth was foretold by Erda), will "see to that end."

To stop at that, however, would oversimplify Wotan's problem and impoverish the drama. Of course, there is a change here. Wotan temporarily accedes to something that has been anathema to him almost from the beginning: the domination of Alberich. And that would indeed be an ending *of a particular kind*. But he says and means something more, of larger significance. In his momentary despondency, there is just one thing he says he *still* wants: "*nur Eines will ich noch: das Ende—das Ende!* [only one thing do I still want: the end—the end!]" Of the things he has been wanting, he has (at least for now) been reduced to wanting this one alone. But what does this mean?

In *Walküre*, Wotan's immediate goal has been to promote the success of Siegmund. He appears to have pursued that goal as a means to regaining the Ring. In its turn, regaining the Ring would enable him to consolidate his power, and that would allow him not only to establish but also to secure a new kind of order in the world. But there is a different way of placing Project Siegmund within a hierarchy of goals. We might view Wotan as having recognized already in *Rheingold* that his overt larger end—the consolidation and perpetuation of his system of law and order, which would make the world an enduringly better and more admirable place—is beyond even his power and contrivance, and thus that what he has striven for from a time in the distant past (well before the opening of the *Ring*) is unattainable. His revised task, therefore, from late in *Rheingold* on, has been that of *finding an ending*. Knowing that his fledgling order must pass, he wants a conclusion that does not simply make a mockery of all he has stood for.

The temporary change in Wotan's attitude at the nadir of his despondency consists in his coming to despair of being able to bring about a *meaningful* ending; for a moment he flirts with extreme pessimism and allows that his own passing can be the triumph of Alberich. That, of course, *would* make a mockery of all he has struggled to achieve, and, as we shall see, Wotan does not continue to believe that nothing better is possible. The line we have quoted is literally correct: he still wants one thing he has been trying to achieve—an ending; but, for the moment at any rate, he has come to acquiesce in the very worst-case ending scenario that he has wanted most to avoid. This, however, is not his final verdict. He is groping toward a positive achievement: that of a *tragic* ending. And he at length finds it spectacularly, three long operas later; for, with great fittingness, his consummation in the flames arising from Siegfried's pyre is his consummation, and vice versa—as is Brünnhilde's.

We readily concede that our proposal about Wotan's deepest aspirations is puzzling, and we shall want to heighten the sense of its strangeness. First, however, we want to motivate it by showing how it illuminates some important moments in the early part of the drama. '*Ende*' and its cognates resonate in the pregnant fourth scene of *Rheingold*. When Erda appears, the rising phrase with which she is associated brings home to us at once that this is a grave and solemn moment. It is an appearance that has deep significance for Wotan and his plans. As Erda proceeds, she tells Wotan that the urgency of his predicament has brought her to him. Three times, with phrases that rise and crescendo to a fortissimo top E, she tells him to "hearken" ("*Höre!*"). Immediately after doing so, she gives what seems to be her main message: "*Alles was ist, endet./ Ein düst'rer Tag/ dämmert den Göttern:/ dir rath' ich, meide den Ring!* [All that is, ends. A dark day dawns for the gods: I counsel you, shun the Ring!]." Its significance is underscored by the weight and intensity of the music to which these lines are set.

There is a familiar puzzle about this announcement, first raised by Wagner's friend Röckel: Why, if Wotan gives up the Ring, do the gods have to be consumed? In fact, of course, Erda's declaration that the day of the gods (like everything else) is to end is not at all hypothetical. She is not saying that the ending of the gods will come if Wotan keeps the Ring (and thereby hinting that the ending could be averted if he gives it up). She leaves no doubt about it: "All that is, ends"—and the gods are no exception. And, she implies, their time is up. The musical gravity of the scene is extraordinary—we the audience, and Wotan too, know that she expresses the world's destiny. She cannot be argued with, or dismissed, and the only appropriate response, even for a "dauntless god," is "care and fear." Her counsel to Wotan, to shun the ring, is obviously given in connection with the prospects of his ending; but its purpose cannot be to try to persuade him to come to his senses before it is too late. Her lines are only heard in the way that generates Röckel's puzzle if one supposes that Wotan could have no motivation to let the Ring go unless, by doing so, he could avoid the end of his order. But, from our perspective, the point is not that he has a way out if he is clever or resourceful enough to take it. Rather, it is that there are *endings and endings*. Erda is reminding Wotan of something he knows, if not fully explicitly: he, too, must pass. The task for him, in view of the inescapability of his approaching ending, is to find *the right kind* of ending—and retaining the Ring would preclude that.

And Wotan responds. First, of course, he does give up the Ring. Then, after Fafner has felled Fasolt, he is left—as Erda warned he would be—in care and fear ("*Sorg' und Furcht*"). His anxiety gives way to a resolution about how to end his doubts: "*wie sie zu enden/ lehre mich Erda* [Erda will teach me how to end them]." We hear these lines, sung to brooding inward music, as carrying a double resonance: Erda will teach him how to end his care and fear by teaching him how to end his aspirations, his projects, everything. So he decides to go to her. At the climax of his revelation to Brünnhilde, Erda will be recalled: after Wotan has sung "*das Ende, das Ende*," we hear the ascending phrase that heralded her original appearance.

Moreover, much earlier in the scene, when Wotan has been describing to Brünnhilde the tortuous path that has led him to his current predicament, he explicitly recalls Erda's warning and its connection to his desire to know of the "end everlasting [*vor ewigem Ende*]." As he sings of Erda, his tone is hushed, almost awestruck; but the following line changes the mood to one of nervous energy, as Wotan becomes more insistent than he has yet appeared in this scene, confessing his desire to know more of this prophesied end. We take this passage to testify to the depth with which Erda's warning has impressed him: in ways of which he is not yet fully conscious, he has come to appreciate the inevitability of his end.

Erda is not alone in explicitly recognizing the coming ending. Loge does so as well. With the lyricism that often accompanies his ironic commentaries, he congratulates Wotan on his luck when one of his enemies (Fafner) murders the other (Fasolt)—a judgment that surely serves to fortify Wotan's sense of unease. Then Loge stands back as the gods enter Valhalla. His mordant remarks ("*Ihrem Ende eilen sie zu* . . . [They hurry toward their end . . .]"), almost demanding to be sung in *Sprechstimme* (as, in his brilliant evocation of Loge, Gerhard Stolze performs them), contrast his own knowledge with that of Donner and Froh, Freia and Fricka—the unreflective lesser gods, who are blithely ignorant of their impending fate. Loge has seen through the sham that this is a triumphant entry, has seen that it is not the consolidation of Wotan's power but the beginning of the end of him and all that he has stood for—and the choices he sees for himself concern what role he will play in the process of ending. (We shall have more to say about him below.)

Wotan is surely different, not only from the clear-eyed Loge but also from the gods who march confidently over the bridge into the new stronghold. Before the official celebration of Valhalla, he has reflected on the consequences of his previous actions in ways that echo Erda: the night is coming. The concerned seriousness of his reflections on the struggles to build Valhalla give way to an even darker mood with the falling seventh ("*Es naht die nacht*"); at this point, we believe, *only* a "great idea" could stir Wotan into the anxious bravado with which he summons the gods to enter Valhalla.

We hear a mixture of emotions and understandings here, neither confidence (or relief) that all is now well, nor firm acceptance that his own passing is unavoidable. Loge's dismissal of the Rhinemaidens' plea for the return of the gold and sardonically celebratory lines about the gods and their splendor are at once at seeming variance and also in deeper accord with his anticipation of the coming end. We sense a dramatic tension in Wotan's case in this climactic moment, between his own grand words about Valhalla and the uneasy intimations of finitude they mask, reflected in his vexed outburst upon hearing the distant cries of the Rhinemaidens. But for him to cross the bridge in the spirit the occasion seems to warrant, the premonitions planted by Erda must be firmly, even brusquely, suppressed.

Majestic as it appears (and sounds), Valhalla's grandeur is all appearance, like the "Rainbow Bridge" leading to it. The permanence it was meant to guarantee was a beautiful dream; but a dream it was and remains. The end of the *Ring*'s beginning is already the beginning of its and Wotan's ending. And try as he might to convince himself and everyone else otherwise, Wotan must know this in his heart of hearts, as Loge does much more clearly. The difference in meaning that this prospect has for the two of them, however, could hardly be greater.

5

Meaning and the Tradition

Having framed Wotan's problem as that of finding an ending, we now want to approach it from a more general perspective by way of reflection on the larger problem of how to think about the significance human life may have or acquire. In this chapter we shall sketch a space of responses to that larger problem, responses that will be familiar enough to most readers from religious, philosophical, and literary sources. By doing so, we hope to set a context in which to locate this problem and a related major theme of the *Ring*. The centrality of these questions to the *Ring*, we suggest, has much to do with the depth and seriousness of its mythology—and with its enduring fascination.

The question of what does or might give human life meaning and significance surely antedates written attempts to deal with it; but literary, religious, and philosophical texts—including the works of Feuerbach and Schopenhauer that Wagner studied—offer a variety of responses. Lives are purported to gain meaning through fulfilling the purposes of a divine creator, for example; or through the attainment of purity of mind, heart, soul, or will; or through the intellectual pursuit of knowledge, understanding, or wisdom; or through the institution and enforcement of principles of justice;

or through the efforts of human beings to help, support, and comfort one another; or through the exercise of human creativity; or through love and the exclusive relationships it engenders. We shall distinguish three main ways of approaching the question: one that sees a source of meaning in an order that is independent of human beings; another that rejects the question entirely, and seeks to deflate it and rid us of the desire to ask it and the craving for an answer to it; and a third that takes the question seriously, but contends that any answer to it must recognize the source of meaning to be in ourselves. (There is, of course, a fourth approach—one that both admits the importance of the problem and denies any possibility of solution. Schopenhauer's pessimism is a prominent version of that approach.)

Mideastern religions and their Western progeny, exemplified by Christianity, have tended to take the first approach. For the devout Christian, the meaning of a human life is to be found in one's relationship to God and one's submission to or accordance with God's will. The ideal life is an offering to God, following the course ordained for it, as a human life in general and as one's own specific life in particular; and the meaning of this life in this world is conceived in relation to the prospect of eternal life—and of either bliss or damnation—in a world to come. Philosophical theologians have explored the contours of this ideal, but the most powerful presentation of it surely occurs in Dante's *Commedia*, with its vivid inventory of the possibilities of human life and their relative positions in the divine hierarchy. In 1855, Wagner apparently read Dante for the first time; and he reported his reaction in a pair of letters to Liszt (who was, at the time, at work on his *Dante Symphony*). Wagner expresses his admiration for the first two thirds of Dante's great poem but advises Liszt that the setting of the last part, the *Paradiso*, is likely to be problematic. This, Wagner suggests, is the weakest section, and he confesses that he has "had to revert to an historical standpoint" to do Dante justice. He concludes:

> In the "Paradiso," the poem seems to me to amount to no more than a "divine comedy" which is ruined for me both as a

> participant and a spectator. The really perplexing problem among all these other questions is always how, in this terrible world of ours, beyond which there is only nothingness, it might be possible to infer the existence of a God who would make life's immense sufferings merely something *apparent*, while the redemption we long for is seen as something entirely real that may be consciously enjoyed.

Wagner has seen why religious answers to the question of the point of human lives are so unsatisfactory, their evident appeal notwithstanding. It is not simply that the existence of a divine creator and lord of the universe is of such dubious plausibility, but moreover that the received ways of elaborating the creator's purposes simply fail to make sense of life.

The problem arises with especial force on reading Dante, not because he is crass or unresourceful, but precisely because of the thoroughness he brings to articulating the theological picture. Dante does not fudge. We enter Hell, learning that the motivations for creating this place of eternal torment were justice, divine power, highest wisdom, and primal love ("*Giustizia mosse il mio alto fattore;/ fecemi la divina podestate,/ la somma sapienza e'l primo amore.* [Justice moved my high maker, in power divine, wisdom supreme, primal love]" [*Inferno* III, 4–6.] As we follow Dante and his guide through the descending circles, we encounter people in whom a single flaw has condemned them to excruciating torments. (One of the most striking examples is Pier della Vigna in Canto XIII, who, falsely accused and blinded, committed suicide. Pier now takes the form of a thornbush, pecked at by hideous harpies; and at the day of judgment, his body will be hung on the thorns, intensifying his agony.) On the mountain of Purgatory, the laboring souls have some hope, for, as they climb, they come closer to bliss. Although they suffer torment, there is a limit to their afflictions, and in the end, their burdens will give way to the great reward.

As Wagner saw, the bliss they are offered must be extraordinary, for it is to redeem the severe penances of Purgatory and to reveal the justice, wisdom, and love behind the horrors of the Inferno. Then, as he puts it to Liszt, Beatrice emerges from "a car out of a church pageant," growing colder and more scholastic as she becomes more radiant. The bliss so eagerly anticipated becomes, in the *Paradiso*, a blaze of light in which theological abstractions correspond to the degrees of luminescence. Despite the extraordinary poetic achievement, it seems to us that Wagner's response was just right. If we return to the gates of hell and reread the inscription, there is no doubt that we can make sense of the infernal circles in light of divine power—but *wisdom*? *justice*? and, especially, *love*?

Of course, we never see Dante's God (the blaze is too bright and the earthly soul must stop short); but nothing we are given in *Paradiso* comes remotely close to explaining how a just (never mind loving) creator would institute the atrocities and penances of the earlier books. Interestingly, a later Christian epic, Milton's *Paradise Lost*, does give a piece of the divine explanation for the sufferings of unredeemed humanity. Apropos of the Fall of Adam and Eve, which God foresees, the Creator shrugs the divine shoulders, asking, with intolerable smugness: "Whose fault? Whose but his own?" Of course, although Milton's official project was to "justify the ways of God to men"—an apparently bizarre enterprise, but one that may have made sense to those who felt that their attempts to work the divine will on earth had been mysteriously frustrated (Milton, like Dante, wrote in political disappointment)—a long tradition of his eminent readers has held that he was "of the devil's party." *Paradise Lost*, magnificent poem that it is, succeeds no better than Dante's *Commedia* in showing how human lives are endowed with significance by way of the sorts of divine purposes and policies to which Dante and Milton give classic expression. They inspire instead the response that a lord of all creation with plans like that would be a chilling prospect.

Theologians and philosophers of religion have fared little better in their attempts to resolve the fundamental difficulties here. If our deeds and mundane sufferings make a difference to our fate in the hereafter, then it is appropriate to ask for the details of how the route to bliss is blocked or delayed, how the ultimate bliss compensates for the tribulations along the way, how denying that bliss to some (if indeed some are denied) accords with the demands of justice (and love). If what we do makes no difference, then our earthly life becomes pointless, an irrelevant prelude to something more glorious which is, inexplicably, postponed for us. In reading Dante, Wagner saw the logical structure of the problem; and we think it far from unreasonable of him to have written it off as insoluble.

It is quite likely that the adult Wagner had many reasons for rejecting the idea that lives obtain their meaning through their relation to the divine will. As far as we know, however, he never seriously entertained our second way of dealing with questions about the meaningfulness of human life. The idea that such questions are not worth asking and that they are wrongly posed or pompously empty, is often accompanied by a celebration of the ordinary. Literary examples abound. Shakespeare's Falstaff, for example, reminds his fellows of the joys of life, joys not to be sacrificed in the name of abstractions. ("What is honor? A word.") Kazantzakis's Zorba the Greek also sounds similar themes. One can hardly imagine spirits farther removed from Wagner's, or sensibilities more foreign to that of the *Ring*.

Those sensibilities are perhaps most evident in the two last novels of James Joyce. In *Ulysses*, Joyce transposes the epic strivings of Homer's heroes to early twentieth century Dublin, where conversation over cocoa in the wee hours or the memory of an early love can serve to affirm the value of a life. Leopold Bloom, who has wandered through Dublin, comes home to his unfaithful wife. He is accompanied by Stephen Dedalus, and the two are, for a short hour, juxtaposed as father and son. Possibly, even probably, their brief intimacy will never be repeated, yet it is intrinsically worthwhile. So too, despite the infidelity, Molly Bloom's upsurge of sympathy for her husband softens the end of his hard journey; and, from her own perspective, despite all the disappointments of her life, including those of her coarse new love, the end is a famous affirmation, a closing "Yes!"

In his late masterpiece *Finnegans Wake* (perhaps best thought of as a Portrait of the Artist as an Aging Man), the pretensions of seeking any grand justification for one's life are even more brilliantly punctured. Joyce's nameless protagonist, dimly accused of some seamy transgression, eventually speaks in his own defense, recounting the accomplishments of a life. He boasts of founding a city, a wonderful metropolis, with civic amenities galore, peace and tranquility. The boast is idle, the city a dream, but the speaker needs no justification. All of the sides of life, grand or respectable, mundane or shameless, are to be accepted for what they are. To defend them is folly, and so, equally, is to ask for their point.

None of this is to deny that parts of human life may be painful, that aging may bring sorrow, and that death may be frightening. Falstaff leaves the stage in *Henry IV, Part II*, to the new king's rebuke ("I know thee not, old man: fall to thy prayers"). The failing flesh of the protagonists of Joyce's *Wake* can only manage an ugly and inadequate expression of their waning desires. And although the morning dawns in leafy beauty, raising the prospect of a walk, a few moments of companionship and joy in nature, the end is very different, hard and chilling. But there is no alternative to acquiescence, and no end, but rather renewal. For Joyce's book is, famously, circular (the book of "Doublends Jined"), and human lives go on, with their mix of joys and pains, without the need to find a point or a meaning.

We have distinguished two ways of responding to questions about how to identify the significance of human lives: one (which we take to be unpromising at best) is to look to some divine order; the other, exemplified in Shakespeare's creation of Falstaff and in Joyce's two last novels, is to reject the question in favor of a comic celebration of the ordinary. Neither would have satisfied Wotan— or his creator.

6

Meaning and the *Ring*

If Wagner could have been persuaded to address himself explicitly to this challenge, he would not have been at a loss for words. An initial response he might have given is prefigured in Wotan's replies to Fricka. It would charge that giving up on the question of some larger meaning in life and settling instead for the acceptance and relishing of the rich if fleeting smorgasbord of experience requires a prior judgment about the significance of the conditions that make possible human life with this celebrated richness. Fricka's failing is to obsess about the rules of morality without worrying about the framework under which the rule of law is possible, or considering whether there might be anything else that matters more. The Joyce-Falstaff counterpart to it is to invite us to celebrate and affirm human lives as they are, without considering either the presuppositions or the limitations of such lives. Unless a social backdrop had been instituted and maintained, for example, there would be nothing recognizable as *human* existence—the lives of members of our species would be (in Hobbes's memorable phrase) "solitary, poor, nasty, brutish and short." Hence the Joycean-Falstaffian celebrations tacitly suppose that larger meaning and significance and point can be attained in and through some human lives after all—namely, those that seek and serve to create and establish the conditions of the possibility of such rich human modes of existence.

But Wagner surely would not have stopped there. He quite conceivably could have claimed that there are genuinely higher ends than a glass of sack or a cup of cocoa, and the companionship of the tavern or the transitory connection of two hitherto independent lives. The democratic tolerance of finding satisfaction in the mundane would strike him as a lazy way of evading a genuine question. Here he could have drawn on examples of admirable higher humanity that have informed philosophical discussion for millennia, such as the life dedicated to theoretical understanding (Aristotle's devotee of philosophy or the great natural scientist); the life focused on extending the scope of justice (the vigorous opponent of slavery or the ardent social revolutionary); the life committed to relieving human suffering (medical practitioners who struggle against diseases in poor nations, social workers in slums); the life of the creative artist (perhaps Wagner would serve as his own paradigm!); and the life dedicated to the expression of love (again, he might see himself in this role). These lives, he might suggest, have point or significance because they realize something of higher value than simple everyday satisfactions. Like Feuerbach, he wants to explore the possibility that there are ways of transforming our natural condition.

As we understand him, Wagner *starts* from the view that there are more and less significant ways of living a human life, taking seriously the question of what grounds or engenders significance. To be sure, his encounter with Schopenhauer profoundly impressed and influenced him; and Schopenhauer is notoriously and avowedly the ultimate pessimist, bent upon making the case that human life not only has no significance whatsoever but that all life is just a pathetic spectacle of meaningless striving, struggling, and suffering. Wagner's professed embrace of Schopenhauer notwithstanding, however, we do not think that the Wagner of the *Ring* even comes close to subscribing to the view that the only significance life can have is the negative significance attaching to pointless suffering, and that oblivion would be preferable to its existence and continuation on any actually possible terms. He may at times have thought that he did; but his music and operatic art—in the *Ring* anyway—say otherwise, far more decisively and convincingly.

But, Schopenhauerian pessimism aside, there are two interesting and important challenges to the view that the exemplars of the previous paragraph could endow human existence with point or meaning—challenges that do not turn on some purported inadequacy of the traditional list. (We doubt whether any additions or substitutions to that list would affect the argument.) Both of them resonate with what is attractive in an approach we (and Wagner) have already rejected: the idea that significance descends from something higher, something beyond humanity—in short, something divine. For in both cases the heart of the concern is a characteristic that distinguishes us from the gods, apparently condemning us to meaninglessness. The first version appeals to the fact of human finitude to make the case that the transience of human life itself, and therefore of the achievements of even the most exemplary of human lives along with it, renders them ultimately insignificant. The second concedes that there are values that would give significance to these lives but denies that such values can ever be sufficiently realized. It assesses human lives generally, however exemplary, as possibly valiant but inevitably flawed struggles to reach an impossible goal.

Here again, we can turn to literature to elaborate the challenges we have in mind. Consider the Faust legend. Goethe's version is clearly the greater work; but the aspect of the legend on which we want to focus is more powerfully expressed in Marlowe's *Doctor Faustus*. In both instances, we begin with an apparently successful but discontented scholar, who reviews his accomplishments and their limitations. Marlowe's Faustus surveys in turn the major branches of potential human accomplishment: Philosophy (the accumulation of knowledge), Medicine (the bringing of relief to human lives), Law (the administration of justice), and Theology (the service and worship of God). None of these satisfies him, and none can be seen as lending significance to his future; that is why he turns to Necromancy and the famous pact with Mephistopheles.

But why is none of the respectable alternatives enough? Marlowe's character sums up his discontent in a telling line: "Yet still thou art but Faustus, and a man!" The slighting reference to his humanity can be taken either as a signal of the finitude of his potential achievements (in the style of the first version of the challenge) or as indicating their incompleteness and imperfection (along the lines of the second). In the context of his renunciation of theology, of course, they also express his determination to be independent of an order of significance stemming from the purposes of some higher being; but, since we have already discussed and dismissed the religious option, we shall say no more about this part of Faustus's attitude.

Should Faustus be so gloomy? One way to understand his search for significance is to see it as aiming at achievements that will endure not only after his own death but after the extinction of the species. To have a valuable life, he might think, one should be able to look down from the perspective of the universe and see significant consequences that flow from that life, to identify an enduring difference that the life has made. Human knowledge, aid to other human beings, the promotion of justice, human love (which does not, of course, figure on the list—an omission that is central to Goethe's version), all are transitory. Even if Faustus passes his knowledge on, even if others appreciate what he has discovered, or build on it, there will come a time when humanity is no more, and, at that point, what he has achieved will no longer matter. If he cures his fellows, or secures for them fair treatment, this will mean nothing if their lives are not worthwhile—and if their lives only gain a meaning from aid to others, we are headed for a regress that must terminate when humankind has vanished. And why will love have mattered, once all lovers are gone?

Many people are moved to despair or desperation by these considerations. We are not—and neither, we believe, was Wagner. Viewing human lives from this bleakly cosmic perspective can easily induce a pessimistic resolve to abnegate all willing (Schopenhauer's recommendation) or a bitter nihilism (perhaps like that expressed by Wotan when he proposes abdicating in favor of Alberich?). Or, alternatively, it may prompt an embrace of the Joyce-Falstaff view, with its dismissal of all lofty aspirations as folly, its commendation of the simpler and more readily attainable delights of human existence to be savored while we can, and its injunction to acquiesce in disappointment and defeat, even in our own passing. But before one opts for pessimism or nihilism, or settles for the celebration of the ordinary, it is worth pausing, for there are serious questions about the Faustian challenge we have reconstructed. Why should we suppose that the appropriate perspective from which to render judgment is that of the timeless observer of the whole universe? Why should the standard of significance require that an accomplishment make a difference that endures for all time? Why should the point of actions that benefit others depend on the uses they make of their new opportunities, or upon these uses together with the further consequences, the ripple effect from them? Cannot there be value in a love's transient reality, that transience notwithstanding? And in its *having been*, even if it is no more?

The first form of the challenge only compels if all these questions must receive very specific answers, and we do not see good reasons for *any* of the responses they would require. But we take the second version of the Faustian challenge—the idea of inevitable incompleteness and imperfection—to be a more serious one. Human attempts at knowledge, one might suppose, are inevitably limited, partial, and distorted. Justice is ever only imperfect. Comfort and aid can only be given in inadequate measures. And human love is flawed and vulnerable to corruption and erosion. Thus, one might suppose, genuine values though these may be, human efforts to realize them are doomed to fail, falling so far short as to be exercises in futility.

While these concerns are more compelling than those that stem from recognition of our finitude, once again the conclusion is too quick. This challenge does not carry the day unless it can be convincingly argued that the best of human efforts do not amount to much—or, at any rate, amount to too little to compensate for their liabilities and shortcomings. Implicit in the considerations about the partial character of our efforts is the idea that we achieve nothing if we are not completely successful. But there is no good reason to think in such "all or nothing" terms. We take it to be perfectly legitimate to respond to the challenge by declaring that the approximations we may actually achieve can be genuinely valuable: the doctors who minister to the victims of plague may alleviate only a fraction of human suffering, but we may nonetheless reasonably view what they do as a significant achievement. Similarly, those who contribute to our understanding of the world or of one another, those whose works of art provide new visions and possibilities, those who bring light into the lives of the people for whom they care, all manage *something*. Contested though it may be, one of the legacies of the Enlightenment is that we can regard exemplary lives as meaningful in terms of their imperfect realization of the values of knowledge, compassion, justice, and love.

There is a different way of responding to the form of Faustian discontent that emphasizes the imperfections of our efforts to realize genuine values. Instead of (or in addition to) finding meaning in approximation (in imperfect realization), one can discern significance in the striving itself (as Faust learned to do). So, for example, one might feel that the work of doctors among a plague-ridden population gains point not because (or to the extent that) they approximate a condition of cure or eradication of the disease, but because of their determination to do whatever they can, however hopelessly inadequate it may be. (Camus explores something like this idea in *The Plague*.) From this perspective, the extent of their success may not be the crucial issue that settles whether what they do has any significance—they may fall radically short, and yet their actions may prove deeply worthwhile. But it *does* matter that they not be simply defeated. If their treatments are utterly ineffective, leaving their patients as badly off as they would have been without them, or if they serve only to make matters worse (as blood-letting used to do), then their striving will indeed have been pointless. We see no good reason, however, to assimilate all cases of imperfection to those of this sort.

With the foregoing discussion in mind, we now can identify a very plausible line of thinking leading to an interesting philosophical conclusion. We shall set it out in a series of steps, to make its logic clear.

- The question of whether and how human life may be endowed with significance is of the utmost importance and deserves to be taken seriously.
- That question need not—and perhaps cannot plausibly—be answered by reference to the purposes of some external agency (e.g., a divine creator).
- The answer also is not dictated by the plausibility of the idea of the perfect attainment and unending perpetuation of the realization of values transcending those of merely natural existence, either in this life and world or beyond them.
- If there is a positive answer, it may—and perhaps even must—be given instead in terms of the possibility of the realization of such values in more limited, imperfect, and transient ways, in this life and world.
- Exceptional significance attaches to efforts that not only realize such values in finitely attainable ways in one's own life but moreover contribute to the possibility of their realization in the lives of others as well.
- What matters most, however, is contributing to and participating in the transfiguration of merely natural and commonplace existence, in ways revealing and expressing its capacity to be endowed with and enriched by such values.
- This conceivably might be done by instituting and maintaining conditions conducive to their concrete realization and perpetuation on a broad scale; but that is difficult at best in the short term, and impossible in the long run.
- This also—and ultimately more importantly—can be done even in failure and defeat, if a transient and imperfect realization of important values finds an ending that preserves

> and even enhances its significance, and so is vindicating despite all.

This philosophical position, we think, is that of the *Ring*. And the final proposition, we suggest, conveys what Wotan gropes toward but never fully grasps—and what Brünnhilde finally understands, and enables them both to realize. If we are right, Wagner belongs with the philosophers, poets, dramatists, and novelists who have responded to one of the deepest questions we can ask. His treatment of it in the *Ring*, we suggest, involves an attempt to conceive the possibility and attainability of a special kind of humanly attainable significance—one that is beyond all optimism and pessimism alike, and that is at once deeply tragic and profoundly affirmative.

If this is correct—and we shall articulate and defend the view below—Wagner both drew on his two main philosophical sources and went beyond them to a distinctive position of his own. The problem of the possible meaningfulness of human life is obviously central to the thought of both Feuerbach and Schopenhauer, the one contending that the problem can be solved relatively directly through the cultivation of a kind of community fostering the transformation of our animal nature into higher forms of humanity, the other dismissing any direct solution as a fantasy. While Wagner takes very seriously the reasons that move Schopenhauer to his pessimistic judgment, he also draws upon some of the possibilities that inspire Feuerbach. In this way he explores a different kind of response to the problem—not a direct solution, but one holding out the prospect of something like victory even in failure and defeat.

While we see how one might diverge in various ways and for various reasons from Wagner's philosophical position in the *Ring*, our interpretation takes it to be an intriguing and powerful view that warrants our respect and deserves serious attention by anyone who considers the questions at issue to be meaningful and important. In any event, it is an animating view that makes the *Ring* much more than a musical drama, fit only for adults of a late-Romantic persuasion and post-Christian sensibility for whom what the Enlightenment offers is not enough. (We suspect that it was because the early Nietzsche saw the Wagner of the *Ring* in something like this way that he responded so strongly and positively to him—and that it was also because Nietzsche subsequently came to see the Wagner of *Parsifal* as having relapsed into a pathological version of the religious approach to the significance of human life, tending toward pessimism or nihilism, that he reacted so strongly and negatively first to the late Wagner, and then to the whole "Case of Wagner.")

We can now explain more clearly what we mean by the problem of finding an ending. Striving to achieve something ultimately unattainable can make sense only if it does not issue in *blank defeat*—in a state of affairs essentially no different from the starting point, or in a conclusion that negates the value that was sought. As we have already suggested, and as we shall argue further in later chapters, Wotan's quest, from late in *Rheingold* on, is to find an ending that is not such a defeat. In his despondency, as he proclaims "*das Ende*" to be the only thing he now wants, he is prepared to embrace *any* ending—even the blank defeat of yielding the field to the likes of Alberich. But that bitter abnegation is not the last word for him—or at least, not yet. And it certainly is not the final verdict of the *Ring* itself.

There is a good deal more about Wagner's position in the *Ring* that remains to be considered. We have so far said nothing about what he thinks matters most, making life worth living and death worth dying—although it is not hard to guess that love (in some form or another) will have something to do with it. Nor have we probed the *Ring*'s treatment of the question of the background conditions against which meaningful lives become humanly possible. These are topics to be taken up as we continue our excursion through the drama in the chapters that follow. We do hope, however, that the foregoing discussion has served both to connect Wagner's *Ring* with important human issues and to link him to other great artists who have explored this philosophical territory.

7

Wotan's Project

Wotan is a god with a past. He regrets part of that past at the end of *Rheingold*; and a naïve construal might suppose that his troubles begin with the decision to build Valhalla, based on a contract he does not intend to keep. In his long explanation to Brünnhilde (*Walküre*, Act II, Scene 2), however, he hints at earlier misdeeds, characterizing himself as one who "longed in my heart for power [*verlangte nach Macht mein Muth*]: impelled by the rage of impulsive desires [*von jäher Wünsche Wüten gejagt*], I won for myself the world." At the beginning of *Götterdämmerung* we learn more about all this, as the First Norn sings of the "dauntless god" who sacrificed an eye, and who broke a branch from the World-Ash. Wotan fashioned that branch into a spear, which turned out to have remarkable power and which he then used to bind the world's denizens by laws and contracts—in ways that were not always entirely aboveboard. And so began a career in which, he has to admit, he was at times "*unwissend trugvoll* [heedlessly deceitful]"—deceitful without giving it a second thought, readily and unself-consciously taking advantage of those with whom he was dealing whenever it suited his purposes to do so, and "acting unscrupulously [*untreue übt' ich*]." Wotan's system of law and order thus was established by means that were very much at odds with its spirit and general character. The fateful bargain with Fasolt and Fafner comes relatively late in this history.

Did Wotan's acts of "heedless deceit" begin with the wrenching of that branch from the World-Ash? There is no reason to think so. The First Norn conjures an image of a being already driven by a longing for power. That longing, Wotan tells Brünnhilde, came when he tired of the delights of "youthful love" (to which, however, he did not exactly become indifferent, and from which he subsequently was far from abstinent). Like Alberich, much later, Wotan turned from love to power; and he manifested that turn in an action that wrested something from its natural surround—the branch that became his spear corresponding interestingly to the gold that subsequently was fashioned into the Ring.

There are obvious parallels between Wotan and Alberich, parallels confirmed by the names introduced for each at various stages of the *Ring*. In *Rheingold*, Loge refers to "*der Nibelung Nacht-Alberich* [the Nibelung Night-Alberich]." Much later, in the riddle duel of Act I of *Siegfried*, the Wanderer (Wotan, in his hands-off, ironist mode) describes himself as "*Licht-Alberich* [Light-Alberich]"; and, one act later, he calls the dwarf "*Schwarz-Alberich* [Black-Alberich]." One might propose that this reflects Wotan's abnegation of power after Act II of *Walküre*, when he seems to give up his determination to try to control the world's future. On this view, "black" and "night" are to be associated with the lust for domination, while "light" is suggestive of the idea that he has freed himself from this urge. But this, we think, would be a mistake. The contrast is better understood in terms of significant differences going back to the distant events recalled in *Götterdämmerung*—and possibly even earlier.

Alberich has been despised, ridiculed, and frustrated—perhaps not only by the Rhinemaidens, for he refers to "your lovely women who spurned my wooing" (*Rheingold*, Scene 3); and both Fasolt and Fafner express irritation (at least) at his past actions (*Rheingold*, Scene 2). When he trades love for wealth and power, it is clear what he intends. He plans to impose his will upon the world, subjecting men and women alike to his power—most crudely by forcing "your lovely women" to submit to his desire, as he brags to Wotan. (His repudiation of love thus clearly does not extend to his craving for sexual gratification—no doubt to be nasty, brutish, and short, but definitely not solitary; although by this point it may well be that he craves more to wield and flaunt power than to satisfy his lust, and that the latter desire is now for him simply another expression of the former craving.) His exchange with Hagen in *Götterdämmerung* makes it apparent that he is driven by a longing for vengeance and a desire to humiliate those who have crossed his earlier endeavors; and the grim vocal lines he sings in this scene provide a naked presentation of how central hatred has become to his psychological life.

Wotan is different. We have no sense of his wanting to use his power to glorify himself, to coerce sexual favors from unwilling women, or to amass a horde of treasures. Nor does he seem to find the exercise of power intrinsically gratifying. Perhaps it is an older and wiser Wotan we now see, for whom power has lost the charm it may once have had for him, at least in prospect. On our view, however, Wotan's original quest—the quest that led him to the World-Ash, and to the sacrifice of his eye—was not for power as such but for something else, to which the power he sought was to be a *means*. To what end? Our answer will supplement the suggestion about "finding an ending" advanced in the previous chapter. But first, we must lay some groundwork.

Wotan is quite willing to acknowledge (at least to Brünnhilde) that he wanted to "rule the world," and takes some satisfaction in having come to do so, however tenuously. (*Walküre*, Act II, Scene 2). Yet we have no sense of grandiose boasting in this confession—the kind of bragging in which Alberich might have indulged—for the musical line is spare and angular, almost offhand. Wotan gives little by way of elaborating his motivations, other than admitting to Brünnhilde that he once had "longed for power [*verlangte nach Macht*]"; but he says something to Fricka as they are about to enter Valhalla that offers a clue. After she asks him what its name means, he replies that its meaning will become clear to her if his dreams come true—or, more precisely: "What my courage, overpowering fear, discovered to me, if it lives triumphant, will be revealed to you! [*Was, mächtig der Furcht mein Muth mir erfand, wenn siegend es lebt—leg' es den Sinn dir dar!*]." This is never spelled out, and of course is never revealed, either to Fricka or to anyone else, since Wotan's designs most certainly do *not* triumph; indeed, the musical setting of his lines suggests that the success of his schemes is very much in doubt (for him as well as for us). But the general sense of his yearnings seems clear enough to us. Wotan aspired not merely to rule the world as it was, but to change it—and to change it in a way that would improve it greatly by establishing a new sort of order in it.

Throughout the *Ring*, we are given many indications of what the world is like when it is not brought into the sort of order Wotan struggles to create. The best side of this primordial state is represented by Erda, and the Norns at their weaving. They have an intuitive attunement to the rhythms of the natural world. They have little, however, by way of articulate knowledge of it, and it never even enters their heads to make anything more of it than it already is and always has been. They simply go with its flow. And more significantly, their mode of existence does not translate into any meaningful—or even viable—form of human life. The haunting ascending phrase associated with Erda echoes the opening music of *Rheingold*, emphasizing her deep connection with the natural state of the world, and its gravity immediately makes us aware that she has a profound intuitive understanding of that natural state, even if that understanding is never fully articulated. The motif immediately establishes her as having a certain kind of authority (of which we shall have much more to say below), but she has no immediate ability to direct the action or to change the world.

Similarly, the opening of *Götterdämmerung* reveals the attunement of the Norns to the primeval world. Although more solemn than the melodies of the Rhinemaidens, their vocal lines similarly grow out of and resonate with the orchestral evocation of the natural state, creating a sense of unity disturbed only when Wotan's breaking of the World-Ash is reported. The shift of mood here marks a change of order, one that prefigures the more radical change in the later *agitato* passage that culminates in their report of the demise of Wotan's own regime, the announcement of the triumph of Siegfried, and the breaking of the rope. (At this point, of course, the Norns have lost their place in the transformed world, and can only descend to join their mother Erda in endless sleep.)

Our first introduction to the primordial world comes at the very beginning, in the form of what can easily be interpreted as the mindless frolicking and blithe cruelty of the Rhinemaidens. The maidens can appear to be eternal adolescents at play, whose shallow immaturity of thoughts and feelings is evident in the taunting of Alberich. The culmination of their unfeeling game is Flosshilde's ear-ravishing but heartless teasing, as she urges Alberich on only to frustrate and humiliate him all the more: ("*Du freitest um zwei/ frügst du die Dritte/ süssen Trost/ schüfe die Traute dir* [You have wooed two; if you asked the third, your darling would bring you sweet bliss]," accompanied by a tender violin solo, and "*Wie dein Anmuth/ mein Aug' erfreut*, . . . [How your charm cheers my eye . . .])."

To borrow Rupert Brooke's phrase, this seems but "love-music that is cheap," a sham of emotion by utterly superficial creatures who are quite incapable of it. Loge would thus be on target in his description of the Rhinemaidens when he refers to the gold that they so ineptly guard as a "toy in the water's depths, delighting laughing children" (with a vocal line that, uncharacteristically for him, lilts in ironic imitation of their own music). When we meet them again, in Act III of *Götterdämmerung*, they are still laughing and teasing, inexplicably and counterproductively switching tactics from seduction to threats when they seem on the verge of winning back the gold. If this childish thoughtlessness represents the world's primordial state, then it is small wonder that a "dauntless god" might want to improve upon it, and think he could.

But the primordial world evidently has either given rise or given way to other sorts of beings as well, of a less innocent nature. There is Hunding, of course; and behind Hunding stand his kin—crude and barbarous people, for whom women are chattel and might makes right, living a life the nastiness and brutishness of which may well have made the shortness virtually guaranteed by its violence a blessing. They may have their loyalties and their code of honor, as indicated by Hunding's narrative and hospitality to Siegmund (however coldly and threateningly given); but life as they live it is only marginally human. The code itself, as the music suggests, is a derivative, botched, and debased version of Wotan's grander system. This form of life seems amply to deserve a Schopenhauerian assessment and verdict: if this is all we can aspire to, then it is better to abnegate the will.

Fasolt and Fafner, upon closer consideration, are little more than larger versions of the same kind of life—outsized creatures of elemental appetite and desire, who live by impulse and brute strength and who regard themselves (rightly) as vulnerable to those who are cleverer. Fasolt's childlike devotion to Freia shows his kind not to be invariably and completely oafish and dim-witted. His affection may not be deep, but it is sincere—the moment where his clumsy reminder of the giants' toil shifts, with a change of key, to confession of a yearning for womanly tenderness and love reveals an unexpected promise in the unprepossessing world from which he comes; and he does have enough sense to see and gumption to insist that Wotan cannot simply play bait-and-switch with his builders. (As he points out, the god obtains his power through contracts and law, and in consequence, he must keep faith—adding, self-deprecatingly but pointedly, that a "stupid giant" is reminding the clever one of this.) But those qualities show little more than potential, hardly amounting to much as redeeming virtues. Fafner has no such virtues at all, and his surly complaints and demands show nothing of the lyricism to which Fasolt occasionally aspires. Even when Fafner gains the Ring, he can think of nothing better to do than use it to turn himself into a dragon, the better to guard his hoard. Hunding and the giants may stand out among the denizens of the primordial world; but they do not exactly grace it, serving rather to show just how much their manner of existence leaves to be desired.

Nor are things much better when we meet the allegedly noble Gibichungs, who represent a superficially more advanced (and all too familiar) version of humanity. Gunther's preoccupation with appearances (for striking a good figure in Rhenish society) prompts him to engage in deception. At best, we might understand his aspirations in terms of some code of honor; but his willingness to acquire the trappings of honor by dubious means makes it apparent that no such code has much salience in his decisions. His sister Gutrune is more appealing, partly because of the sweetly tender theme Wagner associates with her and partly because of her apparently sincere (if shallow) love for Siegfried. Yet she too is prepared to deceive in order to win a husband whom, as she admits, she could not hope to capture on her own merits. The Gibichungs are not innocent weaklings, corrupted by Hagen; they are base to the core, as is reflected in their readiness to jump without hesitation, and with no questions asked, for a trophy wife in the one instance and a trophy husband in the other.

Hagen himself exemplifies an even more pathological possibility in the post-primordial but essentially primitive world of the *Ring*, along with Mime and Alberich (and his subterranean hordes). Each of them is slighted; and each is moved primarily by dark and destructive desires. They may have started with elemental cravings that are natural enough, even if not admirable; but when those cravings are frustrated, their formidable strength of purpose becomes concentrated on expressing spleen and spite, and in taking revenge. None of them can be dismissed as mindless or confused, for there is considerable depth of understanding behind their plots; but their subtleties and cunning are invariably directed to and blighted by their pathologies. That understanding and force of character is particularly evident in Alberich's grim ascending phrases that precede the chilling characterization of "the lord of the ring as the slave of the ring [*des Ringes Herr als des Ringes Knecht*]"—a characterization that will, of course, apply to Alberich himself, as much as to anyone. In similar fashion, Hagen's combination of intelligence, dedication, and malevolence is concentrated in his deeply menacing closing of *Götterdämmerung*, Act I, Scene 2, where his chromaticisms, intertwining with the orchestral suggestions of several motifs, eventually erupt into a rising seventh ("*mir aber bringt er den Ring* [to me, though, he'll bring the ring]").

Whichever of these kinds of beings may have existed in the world's primordial state (and we shall sketch two different versions of the world's *Ur*-history in a moment), our main proposal in this chapter is that Wotan was not content to accept the world—primordial or primitive—as he found it. We suggest that after achieving self-mastery by taming the impulses that had initially driven him, he formed the dream of creating an order that would end the sway of the primitive as well as the stupor of the primordial, transforming the world into a far nobler and more admirable place, in which life could be lived more meaningfully and worthily. From the opening of *Rheingold* to the last Act of *Götterdämmerung*, each of the *Ring*'s four operas provides us with glimpses of the original world *at its best*—while other parts of each show us faces of that world of a less charming nature. Wotan deemed that world to leave a good deal to be desired. He conceived of a new order that would improve upon it, and found the courage as well as the vision and determination to establish and secure it—whatever might be required to do so. He came to the Spring and the World-Ash already in quest, already in the grip of the problem of how to create grander order—and thereby not only endow his own existence with greater meaning for having created it, but also render enhanced life in such a transformed world a more meaningful affair for the world's inhabitants. Valhalla was to be its symbol and beacon as well as its anchor and bulwark.

Or at any rate, this grand ambition would make good sense of Wotan's boast (his anxious boast, we think) to Fricka, cited above, as well as of what he strives both to accomplish and to oppose in the course of the *Ring*—and also of his reaction to his various failures along the way, culminating in his final despair. He had sought (and throughout much of the *Ring*, continues to seek) to impose a new form of order on the world. The result would be a world in which the rhythms of primordial nature have been superseded by the rule of law; in which impulses are brought under rational control; and in which previously prevailing formlessness is given intelligent and admirable form. He fashioned his spear of power from the limb of the World-Ash in order to found a system of laws and contracts because he saw (and continues to see) these as crucial preconditions of the establishment of such an order, as the framework of a world to be proud of, and as necessary parts of a world in which lives are worth living.

Wagner does not tell us anything about the world as the young Wotan found it; the First Norn takes us as far back into the past as we are allowed to go. Yet it is important for the claims we make about Wotan's aspirations that there should be *some* way of extending the story into that earlier world. We shall outline two versions.

First, let us suppose that the primordial state was innocent. It was a world of individuals at play—not just Rhinemaidens, but docile dwarves, gentle giants, happy humans, and guileless gods. The Norns wove their rope, and Erda slept in her intuitive wisdom. Latent in this primeval state were the two principal sources of its disruption. Some of the individuals were stronger, more beautiful, cleverer, swifter, or more skillful than others. In play, it became evident to some that because of these asymmetries, the satisfactions they sought were to be denied them. Alberich and Mime were not born as we find them; their ferocious spite was learned in the school of frustration—not because the primordial state was cruel, but simply because it was heedless. A world of play was bound, sooner or later, to produce an Alberich—one tired of losing and resentful of those who not only withhold what he desires but are amused at his expense, one who resolves to change the game and turn the tables.

This way of conceiving the world's deep past provides a more benign interpretation of the Rhinemaidens than that which we offered above (where we suggested that they could be viewed as shallow, cruel adolescents), and it allows for a very straightforward reading of the opening of *Rheingold*. The wonderful arpeggiating phrases from the initial low E flat provide us with an evocation of a world of natural grace and beauty, yet a world that is static; the phrases roll, caressing the ear, seducing us into thinking that they could continue forever; there is no direction here, no significant change. Even when Woglinde's voice breaks into the primordial harmony, entering on a grace note, she continues the contours of the phrases we have already heard. As Wellgunde and Flosshilde join her, they too are part of this natural, primordial music, singing in lines that seem drawn from it, as if their beauty, and their sense of the world's beauty, could only be expressed in an intuitive, even instinctive, reaction. Instead of chiding them for witlessly singing of the gold (and its powers) in the presence of an interloper, we can hear their lovely arpeggios when the sun strikes the Rhinegold as the tributes that beauty must pay to beauty, natural and unavoidable. Equally unreflective, and perhaps equally instinctive, are their responses to Alberich: not cruel, not teasing, but simply the immediate responses of beauty to ugliness and deformity. They are the mindless voices of this gorgeous primordial world, voices that cannot be in any harmony with those of its inhabitants who fail to exemplify its loveliness.

Alberich's clumping entrance disrupts the smooth flow of the orchestral music with its syncopations, and his awkward, jagged lines are quite at odds with the graceful music we have heard so far. It would be easy to sing those lines with a leer, to suggest that Alberich is already corrupt, but that is not necessary. He can be heard as a jarring voice in this state of mindless grace—one whose vocalizations and whose orchestral accompaniments are never aligned with the natural rhythms, one who is doomed to fail in this primordial world. What we see and hear, of course, is a compressed account of that failure, the clash of ugliness and awkwardness with beauty and grace, and the resulting transformation of mere ungainliness into something more sinister. His vocal lines are almost invariably awkward, just as the Rhinemaidens, whether in joy, panic, or closing lament, are always graceful. Only at two points does Alberich achieve anything like a natural melodic phrase—once in his pallid echoes of Flosshilde's deceptive seduction and once at the climax of his great threat, as the choppy sequences break into the sweeping rejection of love: "*So verfluch' ich die Liebe!* [Thus I lay a curse on love!]." At this second point, Alberich is no longer at odds with nature, and that is because both he and nature have been transformed.

We have been using the opening of *Rheingold* to outline one vision of the primordial state, a vision of the world as originally innocent and unreflectively bucolic. The simple and charming inhabitants of that kind of world might want no more than to flourish and revel in it as it is. In a more thoughtful and more successful individual in such a world, on the other hand (a being who had amply enjoyed but eventually tired of "youthful love's delights"), there might also arise a sense of discontent with the mindless play and an impulse to ask: "Is this all?" That individual might well have understood the possibility (or the probability, or even the inevitability) of the corruption of innocence and the need for a kind of development that would transform rather than deform it. So might begin a quest that would lead to the World-Ash and the transformation of the primordial state by means of a branch torn from it and fashioned into an instrument of power.

Or perhaps it was different. The primeval world might always have been morally heterogeneous, containing not only harmless innocents but also brutish and vindictive barbarians, crude and impulsive giants, shallow and cruel beauties, warped and vengeful misfits, and other such unsavory types as well. We can hear the opening of *Rheingold*, and the opening of *Walküre*, quite differently. The Rhinemaidens can be heard as taking narcissistic delight in their own loveliness, amusing themselves by teasing the misfavored. Lecherous Alberich may enter already smarting from the memory of past frustrations. The stormy opening of *Walküre* can conjure a partial and unstable version of Wotan's attempt at order, as we hear a transformation of the motif associated with his spear and the threatening horn calls that will be associated with Hunding's bellicosity. In response to its blithe cruelties, its Hobbesian tensions, and its swelling malevolence, a reflective and high-minded spirit might aspire to bring this rude world under the rule of law, to settle disputes by principles and contracts rather than by force and thus to foster the conditions under which the inhabitants of this world might turn out very differently, and more admirably. In that event, the world and life within it would be endowed with far greater value—very much to the credit and glory of the one responsible for the transformation as well as to the benefit of those affected. So, once again, the world might come to contain a Wotan.

We do not need to decide which of these possible *Ur*-histories we are to imagine. Either will provide a background for the claim we have proposed: that Wotan comes to the World-Ash intent on solving a problem. That problem—the question of what sort of attainable order might be needed to accomplish this ennobling transformation of the world, and of how it might be instituted and preserved—is what we shall call "the problem of order." This, we suggest, was the issue with which post-adolescent Wotan began—and which eventually came to be transfigured in his mind into the seemingly very different (but, we believe, deeply connected) problem of "finding an ending," as he began to despair of ever discovering a satisfactory solution to his initial great problem and aspiration. He sacrificed an eye to try to achieve a solution to it; and in *Rheingold* it appears initially that he has succeeded. For his World-Ash spear has given him apparent dominion over the world and thus the ability to establish order in it, without which there can only be chaos or blind and grim necessity, devoid of meaning and value. He has sought the power to achieve and safeguard it out of an appreciation of the shallow mindlessness of innocent play (however graceful) and the savagery of disorder.

By the time we meet him, Wotan understands very well the force of the dark instincts that motivate some of his fellows and the need for a comprehensive solution to the problems they present if things are ever to go differently. The rule of law he establishes is intended to tame them, to bind all in a covenant of light. And by introducing a system that requires a more reflective, self-conscious, and responsible mode of conduct, he has made possible a new sort of dignity and worth, building upon but superseding all merely natural existence, which even at its best is wanting in significance. With the building of Valhalla, he was to have consolidated and secured his establishment of a new order characterized by the rule of law and the emergence of richer forms of life.

Even if Wotan had succeeded in his goal, it is interesting to observe that this would have created a problem of a different sort for him: he would no longer have been needed. There would be no place for a Wotan in a world in which the rule of law was complete and secure. He would have put himself out of business. It would have been—would have *required*—the end of him. And we think that Wotan knows this too, even as he continues to strive for the realization of his vision.

8

Wotan's Problem

The realization of Wotan's great vision, of course, certainly would have been an achievement to be proud of nonetheless, even for a god, as the celebration of its apparent advent in the orchestral conclusion of *Rheingold* makes clear. But the celebration is premature at best; for as is evident, the rule of law is radically incomplete. Alberich does not willingly submit to it and so has to be *physically* captured and bound, and his ill-gotten gains seized. More significantly, Wotan's seizure of them has nothing high-minded or even right-minded about it. This is reflected vividly in the orchestral ending of Scene 3 of *Rheingold*, where brief jubilation quickly gives way to menacing music, appropriate to a world that is severely out of joint. Wotan does not hesitate to go outside his own law—or at least counter to its spirit—when it suits him to do so. He is even tempted to keep the Ring for himself; and it takes Erda's intervention to turn him away from that disastrous course.

So already in *Rheingold* we know that Wotan has failed. The rule of law cannot subdue some elements of the natural disorder. The most obvious symbol of this is the Ring itself, fashioned out of material extracted from its primordial condition—not, in the manner of Wotan's spear, as a means to higher ends but out of a pathological impulse to which the primordial state was always vulnerable. This Ring of Power only creates more problems as the new possibilities it represents become known, and as hatred, vengefulness, lust, and greed are amplified through competition for it. Fafner's sudden killing of his brother serves as a portent, as Wotan and the ironic Loge both recognize. Alberich's boasts of what the Ring will enable him to accomplish are never countermanded; on the contrary, Wotan insists that he must have the Ring to ensure that its power will not defeat that of his spear. (A transformation of the music associated with Wotan's spear, into a form in which it sounds uncharacteristically impotent, is heard just before the god is forced to resort to violence in ripping the ring from Alberich's finger.)

The Ring moreover cannot be the only threat to his attempts to impose order. Whatever reasons Fricka may have had for welcoming the building of Valhalla, Wotan had his: it is evident that Valhalla is to be a *stronghold*, the need for which clearly antedates the new problem posed by Alberich's possession of the Ring. There was a history between the carving of the spear and the opening of *Rheingold*—a sequence of events in which Wotan's efforts to solve his problem (the problem of order) presumably met with recurrent obstacles, prompting him to resort to measures with short-term advantages that in the long run only made for further and larger troubles for his project. Dedicated to the creation of a world of law, the god found himself confronted with powers he could not completely subdue and with which he was therefore forced to compromise or battle in compromising ways, thereby leaving and even creating further difficulties, and room for further challenges.

The contract with the giants is a mess—in part because Wotan did not pay much attention to the terms, since he did not seriously intend to fulfill them. But it is important to see that it is not a *gratuitous* mess. Wotan has entered into it (at Loge's suggestion) as a response to earlier difficulties. His fantasy, as Scene 2 of *Rheingold* opens (and Wotan sings with greater confidence than he will ever again achieve), is that *this time he has it*: this time the pieces are all in place, and the final imposition of order on the world will now become possible. By the fourth scene, of course, Wotan knows that this is not so, and that Valhalla—perhaps like other ventures before it—has not solved his problem. He now comes up with a new dream: the dream that Fricka will frustrate in *Walküre*. So, as he tells Brünnhilde, he has been "heedlessly deceptive" not because he was pursuing egoistic goals in the style of *Schwarz-Alberich*, but rather—precisely—because he was so intent on succeeding in his long attempt to bring stable order and new meaning into his world.

Here it may be helpful to compare the *Ring* with Shakespeare's *King Lear*. The fairy-tale beginning of *Lear* ought to strike us as arbitrary: why is Lear bringing his court together to observe a ceremony in which the kingdom will be divided among his daughters? Lear himself tells us:

> We have this hour a constant will to publish
> Our daughters' several dowers, that future strife
> May be prevented now. (I-i-39–41)

By the end of the play we understand the depth of the strife Lear was so concerned with preventing (even though he was far from imagining how dreadful it would actually turn out to be). If there was original folly in Lear's division of his kingdom, it did not stem from his sowing the seeds of turmoil but from his removing all checks on their monstrous growth. The subsequent developments make vivid the ferocity of naked human impulses; and, with the death of Cordelia, the play's brightest light, the only possible verdict seems to be that rendered by Kent: "All's cheerless, dark, and deadly" (V-iii-343). Lear and Wotan (although Lear much more naively than Wotan) began by taking up different versions of the same problem—both of them fearing, and then finding, that the condition of the world in its post-primordial state is vulnerable where it is not already debased, and both attempting to create and maintain an order superior to the state of affairs that would otherwise exist. For Lear, that problem arises as he "crawl[s] towards death," believing that he need only find a posthumous means to continue the order he has consolidated and overseen (through the force of what the play reveals as, even in its decline, an indomitable will).

As a means to that end that would also enable him to achieve what he imagines to be a fitting ending, Lear comes up with an idea that proves disastrously self-defeating, of the public performance of a kind of contract (of love professed and therefore presumed to be assured). While this earns for him and the play the name of tragedy, however, and obviously is a catastrophic misjudgment, we are given sufficient insight into the strength of the corroding forces to conclude that nothing else would have been likely to avail for his larger purpose. Can we really believe that if Lear had been wiser and had demanded no public display, and Cordelia and France had settled down in their "richlier third" (or even had been given the whole kingdom by a still wiser Lear, who saw and tried to thwart the ambitions of Goneril, Regan, Cornwall, and Edmund), all would have been well?

The *Ring*, by contrast, reveals Wotan twisting and turning in an attempt to find a way to resist and overcome the kinds of disorder that have arisen in the world with the loss of any primordial innocence it may once have had and to which it remains constantly susceptible and vulnerable. His inability to do so leads him to conclude, in his despairing exchange with Brünnhilde, that there can be no solution, and that the world must simply be left to the untender mercies of Alberich and the as-yet-unnamed son he has contrived to sire. But the problem continues to exercise Wotan, even in his failures.

From the mid-point of *Walküre* on, we suggest, the increasingly explicit focus of Wotan's judgment is how to prepare for something that goes beyond his own doomed strategy of solution— how to end the system without simply negating it and making way for a return to denatured chaos and degradation. Indeed, we suspect that he has been implicitly committed to finding some such ending since the encounter with Erda in *Rheingold*. The idea of somehow managing to wipe the entire slate clean enough to restore the world to the condition of some innocent primordial *Urwelt* is far from his mind, at least as long as he remains on stage. Despite his respect for Erda's wisdom, he would seem to be constitutionally incapable, even at his wits' end, of being attracted to the prospect of endless mindless play. Even at *Twilight* time, if that is the only alternative or best available outcome, he prefers oblivion.

So in the end, it seems, Wotan fails. He fails to solve the problem (of order) he has set for himself; and, as we have already suggested, throughout much of the drama he is conscious—at first dimly, later more clearly—that failure is inevitable. So far, there seems to be no difficulty: perhaps there are enterprises so large that even gods may fail at them. But Wotan's failure is a larger one, involving more than just the passing of the civil order he attempted to establish in the world. He and the other gods not only do not prevail; they are consumed in the final conflagration. The ending that is to be desired, that would have some sort of positive rather than merely negative significance, thus presents an even more formidable challenge; for it would have to make sense in a way that makes no appeal whatsoever to any sort of enduring reality of divine beings and purposes.

Indeed, one may well ask: what remains of divinity itself, if gods are not only limited in power and individual duration, but finite in the sway of their very godhead as well? Throughout the *Ring*, characters sing of the "*ewige Götter* [eternal or immortal gods]." And yet the Third Norn tells us, in the Prelude to *Götterdämmerung*, that "the end of the eternal gods eternally is at hand [*der ewigen Götter Ende dämmert ewig da auf*]." Their imputed "eternal" nature is no such thing—or at least, is not what it is generally taken to be.

One way to respond to Wagner's practice of inserting "*ewig*" ("eternal") at key moments of the drama would be to suggest that this is simply a means of drawing attention to the portentous character of what is being reported or foretold—a strategy of underlining, akin to the solemnity or strong accents Wagner often provides in his musical settings of the word. But we think it is possible to do better than that, and to see him as aiming at a more subtle meaning. In one of his most philosophical letters, Wagner provides clues to his usage of this key term. Writing to Röckel in 1854, he explains: "'*Ewig*'—in the true sense of the word—is that which negates finitude (or rather: the concept of finitude): the concept of finitude is unsuited to 'reality,' for reality, i.e., something that is constantly changing, new and multifarious—is precisely the negation of all that is merely imagined and conceived as finite." The interpolated interpretation of reality, in terms of change, hearkens back to an earlier passage in the same letter, in which Wagner had offered the following characterization of the real: "to be real, to live—what this means is to be created, to grow, to bloom, to wither and to die; without the necessity of death, there is no possibility of life." Wotan expresses a similar view early in *Rheingold*, when he reprimands Fricka for attempting to hold him to a constant course: "All who live love renewal and change: that pleasure I cannot forgo!" (Ironically, but also perhaps significantly, this phrase is linked by the accompanying orchestra with Valhalla, which in Wotan's mind at this point is to be the culmination of his quest for order.)

One aspect of Wotan's character that satisfies Wagner's description is this very quality, writ large in his aspiration to change and renewal on a grand scale. He would transform the entire world, "negating finitude" by transforming and thereby transcending the limitations of the world as he found it, giving it a meaning that does not reduce to mere life and death on primordial nature's or primitive humanity's terms. Moreover, he eventually embraces the idea that not only his preferred kind of order, but also he himself and the rest of the gods along with him, must perish. And this requires a different mode (if one can be conceived) of opposing or negating finitude—for the ending he seeks is one that still allows for the possibility of deathless significance. In any event Wotan himself is eminently deserving of the epithet "*ewig*" even though his powers are limited and he must perish, because his efforts do involve overcoming finitude, in a manner that transcends his own existence, and even have a kind of cosmic significance. (Whether the same epithet applies to Fricka, Donner, and the rest with anything like the same significance, other than by courtesy of their association with Wotan, seems much more dubious.)

Wotan's confessional dialogue with Brünnhilde signals a change, but it is continuous with the course he has been pursuing before. His long and painful revelation marks a further phase in his development as he becomes increasingly aware that his task is not to struggle ever more ingeniously to impose an order based on law, but to find a way for that order to pass—and for the gods to pass along with it. It represents a last great step in his evolution to grasp the relation between the nature of his "eternal" divinity and embracing the right kind of ending. In any event, he and we are dealing with the termination of the rich history of a god who has tried to make something of the world, rendering it a better place than it had been at its previous best (of which Erda is the representative), and better by far than the alternative represented by the likes of Hunding, let alone that envisioned by Alberich. The conditions under which the action of the drama unfolds stem either from the problem of how to effect and preserve such an ennobling transformation to which Wotan has dedicated himself (the problem of order) or from his own earlier efforts to address it—and then from the need to transform that very problem itself, if it is to be rendered susceptible of satisfactory resolution.

Let us recapitulate. When we first meet him in *Rheingold*, Wotan supposes that he can achieve a lasting solution to this problem in its original form, by using Valhalla as the instrument through which the rule of law can be universally accomplished and secured. After the fashioning, capture, and loss of the Ring, his intention is that it should be recovered by the actions of a being who would be free of the (contractual!) constraints under which he finds himself, to avert the threat it poses even to Valhalla—and so to the order he is seeking to secure. But Fricka teaches him, to his great chagrin, that his hands are tied even more thoroughly than he had thought. The problem of order thereafter seems to admit of no direct solution.

After his bout of despairingly nihilistic acquiescence in any kind of end to it all—even in the form of the triumph of Alberich—

Wotan comes up with a new and ingenious way to deal with this problem, involving its transformation into the problem of finding a fitting ending, thereby in a sense dissolving rather than solving it. He comes to recognize that he can save neither himself nor his order, and that the best he can hope for is an ending that preserves some version of the meaning for which he has striven. It is in this quandary that we now find him. He does not know how to do this. He realizes, however, that its achievement will depend on his *not* actively bringing it about. He will come to hope, implausibly, that Siegfried will solve his problem for him. But this is no task for a Siegfried. It requires a Brünnhilde.

We began with the question of the sorts of judgments that are made in the *Ring*, and we can now say more explicitly what the focus of judgment should be. Many of the interesting judgments of the tetralogy focus on Wotan's problem of order, and we have already canvassed some of the judgments that are at issue. One is that stable admirable order can be achieved in such-and-such ways (by building Valhalla, by siring Siegmund and Sieglinde). Another is that such order is impossible, because any strategy will turn out in its implementation to be self-defeating. Fricka's judgments are out of focus for, as we have seen, her moral assessments only arise against a particular background—the framework of laws and principles that Wotan has guaranteed—and they are out of place in a discussion in which the maintenance of that framework is at stake.

Alberich's judgments, like Fricka's, play no constructive role in advancing Wotan's problem of order. This is not because Alberich fails to grasp the importance of what Wotan is about, but because his alternative is so radically different. What Alberich seeks is not some different meaning-enhancing reordering of the world that would be superior to Wotan's; for in his resentful and vindictive bitterness, nothing matters except vengeful domination. Yet he is astute enough to see that thwarting Wotan is crucial to his own pathological aims, and consequently he can be expected to pounce on those features of Wotan's strategies that prove self-defeating.

Just as Fricka's judgments may impinge on Wotan's larger plans even though she is pursuing her own limited goals, so too we find Alberich offering judgments in the hope of realizing his ambition. He is acute when identifying a weakness will help his cause, and he distorts the situation when doing so seems to serve him best. When he and Wotan meet in *Siegfried,* Alberich offers a double judgment that elaborates his charge (made in *Rheingold,* Scene 3) that in wrenching the Ring from his finger, Wotan sins against "all that was, is, and shall be." The first part of it is the accusation that Wotan broke his contractual obligation in taking the Ring from him; and the second is the contention that the god cannot take from Fafner what he gave in payment. But his judgments are offered to no effect. Wotan has long accepted the second point, and so says nothing in response to it; and he dismisses the first by declaring that Alberich was always outside the scope of contracts—an outlaw whom the spear subdued not in virtue of its legal force but because of its power as a weapon. (The musical setting of Wotan's lines here conveys a massive calm, born of his transformation into the detached Wanderer.)

There are other characters in the *Ring*, however, for whom Wotan's problem of order is a matter for judgment as well, and whose judgments are of more significance and consequence. This is at least in part, we suggest, because their judgments have greater authority, of one sort or another. We shall start with a character (slighted in many discussions of the *Ring)* from whom Wotan learns much.

9

Loge

It is hardly an exaggeration to say that *Rheingold* is Loge's opera. Alberich sets the drama in motion, is duped, and suffers defeat; Wotan broods and connives, eventually leading his fellow gods into Valhalla. But Loge connects the incidents, bringing Alberich's theft to Wotan's attention and masterminding the scheme through which Wotan (temporarily) gains the Ring. At each stage, his clarity of vision contrasts with that of the other participants. He knows how to tell his story so as to arouse the cupidity and uncertainties of the giants (Fafner, in particular); he recognizes what the loss of Freia will mean for the gods; and, as already noted, his final judgments foresee large parts of what is to come. Indeed, the thought he entertains at the end of *Rheingold*, of turning himself back into flame and "destroying those who once tamed" him ("*Sie aufzuzehren die einst mich gezähmt*"), will be fulfilled at the end of *Götterdämmerung*. Wotan had effectively overpowered him, forcing him into service. Small wonder, then, that Loge takes a certain satisfaction in doing Wotan's bidding in ways that Wotan will learn to regret. Once in Wotan's power, his tactic was to assert himself by becoming clever; and become clever he did—a good deal more so than the nobler Wotan, whose power (wrongly) seemed to make cleverness unnecessary.

Loge takes a bemused interest both in the particular puzzles that confront Wotan and in the general problem of order. When he first appears, his task has been characterized as that of providing a substitute for Freia that will induce the giants to forgo their contract, and he begins by seeming to dodge that issue. Instead of delivering what Wotan had been hoping for, he meticulously specifies his role in previous conversation and agreements: he made no contract, he promised to *try* to find a substitute—and indeed he has done his best. The entire presentation is aimed at creating the impression that he has failed—precisely so that when the substitution is suggested, it will appear not to be an effort to evade the bargain but rather an alternative that will provoke spontaneous interest in his entire audience, the giants included. Convinced that Loge has failed, the lesser gods berate him; and after intervening on his behalf, even Wotan chides him for his intransigence. Thus begins one of the most musically rich and dramatically dense passages in *Rheingold.*

In his narration "*Immer ist Undank Loges Lohn!* [Ingratitude is always Loge's reward]," Loge purports to have achieved three things: to have discharged his promise to Wotan (even in the strong form that required success in his quest); to have kept a promise he made to the Rhinemaidens; and, further, to have come up with the best response to the general problem of order. Which of these things he is interpreted as doing (if any) will depend on the assumptions made by his listeners. The intertwining of musical motifs that variously suggest the primordial world and its innocent delights, the lure of gold, the delights of love, the fateful intervention of Alberich, and the possible return to an earlier state of harmony allows for Loge's complex story to find climaxes at many different moments. He is in complete control of this narrative and can play on his audience with the full resonances of the orchestra.

One standard way of thinking about Loge is as a trickster—in the context of his narration, a masterly trickster—as if he were bent on deception; but this, we believe, is a mistake. Loge is the embodiment of cleverness—or, to put it more nicely, of the fine adaptation of means to ends. Like *Homo economicus*, the embodiment of theoretical rationality, he is brilliant at calculating the ideal way of achieving a goal that has been set. He has no intention of his own to induce false belief by the cunning presentation of something true or to advance his own agenda. He is a piece of external equipment for Wotan to use, and his own purposes or aims typically have no bearing on how he makes his presentations. (As we suggested above, he does have resentments and hankerings, but these are made neither more nor less likely to be satisfied by his modes of speech.) There is no significant difference between the way he is employed in *Rheingold*—as a source of factual insight—and the manner in which he figures in later parts of the drama (as fire). But it is at least arguable that in doing Wotan's bidding, he sees that the god is setting himself up for a fall, and that he is at least amused and, quite possibly, satisfied by this, by gaining a dutiful servant's revenge on his master.

Loge's promise to Wotan can only be kept by his providing a substitute for Freia (if we subscribe to the strong version in which he agreed to *find* one, not just to *try* to do so). But nothing counts as a substitute unless the giants will take it to be one. Hence Loge must lead them down a path that will induce them to fasten on a particular thing (the Rhinegold) as potentially worth more to them than Freia. (Of course, the giants do not respond identically to Loge's recitation; Fasolt remains doubtful of the greater value of the gold.) Without embellishment, Loge explains how Alberich stole the gold and implies that he has promised to appeal to Wotan, the guardian of law, for help in returning it.

This is the first of four occasions on which Loge indicates the possibility of restoring the Rhinegold—a possibility that comes to be appreciated in *Götterdämmerung*, where Waltraute reports to Brünnhilde that Wotan has come to hope for this outcome and pleads with her to give up the Ring that Siegfried has given her. (We shall examine this scene in more detail when we come to consider Brünnhilde's own development.) We take it that Loge sees clearly how restoring the gold would contribute to the realization of Wotan's aspirations—or, more exactly, how failure to take this action will result in the obstruction of their realization.

Wotan, however, is preoccupied with the immediate problem of evading the contract for Valhalla—understandably enough, since the loss of Freia would lead to the gods' aging and decay, as well as being dishonorable on his part. (For, as Fricka correctly points out, giving Freia to the giants as payment for services rendered would be treating his sister-in-law as a mere chattel.) He therefore consistently dismisses Loge's suggestions as frivolous and irritating—and in doing so displays a familiar and all-too-human trait: the tendency to seize upon a short-term expedient as a means to the attainment of some larger purpose, and to proceed with it even though it may be clear to others (and may eventually become clear to oneself) that doing so actually compromises or undermines the attainment of that very purpose. Loge is the clear-eyed onlooker who sees the structure of the situation—and is ignored.

We would go further in praise of Loge. He understands that the problem of reinforcing and extending Wotan's system of laws and contracts is insoluble, and he recognizes this well before Wotan comes to an explicit appreciation of the point. The local difficulties can be solved by giving up Freia and returning the gold to the Rhinemaidens, although this will have the consequence of weakening the gods (they will become "old and gray"). Other approaches will only make matters worse and hasten the inevitable end. Wotan, in short, has gotten himself into a hopeless bind, and that is all there is to it. All that remains is to play out the hand. Such, we suggest, is the upshot of Loge's judgment.

And he is right. Loge is an epistemic authority with respect to the issues of means and ends that pertain to the focal questions about instituting and maintaining order. Of course, his directive authority is limited. The lesser gods (Fricka, Donner, and company) recognize that he is clever, but they have little appreciation of the genuine issues, or even of what they are. They march merrily off to Valhalla, oblivious of the problems with which Wotan must wrestle and of their own vulnerability. And, like the giants, they have an instinctive distrust of "cleverness." ("*Loge heisst du,/*

doch nenn' ich dich Lüge [You're called Loge, but I name you Liar!]" is Froh's reaction.) Loge's directive authority, such as it is, stems from Wotan's recognition of him as an epistemic authority with respect to some issues that bear on his projects (the gold could be used to pay off the giants, and it could be obtained by robbing the robber). Yet he does not realize that Loge has a clearer view of the possibilities and consequences than he does, and he is not willing to take Loge's advice about everything (with respect to the return of the Rhinegold in particular). This may be partly because he shares some of the prevalent distrust of Loge; but, we think, it is more importantly because, through most of *Rheingold*, Wotan is focused on the immediate problem of what to do about the bargain with the giants—and Loge irritatingly keeps telling him things he does not want to hear.

Loge is rather like the perfect consigliere—or the economic advisor steeped in the methodology of positive economics. Provided with a definite issue of policy, a set of constraints, and a statement of available resources, he has the technical skill to analyze the problem and to identify the optimal strategy for working toward the goals that have been set. When asked to stand back from the issues and to consider whether the ends involved are worthy ones, or what ends should be adopted if those originally set prove unattainable, he has nothing to say. He is an expert on matters of means; ends are not his bailiwick. If Wotan were to inquire whether there might be some viable way of going beyond the order of laws and contracts, or at least of bringing about an ending that would validate what he has been trying to accomplish, Loge would have no answer. If others, including Wotan, want to distinguish one ending from another, that is their business; once they have worked out what they want, they can engage his services.

We can easily imagine what Loge would say if his attitudes were made fully explicit. It might go something like this: "Your problem, Wotan, is to make the rule of law and contracts fully applicable in a stable fashion. Strictly speaking, that's impossible, because the nature of the beings with whom you are dealing and the resources available to them, as well as the history of past compromises (including some of your own actions), guarantees that the sway of law and contract must remain local, and even diminish with time. You may try various ways of continuing your efforts to solve the problem, including fobbing off the giants with the gold and setting yourself up in Valhalla, but this will only precipitate further instabilities that will bring your order to an end. The best thing you can do is limit the damage already done in the breach of contracts—that is, return the gold to the Rhinemaidens and give Freia to the giants. To be sure, this will enfeeble you, and in the end will contribute to your overthrow, but this is the approach that will be most likely to defer your inevitable decline and fall."

Wotan is different from his dull-witted fellow gods in recognizing the correctness of much that Loge says; he identifies Loge as an epistemic authority and so accords him some directive authority. But he either misses the larger judgment we are ascribing to Loge or refuses to acknowledge and accept it—perhaps as being beneath him. And that is a good thing, not only dramatically speaking, but also because acceptance of Loge's judgment might have prevented him from undertaking the quest for an alternative way of framing the issue. At the end of *Rheingold*, after the decisive intervention by Erda, Wotan is groping for some reconception of his predicament, formulated first relatively crudely in the idea of a hero who will do what he cannot (win the gold and the Ring without breaking any contract). We hear the trumpets sound the first appearance of the Sword motif at the moment where the stage directions indicate that Wotan is "as though seized by a great idea"; and this allows him to pull himself out of his funk and issue his invitation to Fricka to follow him into Valhalla.

Do the later developments in the *Ring* vindicate Loge's judgments? Clearly, there is a sense in which Loge proves right. The twists and turns of *Walküre* and *Siegfried* can be understood, at least from one perspective, as complex sequences of events that embody imaginative strategies for tackling the problem of order in its latest and most salient version, involving the possession and repossession of the gold and so of the power that it gives. Project Siegmund is the first of these strategies. It eventually gives way, as we shall see, to Project Siegfried. These attempts fail in various ways: Wotan learns, painfully, that he cannot simply manipulate Siegmund as a gold-retrieving marionette; and in *Götterdämmerung*, Siegfried falls to the wiles of Hagen (and Alberich).

Just before Siegfried's death, the hero encounters the Rhinemaidens and is offered precisely the same option Loge suggested to Wotan many operatic hours earlier. Once again, the Rhinemaidens behave like thoughtless and impulsive children, beginning by teasing the hero with playful seductiveness. This actually produces an effect: Siegfried responds by inviting them to return to the surface and offering them the Ring. But then they foolishly issue threats—a course of action that has the opposite effect upon the boy who knows no fear—and he withdraws the offer. Naïf that he is, Siegfried has no understanding of what the request means or why he should grant it. If he had been able to know, of course, he would have to have been an extension of Wotan, and so his obtaining the Ring would be no solution to Wotan's difficulty at all. Not knowing, however, he can understand neither the solution nor even the problem. Thus it is left to Brünnhilde to carry out Loge's original proposal—and indeed to involve Loge in the ending of the gods' order he considered at the end of *Rheingold*.

The relief we feel (and Wagner's music conveys) at the restoration of the gold invites the question of whether anything has been gained by the long delay. From Loge's perspective, one might understand the action as a long series of imaginative but misguided and futile struggles to find a better way that does not exist. That is not the only perspective, however; and it would be shallow—as Loge is shallow—to insist that Brünnhilde simply does exactly what Loge proposed to Wotan in *Rheingold*. Events do not have a constant meaning or value that is independent of the contexts in which they occur. As we shall argue below, what happens at the close of *Götterdämmerung* bears the weight of all that preceded it. And from that perspective, matters come to look very different.

Loge is unable to help Wotan with the questions that presumably have begun to trouble him by the end of *Rheingold*—questions not so much about how to attain given ends with the means available as about what ends to pursue. Wotan's recognition of the necessity of a redirection of his quest at this point is signaled by the resolve to go to Erda, who now (for a time) replaces Loge as his chief counselor. Wotan has absorbed much from his former advisor; but he will prove nonetheless to be far less adept as a reasoner than Loge. He is soon to make the important mistake that Fricka brings to his attention, for example—a mistake that Loge never would have made, and that he surely would have pointed out to Wotan much earlier and more precisely (and less painfully too) had he been on hand to do so.

Loge himself ends *Rheingold* reduced to the role of ironic chorus. He comments on the gods' blindness, suggests that "it wouldn't be stupid [*nicht dumm*]" to burn them up, and concludes this brilliant speech by asking "Who knows what I'll do?" The question need not be heard as rhetorical. If we are right about Loge, he himself may not know what he will do—his knack, as befits the embodiment of reasoning about means, seems to be above all to avoid doing what is stupid. But his kind of usefulness will be needed again, even if his judgments will be neither wanted nor heeded. Wotan will yet again find a purpose for his former instrument; fire, like reason, can be adapted to very different ends. Indeed, both Wotan and Brünnhilde will employ him in this way, giving him the chance to play the part he envisions for himself.

Loge sings twice more. One brief phrase reminds Wotan yet again that the gold has been stolen from the Rhinemaidens. The second and longer phrase sarcastically reverses the *sotto voce* judgment of the imminent end (once again, Loge is at his most lyrical when he is being ironic—as if the sober calculation in which he excels were ill-suited to shapely melodic lines). The lamenting Rhinemaidens are urged to rejoice in the splendor of the gods, and the stage direction tells us that the gods laugh. Not all of them, we think. For Wotan knows (whether or not Loge knows that he knows) that things remain very unsettled, and that, as the Rhinemaidens sing, the newfound splendor is indeed "false and foolish [*falsch und feig*]."

10

Erda

Wotan turns to Erda after she makes her first appearance, arising from her sleep to deliver striking judgments. Plainly, she has some authority with respect to those judgments, for he concedes the Ring to the giants in response to her warnings, and, more importantly, comes to see her as a crucial source of illumination. Between the operas he has come to know her (in more senses than one); and the god we hear about in Act I of *Walküre*, and whom we meet again in Act II, is much the wiser for it. His relationship with Brünnhilde betokens his commitment to absorbing the wisdom Erda has to offer.

Erda's utterances in *Rheingold* fall into two categories: express directives (for example, Wotan should abandon the Ring) and factual statements that take a broader view of things than Wotan (or any of the other characters) has yet managed to achieve. There is a connection between these two kinds of pronouncements: we are given the clear sense that Erda knows what to command because her knowledge is so vast. She has wisdom about ends (and endings) because she has a synoptic sense and synthetic view of history. Indeed, after issuing her command with respect to the Ring, she declares that she knows "everything [*Alles*]." The beauty and gravity of her musical phrases reinforce our—and Wotan's—sense that this is no idle boast.

Yet Erda's declaration is puzzling in at least three ways. First, if she knows everything, then she must know that Wotan will give up the Ring, and indeed that she will play an instrumental role in leading him to give it up; but this is hard to reconcile with the sense of urgency she expresses. Second, she announces that all things end. In context, it is natural for Wotan (and the audience) to apply this to the order he has been trying to fashion; but the generalization, if true, applies to Erda herself and her knowledge. Third, when we meet her again in *Siegfried*, she expresses confusion. Wotan calls her up with the ostensible purpose of obtaining information, but the roles are reversed. He not only summons her (whereas earlier she had come to him unbidden), but moreover now seems to be the one with the knowledge; for example, he informs her about the fate of their daughter, Brünnhilde. Her responses to Wotan's questions are to redirect them to beings (the Norns) who were earlier characterized as more limited than she. (In *Rheingold*, the Norns are messengers who inspire Wotan's dreams; but the abandonment of the Ring was so important that Erda felt she had to convey this information herself.)

Perhaps these questions could be dismissed as trivial, and it would be more appropriate not to attend to the specific lines Erda is given but to the *atmosphere* she brings, with its resonances of the primordial state and premonitions of the gods' destiny. The magnificent first scene of Act III of *Siegfried*, whose concentration of themes suggests the world's past, Wotan's journey, and the loves for Erda and especially for Brünnhilde that have illuminated his way, can be heard as beautiful recapitulation and serves as a way of reminding us of what has been and preparing us for what is coming. This is undoubtedly part of the scene's power. But we think that more is going on. The details of this last encounter between two great figures of the passing order genuinely matter; and the Wanderer's uncharacteristic intensity and Erda's perplexity tell us interesting things about both of them. So we shall take the questions of the last paragraph to be worth considering.

One obvious way to cope with these puzzles is to fix a particular limit to Erda's knowledge, making it extend just as far into the future as will the order that Wotan has been struggling to make universal. In this spirit, we could suppose that at the moment human freedom first expresses itself in the decisive confrontation between Siegfried and the Wanderer, the Rope snaps, leaving the Norns unable to foresee subsequent events and depriving even Erda of predictive power. But this interpretation does not fit with the knowledge the Norns actually have in *Götterdämmerung*: the second Norn narrates how a "dauntless [*kühn*] hero shattered the spear in combat" (using the same word that had previously been applied to Wotan at the World-Ash, as his own period of dominance began). And the third Norn predicts that Wotan will bury the "sharp-pointed splinters" in the fire-god's breast, thus beginning the conflagration that will consume the gods. Nor will it account for a crucial difference between the Norns and Erda: the Norns know the story of Brünnhilde, whereas Erda evidently does not (until Wotan tells her).

We think it more illuminating to think of Erda as possessing intuitive, inarticulate wisdom. She sleeps; and in her sleep, her judgments are informed by the broad currents of life and the world as they have always been. We should not think of her as a mistress of detail but as having a wonderful power to synthesize—a power that issues in judgments about the relative value of particular kinds of goals and about the significance of different kinds of endings. Loge might have been able to tell Wotan about the expected consequences of his options at the crucial moment when the giants demand the Ring as the final piece of gold (although he would not have been able to take a stand on the value of the various possible outcomes). But Erda, without knowing any of the details, can tell Wotan both that his order must end and that the ending produced by retaining the Ring will be the wrong ending—a blank defeat that will deprive his strivings of significance.

When Wotan summons her in *Siegfried*, however, Erda lacks the basis for the kind of synthetic judgment that would inform him. Whether current events are headed toward the right kind of ending will depend on many things she does not know—things that turn on the actions of human beings. Those things have not been reported to her, and we have the clear sense that these new, free beings are opaque to her. Perhaps Brünnhilde, whom Wotan has sent into the human world to retrieve the dead heroes, will be able to help. Or perhaps the Norns have foreseen more. Her evasive replies to Wotan express her awareness of her own lack of any basis for judgment. She understands—even if Wotan does not—that the world is changing. Musically, there is no longer a connection to the primordial world, so strong and evident in the phrases that accompanied her in *Rheingold*, underscoring the sense that this new world has rhythms that go beyond hers. Thus, she no longer has intuitive access to the features that would enable her to answer the question he is really asking. (We shall be more explicit shortly about what that question is.)

Why has Erda lost authority? In part, as Wotan points out to her, it is because the end of his dominion means the end of her power to know—an end signaled in her failure to recognize his change in his will. In part, it is also because his "taming" of her (and the subsequent birth of Brünnhilde and the other Valkyries) has taken something from her, just as Wotan's fashioning of his spear from a branch of the World-Ash took something from the tree, and diminished it. In her replies to his questions, we can hear the dilution of her primeval wisdom—the knowledge of ends and destinies is now distributed among different individuals (the Norns, Brünnhilde, Wotan himself) who have weaker versions of what she once possessed. He was the first to know her and the first to draw knowledge from her; in this way, he was the beginning of the end of her reign—just as the manner of the beginning of *his* reign was also the start of its own end. Wotan absorbs Loge's knowledge of how to adapt means to ends, going beyond him and reshaping him to new purposes; similarly he seems to have absorbed Erda's own judgment about the end of the order of the gods—and in doing so, to have stripped from her some of her intuitive power.

At the end of *Rheingold*, Erda was clearly wiser than Wotan. But when he summons her in *Siegfried*, her old ability to make intuitive judgments about the value of ends and of endings seems to have given way to a diminished version of this capacity. He is no longer at the mercy of her decisions about when to appear and when to vanish. Now it is he who chooses when she should awaken and when she should return to her dreams. She retains grandeur, but it is of a different kind. No longer solemnly and immediately authoritative, the music of her first responses breathes with an autumnal tenderness and sweetness, a resignation to the passing of the world with which she has been so deeply in tune; only as she learns more of the new dispensation, more about the doings of those who are beyond her insights, does the gentle acceptance give way to impassioned protest (reaching its climax with the condemnation of falsehood—[*Meineid*]—in a descending interval of a twelfth from a high A flat). Wotan's response is not angry self-defense but reassuring explanation. As in the case of Loge, Wotan's absorption of Erda's special understanding leads to a reassignment of role: in an echo of his loving farewell to Brünnhilde at the end of *Walküre*, he commits her mother to "ageless sleep"—the first *Dämmerung* of the most primordial of the *Götter*. Erda no longer is or has the answer. For Wotan (and for us), this tap root has been cut.

The mark of Erda's authority is evident in Wotan's trajectory from the end of *Rheingold* to the third act of *Siegfried*; and her admonishment that the end must be accepted is an important part of the wisdom he comes to acquire. Wotan abandoned the counsels of Loge in favor of those of Erda, superficially in his decision to allow the giants to take the Ring, and much more deeply in his reconception of what he is about. Having begun by taking his goal to be that of ensuring the wider sway of his system of laws and contracts—a goal that was specified first in an attempt to persuade the giants to release him from the contract for Valhalla, and subsequently in the acquisition and retention of the Ring—he comes to envision a quite different course of action. Initially, it is framed in terms of a higher type of justice, requiring the continued pursuit of the Ring: Siegmund is to do what the god cannot, and the incestuous relationship with Sieglinde is supposed to demonstrate vividly the power and justification of the hero to disregard divine regulations. Fricka's uncomprehending correction reveals to Wotan that this is a muddle and that he himself must not permit it; and so it comes about that, recalling Erda's announcement of the inevitable end, he bitterly describes himself as willing the end.

By Act III of *Siegfried*, however, he has fully accepted Erda's judgment and her former authority. Just as her initial judgment of the inevitable end of the gods' order is set against a benign, peaceful version of the motif we associate with her (a theme that, up to this point in the scene, has been charged with menace), so too Wotan's promise to reveal his will ("*Dir Unweisen/ ruf' ich's in's Ohr* [You unwise one, I tell you now]") is set against a similarly soothing version. In both instances, too, the descending motif that follows (often associated with the decline of the gods) appears in a beautifully resigned form.

But why does Wotan call Erda out of sleep? His vocal lines are insistent, urgent, very different from those of the ironist who has figured in the earlier acts of *Siegfried*—and there are other emotions, too, echoes of love as he calls her name. He claims to want her knowledge. At the same time, he announces that her wisdom is at an end, endorsing her own judgments about her confusion and the clouded state of her mind. Small wonder that she chides him ("You are not what you say you are!"), demanding to know why he has wakened her, for his ostensible aims do not seem to make sense. But we think that Wotan has three purposes. One is valedictory: by explaining his will to her, he acknowledges her old authority, acknowledges too what he has gained from her and what she has given him, acquiesces in her judgment that his order must end, and bids her farewell. A second is probative: he is testing her, and her inability to provide him with information signals both the passing of her wisdom and the coming end of his own dominion. He suspects, of course, that Siegfried's success in killing Fafner and in regaining the Ring already marks the beginning of the transition; but Erda's confusion is further confirmation.

Beyond this, however, Wotan has a genuine question. That question concerns just the kind of issue on which Erda is authoritative.

What he wants to know is whether he has found the right ending. Will the advent of Siegfried give significance to all his strivings? Even if Erda's vision is limited, there is a chance that her intuitive understanding will provide reassurance. But Erda cannot answer that. The significance of Wotan's long quest for a grand new order cannot be assessed without knowing how the world will proceed in its new state. And that will depend on the actions of free beings—the beings whom Wotan has seen as his successors—and the course of events cannot be extrapolated from the rhythms that Erda intuitively understands.

Thus it is left for Wotan to declaim what he believes—or at any rate, perhaps, what he hopes. (One of the residues of the passionate god in the more contemplative Wanderer seems to be the tendency to transform hope into anxious belief.) So he tells Erda: "*Die du mich gebar'st,/ Brünnhild'/ weckt sich hold der Held:/ wachend wirkt/ dein wissendes Kind/ erlösende Weltenthat* [Brünnhilde, whom you bore to me, the hero will lovingly waken: waking, your wise child will work a redeeming world-deed]." This is, of course, rather vague. What sort of "redemption" is he talking about, and what exactly is this redeeming deed supposed to be? Loving Siegfried? Returning the Ring? Something else? We think Wotan does not know. He has *hope* for something of enormous significance but has no idea what that might be. He would have liked Erda to have been able at least to confirm his great (if indeterminate) hope, but she cannot—or, at any rate, does not. So, despite his apparent confidence, there is an anxiety behind this passage, as indeed there has been from the opening of the scene—an anxiety that emerges on the extraordinary harmonic change at the final syllable of the mysterious "*Weltenthat* [world-deed]." Acquiescent in many things, including his own passing, he still yearns to know what lies beyond and whether it will vindicate his strivings.

Wotan has moved beyond Erda as an authority, as he moved beyond Loge. But there is a Socratic sense in which she remains wiser than he: she has a firmer grasp of the limitations of her knowledge.

11

Wotan's Judgments

Wotan judges the world and he judges its inhabitants. We have begun to trace the course of the former type of judgment, but it is important to understand Wotan's changing attitudes in the context of the verdicts he issues on particular individuals. In some instances—Wotan's final words to Mime, for example—there are no significant connections; the advice to the dwarf to guard his own head well, set against the orchestral motif we associate with Loge, simply confirms Wotan in his new role as mocking ironist. By contrast, Wotan's dismissal of Hunding, delivered to deadly effect as the music slows and moves from the motif associated with the *Wälsung* to the descending figure that recalls Wotan's commitment to the rule of law, brings vividly before us the wrenching pain of his desertion of Siegmund, and of the dashing of the hopes that have foundered on Fricka's reminder to him of the rules he has set and in which he now finds himself trapped. The last command, "*Geh! Geh!* [Go! Go!]," can hardly be sung; it seems torn from the singer's throat. Even more significant, as we shall see (in Chapter 13), is the judgment of Brünnhilde in Act III of *Walküre*, where Wotan's reaction to her plays an important role in his perception of how the problem of order should be addressed.

Because Wotan's judgments are so intricate and central to the drama, it will be helpful to be as explicit as possible about the content and structural relations among views he adopts at various stages. We shall therefore recapitulate some points that have been scattered through earlier discussions, assembling the major judgments Wotan makes. We distinguish two levels of judgment. The most important claims to which Wotan is committed—*framing* judgments, as we shall call them—provide a relatively enduring background against which he searches for solutions to the problems that arise for him. In the context set by the framing judgments, Wotan arrives at other convictions—sometimes held for only a relatively short time—that often inspire specific actions. As he twists and turns, trying to honor—as well as sometimes to wriggle out of—the commitments registered in the framing judgments, he is sometimes moved to conclude that his predicament is impossible; and such conclusions at times occasion or even force a change of frame.

At the beginning of Scene 2 of *Rheingold*—indeed, earlier, from his visit to the World-Ash and even from the point at which he began his original quest—Wotan appears to subscribe to a broad normative judgment that sets the widest frame for his endeavors:

> Life needs to be (made) meaningful if it is to be worth living.

Wotan also believes that the world must become a better place than it is to begin with if life in it is to be meaningful. He further appears to suppose that an essential condition of the world's becoming a better place is that an admirable order be established in it—and moreover, to believe that making the world a better place would be an excellent way of making one's own life particularly meaningful. It is hardly surprising that he reaches the conclusion:

> It is important that an admirable order be established.

This commitment—to the idea of providing an admirable order for and in the world—frames all the particular judgments that lead him to action in the first three parts of the drama.

As we have suggested earlier, Wotan's original concern with the possibility of the meaningfulness of this life in this world, which led him to the basic judgment that life needs to be *made* meaningful, was founded in dissatisfaction with the world's primordial state. We can imagine the god recognizing the limitations of the mindless play of the Rhinemaidens and appreciating that the primeval state has within it the seeds of hideous pathologies: it allows for the emergence (or corruption) of Alberich and for the brutal harshness of the likes of Hunding. So we can understand that Wotan's basic normative judgment should have led him to believe in the importance of transcending the world's primordial state; that it is important to avoid the corruptions of the primordial state; and (most importantly) that achieving an order that transcends the primordial state—an order both durable and ennobling, with safeguards against relapse into the primordial state or any corruption of it—would be a truly divine achievement, worthy of the greatest of gods.

Moreover, Wotan has had a specific idea about what such an admirable stable order would be like, and throughout the history that has led up to *Rheingold* he has been pursuing it. Indeed, by the time we first meet him on stage, the commitments just reviewed have led him to embrace a framing judgment that will motivate his actions through most of the first of the four operas:

> The kind of durable admirable order that would transcend the primordial state, and would be resistant to corruption and relapse, can only (or best) be achieved by extending the scope and sway of laws and contracts throughout the world.

In the past, however, Wotan has made some derivative judgments that have embroiled him in various kinds of difficulties. (He has had *reasons* for needing a stronghold from which to be able to "rule the world" in this manner and to this end.) Thus his problems in realizing this objective have led him to conclude that a stronghold (Valhalla) must be built. This strategy turned out to require making a contract with the giants Fasolt and Fafner, stipulating (at their insistence) that they would receive Freia in compensation for their efforts in building Valhalla. Now that they have completed the construction, Wotan's belief in the importance of the rule of law commits him to holding that the contract with the giants must be kept by giving up Freia — or by finding a substitute that the giants will accept in place of her. When he learns of the theft of the Rhinegold and the forging of the Ring, Wotan realizes that the possession of the Ring by anyone not prepared to acknowledge the rule of law — as Alberich, its current owner, who acquired it by theft, clearly is not — presents a substantial threat to everything he is trying to achieve. He draws the obvious conclusion that the Ring must be wrested from Alberich and must be retained.

While regaining the Ring might be relatively straightforward, however, retaining it would be quite another matter. For as Loge sees from the start and others eventually come to appreciate, it would make a mockery of the rule of law, even in the absence of an established legal context or valid contract at the time, to emphasize the supremacy of law and yet not recognize the right of the Rhinemaidens to the gold. Even if they are careless creatures of nature, the gold was theirs, there was nothing wrongful about their possession of it, and the only consistent extrapolation of the rule of law to a broader domain would demand that the Ring — into which the gold has been fashioned — must be returned to them. But it turns out that Alberich's gold in its entirety—Ring included — is the only substitute for Freia the giants are prepared to accept (Loge's correct judgment again).

Wotan's commitment to keeping his contract with the giants — either by giving up Freia or by giving the giants a substitute they find acceptable — thus leads him to recognize that the only way to avoid losing Freia is to give the giants the Ring. Observing the lassitude that overcomes the gods during the interval when Fasolt and Fafner have taken Freia as hostage, however, Wotan is brought to a vivid recognition of what the effects would be if Freia were to be abandoned to the giants. In addition to the unpleasant personal consequences for the gods (including Wotan himself), the weakening of his power would doom to failure his attempt to achieve the rule of law. Hence, he also has to think that Freia must *not* be relinquished.

At this stage, it is apparent that the whole project is impossible in multiple ways. For, as we have seen, the attempt to establish and extend the rule of law has committed Wotan to seizing the Ring from Alberich and to keeping it, and *also* to returning the gold to the Rhinemaidens—and plainly he cannot do both. Nor can he keep the Ring, keep Freia, and still honor the contract with the giants. Understandably, the latter problem is at the center of his thoughts during most of *Rheingold*; but as Loge sees (and irritatingly points out), the incompatibility between retaining the Ring and dealing justly with the Rhinemaidens is equally troublesome. After Erda's intervention, Wotan abandons the thought of keeping the Ring. He gives the giants the gold and thus achieves two of the things he thinks have to be done: satisfying the contract with the giants, and retaining Freia. Yet, as he is now quite clear, this leaves his major objective—the establishment of a stable order based on the rule of law—unsecured and endangered.

At this point, we discern an important shift in Wotan's attitudes: there is both an explicit continued commitment to securing the rule of law that motivates Project Siegmund, and a vague, intuitive, displacement of that framing judgment in favor of something different. The rule of law can only be assured if the Ring is no longer in dangerous hands. So Wotan comes to fix on the idea that the Ring must be wrested from Fafner (now a dragon). It would be inconsistent with his commitment to laws and contracts for Wotan to do this himself. But he has had a "great idea": *someone else* can do it *in his stead*—although it would have to be someone of exceptional prowess and virtue. That idea takes shape in a new judgment: that some hero must defeat Fafner and obtain the Ring. Between the first and second operas, Wotan has undertaken to supply the needed hero, and by the opening of *Walküre*, the "great idea" has taken the more specific form of the belief that Siegmund must defeat Fafner and obtain the Ring—the belief that underlies what we are calling "Project Siegmund."

Fricka's contribution to Wotan's development consists in her making it clear to him that this judgment—a judgment that has guided many of Wotan's actions between *Rheingold* and *Walküre*—cannot be reconciled with his commitment to achieving a stable order based on law, because Siegmund is not truly independent of Wotan but rather is an instrument of his will. The whole point of the project was, of course, for the Ring to be returned without any violation of law on Wotan's own part. But when he comes to appreciate that Siegmund's actions are, in the pertinent sense, simply his own by remote control, Wotan recognizes that the detour through Siegmund is pointless and provides no genuine solution to the problem that has been at the forefront of his mind.

Yet another equally deep and intractable difficulty has eluded his serious attention. Wotan is committed to the imperative to return the gold to the Rhinemaidens; and this part of his difficulty in keeping all his commitments has been left unresolved. It would not be addressed even if Project Siegmund were to succeed and Wotan were thereby to regain the Ring. (This, of course, is what Loge sees so clearly.) On the face of it, then, Wotan is just thoroughly confused. In the early parts of *Walküre*, the stress on the urgency of regaining the Ring suggests that he is still supposing that it will return to *him* rather than being used by Siegmund or given back to the Rhinemaidens. Even in the long exchange with Brünnhilde, Wotan seems obsessed with gaining the Ring for himself: "From him [Fafner] I must wrest the Ring . . . [*Ihm müsst' ich den Reif entringen . . .*]." The failed plan thus appears to be set against the background of securing the order of laws and contracts, protecting against reversion to the primordial state and also (more immediately and urgently) against the dark powers with whose threat to that state he has long been concerned—powers personified in the current context by Alberich, with Hunding and Hagen to follow.

If that were all there were to Wotan's intentions, then he would be continuing to miss the point, for nothing in Project Siegmund addresses the need to keep faith with the Rhinemaidens. But Wotan's turn to Erda has marked a shift in his aims. His pursuit of a system of laws and contracts was based on a felt need for *some* kind of stable order to allow for possibilities of meaningful human life (recall his broadest framing judgment). In effect, Wotan had begun by translating his sense of the need for stable order into the more specific project of establishing the rule of law, by supposing that only laws and contracts will serve to tame the dark forces of nature in one form or another (whether that of Alberich's vile and vicious tyranny or of the base and brutal Hobbesian world of Hunding and his kin). Wotan has assumed that if the rule of law cannot be established, the only likely alternatives are grim (alternate visions of Dark Ages; the cheerlessness and cruelty manifest in *Lear*).

At the nadir of his hopes, Wotan's apparent assumption of this bleak vision of what a world without omnipresent law would be like combines with the failure of Project Siegmund to yield his bitter conclusion that the triumph of darkness is inevitable. But the turn to Erda suggests his openness to exploration of other ends and values, and his growing readiness to question whether the establishment of law is really an indispensable precondition of meaningful life. The questioning is most evident in the character of Siegmund himself, who has been bred to transcend the order of mundane laws and customs. Out of the dialogue with Fricka come two important ideas: Wotan's own emphasis on the importance of a being who can *transcend* his own order, and Fricka's point about *freedom* as an essential attribute of any such being. The combination crystallizes Wotan's doubts about whether the rule of law is necessary. Liberating himself from his assumption, he will also abandon the commitment to the rule of law while retaining the even more general framing judgment that some kind of durable admirable order must be found. So, instead of fixing all his hopes on establishing the sway of law, Wotan will now seek different realizations of the order that he takes to be necessary if life is to be meaningful.

In fact, Wotan's exploration of possible ends (begun in the turn to Erda) generates a different way of conceiving Project Siegmund—one that connects to his general search for order. (Thus Project Siegmund turns out to be an attractive option, whether Wotan is seeking to maintain the order of laws and contracts or simply trying to achieve *some* durable, admirable order.) Quite independently of his commitment to laws and contracts, Wotan should see Fafner's possession of the Ring as a problem for *any* form of stable order, since in the wrong hands the Ring could be used to wreak havoc with any form of admirable order. And Wotan should thus be interested in wresting the Ring from the dragon to protect whatever type of order he can achieve, or whatever type supplants his own.

Yet Wotan cannot coherently abandon his previous assumption that law was needed to avoid a bleak and hopeless world, give up the commitment to the universal sway of law, and, with his new freedom, simply seize the Ring from Fafner, either in person or by proxy, and hope for the best. For that would not be a move in the direction of some new form of order but rather would fly in the face of all he has striven for, signifying his own endorsement of the "law of the jungle" as the only law—as Alberich points out to him in the second act of *Siegfried*. Even if Wotan were to arrange for the Ring to be given back to the Rhinemaidens, the result would still be failure: after all his struggles, he would be resigning himself to settling for the primordial state as the best of possible worlds—bland and meaningless as it is (at its best), and also permanently vulnerable to corruption and decay into something far worse.

At this juncture, therefore, Wotan may be ambivalent; but whether he adheres to his old commitment to the rule of law and is continuing to seek an order based on laws and contracts or acquiesces in its demise in favor of some alternative admirable order that will ultimately allow for meaningful human lives, he has come to have reasons for believing that a free being, truly independent of his will, and therefore capable of opposing it, must be created to defeat Fafner and obtain the Ring. In the despair that marks Act II, Scene 2, of *Walküre*, Wotan laments that he cannot see a way to fulfill this imperative: "*Knechte erknet' ich mir nur!* [Servants are all I can produce!]" This is why the failure of Project Siegmund seems so complete. For if any stable order depends on an action of a free being, and if there is no possibility of producing a being who is free in the appropriate sense, then the situation appears hopeless.

Ironically, while Wotan is expressing his despair, he is initiating a process that will unwittingly produce (where he least expects it) the very thing he seeks: a free being who is more than capable of opposing him—even if initially only out of deep devotion to the fulfillment of his (true) will. Over-generalizing from Fricka's characterization of Siegmund as the extension of his own will, Wotan responds to Brünnhilde's protests by asking her how she dares challenge him since she is and can be nothing more than a "blindly following extension of my will [*meines Willens blind wählende Kür*]." Love for her father and compassion for his despair begins the process of Brünnhilde's transformation into an independent agent—a process that will be completed by her recognition of the nobility of Siegmund and Sieglinde and of the strength and praiseworthiness of their mutual love.

Thus Wotan is wrong (even before Siegfried is more than a gleam in anyone's eyes) to judge that the free being required by his plan is impossible; and his mistake in judgment leads him into a psychological state whose expression in his bitter words to Brünnhilde sets in motion the very outcome he has dismissed. Believing that he cannot produce a free being, he expresses his dejection and anger in ways that cause Brünnhilde to act against his explicit directive—thus (ironically but serendipitously) beginning her transformation into just the sort of being he had deemed impossible. (The expression of his emotions often results in events that he ultimately wants, even though he does not see, intend, or even imagine that those consequences will occur. In due course, we shall explore this point and its bearing on the notion of freedom Wagner employs.)

When Wotan does come to think that he can hope for the achievement of an admirable and durable order, he bets on the wrong horse: Project Siegmund gives way to Project Siegfried, as Wotan comes to the idea that Siegfried can and must become truly free as well as valiant—and so capable not only of besting Fafner but also of defying Wotan himself. The ability to defeat

Fafner is important because the threat posed by the Ring requires that some being must be able to regain it; and the ability to defy Wotan is equally important because this is essential to the freedom of the hero (the point Wotan has absorbed from Fricka). Once again, however, Wotan is shortsightedly obsessing about a part of the general problem of creating admirable order while ignoring the complications. Just as earlier he had focused on the need to repay the giants and ignored Loge's advice about the claims of the Rhinemaidens, he now worries far more about the hero's obtaining the Ring than he does about the likelihood that a better order will actually ensue.

Wotan is mistaken in concluding that Siegfried is the Great Hope; but he is not alone in his misjudgment. Brünnhilde herself takes over from him the idea that the crucial free actions involve the defeat of Fafner and the reclaiming of the Ring, and that this is to be accomplished by Siegfried, Sieglinde's yet unborn son. Thus, in the passage that precedes Sieglinde's magnificent exclamation "*O hehrstes Wunder!* [Sublimest wonder!]," Brünnhilde names Siegfried, and foretells his role as the hero who will re-forge the sword. In the last scene of Act III of *Walküre*, she discloses to Wotan the continuation of the *Wälsung* line. His immediate reaction is to dismiss any project of assisting—a response born of anger that is also absolutely essential for the subsequent judgment to which he moves in his valediction to Brünnhilde. (Here again, as we shall see, the conditions of freedom are realized because Wotan's emotions—not his forethought—produce the outcome he ultimately desires.) Accepting her plan that the rock shall be guarded by fire, he assures her that the man who will wake her (and to whom her human life will be bound) will be the envisioned and desired hero: "one freer than I, the god! [*der freier als ich, der Gott!*]."

In the last scene of *Walküre*, both Wotan and Brünnhilde accept the idea that what is needed is a free being who can defeat Fafner and secure the Ring. Thoroughly convinced by Fricka's points about his training of Siegmund, Wotan judges that the fulfillment of this idea depends on his doing nothing to assist Siegfried. In consequence, from this point on, he becomes little more than an observer rather than a shaper of the action. His last major act is to create the conditions under which Siegfried alone will be able to win Brünnhilde. (Appropriately enough, Loge is the instrument of this final intervention.) And his last act on stage, an opera later, is his heartfelt but inadequate attempt to step out of his Wanderer role and teach Siegfried a thing or two—which Siegfried uncomprehendingly, easily, and devastatingly brushes aside.

12

Project Siegfried

But not yet. Before Siegfried thus demonstrates his independence of Wotan's will all too vividly and thereby effects the Wanderer's final exit from the world's affairs, Wotan professes to Erda that he accepts the end of the order of the gods. He explicitly abandons the project of bringing about a stable admirable order by way of establishing a system of laws and contracts. We suggest that Wotan's questioning of his original assumption that only the rule of law could provide the admirable order that would make meaningful life possible—the questioning that makes it possible for him to hope for an alternative form of order—began with the original turn to Erda (at the end of *Rheingold*), strengthened in the training of Siegmund (between *Rheingold* and *Walküre*), and went beyond mere contemplation by the end of *Walküre*.

Project Siegmund was ambiguous between an attempt to establish the rule of law and a venture toward some *other* type of order that would also satisfy Wotan's fundamental framing judgment that life needs to be made meaningful to be worth living. Project Siegfried, on the other hand, requires the abandonment of his old preoccupation with lawfulness. A moment's reflection, of the kind of which the Wotan of *Walküre* is eminently capable, reveals that the existence of a free hero, able to gain the Ring from Fafner and capable of defying Wotan, does not comport well with the establishment of a universal order based on laws and contracts. Wotan's new insight is to see that this circumstance, while it does not bode well for the rule of law, is also an opportunity with respect to a different kind of admirable order. The free hero, Siegfried in prospect, may create an order that allows new possibilities of meaningful life. Wotan, in short, has come to accept that a further alternative to the world-possibilities considered so far—both the order based on laws and contracts and the reign of the dark forces that laws are intended to check—would be *a world governed by free and noble beings*. This leaves in place the importance of the appearance of the free hero, now recast as the necessity of a genuine hero who would be truly free and independent of anyone else's will (including Wotan's) and who would be capable of the greatest feats of valor (such as defeating Fafner). That is what Siegfried is to be.

Once the thought of the hero has become detached from any idea that this hero will carry out Wotan's original plan, contributing to the establishment of the rule of law, it is not hard to recognize two important further judgments. First, the appearance of Siegfried, as a hero of the appropriate type, must spell the end of the rule of the gods and of Wotan—and therewith, of Wotan's kind of order. Second, the dream of a divinely ordained world-order based upon laws and contracts is to be replaced by the goal of a noble *human* order anchored in the sway of heroic virtue. If this can be achieved, then despite his own failure—and the passing of his own order—Wotan will nonetheless have prepared the way for a fulfillment of his deepest aspirations (even if not in the manner originally intended). One important framing judgment will have been abandoned in favor of something different; but the ultimate sources of that framing judgment—the aspiration for a durable, admirable order and, by means of it, the creation of the conditions that make meaningful life possible—remain in place and are to be satisfied through the change of perspective. The goal of making the world a better place survives the alteration in the god's thinking with respect to what this will require. Moreover,

Wotan's own existence and strivings will still have been endowed with significance, for they will have contributed to the possibility of reaching his most basic goals, even if not as directly as he had originally intended.

Wotan commits himself to the passing of his order and its replacement by the sway of heroic virtue in his final scene. Confronting Siegfried, he declares that the awakening of Brünnhilde, by one having the exceptional and yet distinctively human virtues this will require, will mean the end of his rule: "*wer sie erweckte,/ wer sie gewänne,/ machtlos macht' er mich ewig!* [whoever awakens her, whoever wins her, makes me powerless for ever!]." If we suppose that Wotan's judgments, as modified, now require commitment to creating a truly free being, then we can view him as trying to solve the problem of admirable order in a way he has not previously anticipated, in the belief that a counterpoise to the vengeful and destructive egoism of Alberich and Hagen is the dominance of a contrasting set of (heroic) dispositions and qualities—even though it spells his end, and indeed requires it.

Wotan's own valiant earlier efforts to institute and secure an admirable sort of (divinely ordained) order may thus be seen as a preliminary advance beyond the primordial state and the bleakness of its degeneration into greed and need (variously demonic), toward something that will transcend them all: the *heroic*. Siegfried is to be its avatar and the agent of its advent. Wotan's divine (but, as it turns out, transient) order thus assumes the significance of a transitional stage that must give way to something nobler still; and the god will have found an acceptable ending.

This becomes Wotan's new dream and hope, inspired in him and ecstatically shared by Brünnhilde in the last act of *Walküre* (although Wotan does not clearly articulate it until his exchange with Alberich in Act II of its sequel). With this vision, Brünnhilde rapturously greets the hero at the end of *Siegfried*. The enthusiasm that Wotan and she share makes perfect sense, for the vision answers to something fundamental in both their natures. Indeed the Brünnhilde of *Walküre* would be a fine exemplar of the vision herself were she not a god, and were she not also bound to a kind of absolute obedience that is at odds with a crucial feature of it: its proud independence of spirit. She comes closest to it, prior to the end of *Götterdämmerung*, precisely when she casts off that bond and so invites (and earns) Wotan's wrath and de-deification of her.

Yet when Brünnhilde awakens, it is not to a new life as co-exemplar of human heroism with Siegfried—even though her own ending, an opera later, certainly has something of the heroic about it. For Wagner has her almost immediately vault over and beyond Siegfried's brand of heroism and into another possibility that is only fully realized when transposed from the realm of the divine into that of the human. It is, of course, *love*—human love, which not only exists under the shadow of death, but lives and burns all the more brightly in that very shadow. Brünnhilde's great significance in the *Ring* is her evolution into one of Wagner's several supreme embodiments of his vision of the ultimate in human love. Indeed, her eye-opening and will-liberating discovery of the possibilities of love, in her encounter with Siegmund, begins her own transformation, even if she is initially led—by both her own warrior-like predilections and Wotan's focus on the heroic ideal—to esteem the qualities Siegmund displays and that Siegfried is literally conceived to epitomize; but that is because her sensibility has not yet caught up with her recent revelation.

Once the new order arrives, then, the heroic alternative—the idea that what will replace Wotan's rule of law is the triumph of heroism—is accompanied by a second option: the possibility of *an order based on the sway of love*. Looking down from Valhalla, Wotan could conceivably reconcile himself to the idea that the rule of heroic virtue, as well as the rule of laws and contracts, is best replaced by the rule of love. In that event he might be able to see himself not as having failed but rather as having played a significant initiating role in a complex, multistage, process leading eventually to the realization of his goal of instituting the conditions for meaningful life in this world. We shall suggest, however, that for other reasons he does not do so.

Brünnhilde's dawning new capacity for love is a very different thing from the heroism that is Siegfried's primary stock-in-trade, and also from the adolescent style of love he brings to her—even if he himself begins to discover the possibility of a richer love through her, and perhaps at the end has grown enough to be capable of realizing it with her. It is different from Wotan's love as well, in its various significant forms, including that to which he rises so movingly at the extraordinary conclusion of *Walküre*—although it is both fair and important to recognize that Brünnhilde's achievement owes much to her lessons in love both from Siegmund and from her father. (When we focus on her development below, we shall consider the various ideals of love that are pertinent to understanding her judgments. For the moment, however, we continue to concentrate on Wotan's trajectory.)

Siegfried and Brünnhilde thus offer two different potential solutions to Wotan's problem of bringing about a durable admirable order—one cast in terms of the ascendancy of heroic virtue (Wotan's official solution during *Siegfried*, and perhaps already at the end of *Walküre*), the other in terms of the sway of love. Wotan would surely be right to think that both heroic virtues and love might have positive effects on human affairs and relations. Yet it is made painfully clear in the course of *Götterdämmerung* that however much can be said in favor of them, neither heroism nor love is likely to promote much in the way of *stability*, and indeed both are far more likely to destabilize just about any kind of order based upon general rules, regardless of their relative justice or injustice.

Once Brünnhilde's option is on display, however, Wagner invites us to consider whether love may be enough—enough, that is, to live and die for, and to live and die by, even if not enough to establish and secure a stable social order. If we start from what we take to have been Wotan's fundamental problem of whether and how life might be given some point and meaning, then love may turn out to provide a kind of solution, even though it is incapable of realizing and securing Wotan's preliminary aspiration for a stable and admirable order. It is not a happy solution, if either heroism or love—and it turns out to be love—may be the best we can achieve, since both tend to self-destruct. This is, after all, tragedy on the grandest of scales. Seen with the right eyes and attained sensibility, however, this could prove to be a solution nonetheless—and a powerful one at that. The attainment of this sensibility is a real and difficult accomplishment. It is the work and great achievement of tragic art.

Any treatment of Wotan's judgments after the end of *Siegfried* must be even more speculative than our account of his earlier intellectual and emotional odyssey has been, in view of his absence from the stage after his Wanderer's encounter with Siegfried. That meeting makes clear that even for a god who has acquiesced in his own passing, the end comes hard; but it leaves entirely open the possibility that he can console himself at that point with the thought that Project Siegfried is well and truly launched, and that the establishment of a noble human order of heroic dimensions and lineaments might be realized. The death of Siegfried certainly shatters whatever might have been left of that hope by the end of the penultimate scene of *Götterdämmerung*—as well as apparently spelling doom for the other possible solution to the problem of order, represented by the rule of love. But we know (from Waltraute, considerably earlier) that Wotan has been in a deep depression for quite some time. He did not return to Valhalla, pile up the logs from the World-Ash, summon gods and heroes to join him—and then deliver a stirring oration on the inevitable passing of their order. Instead, we are told, he sits, unsmiling and silent, clutching the splinters from the spear in his hand, while gods, heroes, and Valkyries are "consumed by dismay and infinite dread [*uns alle verzehrt/ Zagen und endlose Angst*]." What has happened?

We consider two possibilities, corresponding to the two possible solutions. One interpretation of Wotan's gloom is to suppose that he stays with the commitment to replacing his order of laws and contracts with the rule of heroic virtue. On this view of the matter, unlike Brünnhilde, he does not make the transition from thinking of the new order on the model of heroic virtue to conceiving it in terms of the sway of love. When he has the opportunity to size Siegfried up, he realizes that his high hopes for him—as prospective founder of a new heroic order surpassing his own efforts—are in vain. Whatever his merits, Siegfried is terminally naïve, hopelessly superficial, and foolishly brash; and while this may not matter in the wilds, in the far trickier world of human interaction with others—especially with people of a differing stripe and greater cunning—it is a fatal combination. Because of his naïvete, superficiality, and brashness, *this* hero cannot deliver the new order Wotan yearns for—but he has needed precisely these attributes to carry out the first part of the task Wotan has envisaged for him, to transcend the god's own order. If our first possibility is on the right track, once Wotan grasps the contradiction, he despairs.

The alternative is to suppose that he goes one step further. Before Siegfried ascends the rock and awakens Brünnhilde, Wotan is committed to heroic rule as the replacement for his own (failed) order. It is possible, however, that sooner or later he responds—as we, the audience, presumably are meant to do—to what happens next, seeing the expression of Brunnhilde's love as even more splendid than the heroic virtues on which he has been focused. At that point, on this alternative interpretation, it dawns on him that the right way to achieve the admirable order at which he has been aiming is through the sway of love. But he is surely wise enough to see something of which Brünnhilde only harbors vague premonitions—that the love of Siegfried and Brünnhilde is vulnerable to the same kinds of corruption that threatened his order of laws and contracts, and that love is no match for the greed, envy, and wickedness of the world. The most salient threat is posed by those who truly reject or are incapable of love. Once again, Alberich emerges as the focus of Wotan's concern, as he begins to see that the possibility of a relapse to the demonic order the Nibelung envisages is intensified by the continued existence of the Ring. Wotan's anxiety stems from his appreciation that the sway of love is unstable, and he comes to the desperate hope that the problems may be mitigated if the Ring is returned. By the beginning of *Götterdämmerung*, he has become convinced of the idea that the sway of love will be unstable unless the Ring is returned to the Rhinemaidens.

A clear-headed Wotan would also appreciate that he can neither interfere to bring about the return of the Ring (the point, after all, is that his reign and his power are at an end in any event) nor genuinely hope that Brünnhilde will voluntarily return the Ring. For he has cut her loose and set her adrift on the uncertain seas of mortality, condemned to cast her lot with whatever mortal hero happens along and passes the Fire Test. If his sources are any good, he must know that Siegfried has done so, and he must further know of Siegfried's gift of the Ring as the emblem of his love for her. If his sources were also good enough to give him some inkling of how she feels about it all, he must know that she would consider giving up the emblem of that love to be giving up love itself, which for her would be quite impossible. If love really is now to replace heroic as well as civic virtue as the supreme value—as it has in her case—and so is to be given precedence over all else, then Wotan must accept the consequence that Brünnhilde should not return the Ring.

So what hope is there for Wotan's dream of not only achieving but also stabilizing an admirable order? Apparently none. For at this stage we cannot imagine him even contemplating some further strategy such as some new set of free beings who would transcend Brünnhilde and Siegfried, as they transcended him. Wotan can think of no way out. No wonder he sits with the kindling piled around, in a state of thorough dejection. On this interpretation, he has come back to his earlier pessimistic assumption, the belief that there is no real alternative to laws and contracts as the foundation of a stable order, and that otherwise the world will be bleak and cheerless and life stunted. The possibility of that alternative has now passed, with the triumph of the hero and the shattering of the spear.

So, it seems, Wotan must abandon his hope of fulfilling his basic normative judgment that life, to be worth living, must be made meaningful. The difficulty he ignored in *Rheingold*—the problem Loge saw, that the commitment to the rule of laws and contracts required the return of the gold—has come back to haunt the transformed world, and Wotan sees nothing better than for the Ring to be returned (and so denied to the Dark Forces). This is to wipe the slate clean and to become resigned to the conclusion that law, heroism, and love are all unable to provide a viable solution to the problem of achieving and securing the kind of order apparently required to banish the alternative specters of emptiness and degradation, and so to save life and the world from themselves. Since Wotan continues to think that a durable admirable order is a precondition for meaningful life, he must conclude that the failure infects his aspirations at the most fundamental level; and that all of his striving has been in vain.

13

Wotan's Dilemmas

We have been reconstructing the course of Wotan's judgments throughout the *Ring* in the hope of making them and their relationships as clear as possible. To this point we have focused largely on the earlier parts of his trajectory. We now shall explore the course of its later stages more closely, starting with an obviously important moment: Wotan's judgment of Brünnhilde in Act III, Scenes 2 and 3, of *Walküre*. In this almost unbearably painful passage, Wotan's harshness is initially repellent. Yet if we listen carefully to his arraignment and denunciation of her, his tone is almost consistently an indignant defense of wronged justice: Brünnhilde has broken faith with him, and with herself as well, denying her own nature as his creature, as the instrument of his will. Plainly the earlier conviction that his only power of creation is to generate dependent beings pervades his verdict, and when he sings of the inevitability of her banishment from the company of the gods ("*Nicht send' ich dich mehr aus Walhall* [No more shall I send you forth from Valhalla]"), he does not mourn their separation but simply declares the inevitable consequences of a just resolution. (Although these lovely melodic lines could easily be charged with the sentiments that will arise in him later—and they will be treated differently in the orchestral transition that prepares the mood of the third scene—it is important to honor Wagner's stage direction: the god remains angry (*zornig*), not sorrowful (*pathetisch*).) Denying what she has been, Brünnhilde can only remain what she has chosen to become: an outcast, mortal woman, prey to the debased concubinage we have already glimpsed in the first act.

In his initial pronouncement of Brünnhilde's fate, Wotan confronts her as the hard voice and arm of the law he feels compelled to be. But when the eight Valkyries offer their shallow protest, his state of mind intensifies into rage, and even wrathful cruelty, driven by the pain he feels at Brünnhilde's betrayal. We shudder with her at his madly vindictive provision of detail as he announces to his long-beloved daughter that she will "sit by the hearth and spin, the butt and plaything of all who despise her [*am Herde sitzt sie und spinnt,/ aller Spottenden Ziel und Spiel*]." These chilling lines conjure the image of Sieglinde's plight and recall her description of her wedding feast in Hunding's hut. And we may well suppose that it is to precisely this cruel fate, of which she is well aware, that Wotan in his fury means to condemn her. It is a fury that clearly is being fueled by a good deal more than Brünnhilde's action alone, reflecting the depths of his anguish at the impossibility of his own situation and the devastation of his hopes and dreams.

Brünnhilde's wonderful question "*War es so schmählich, was ich verbrach?* [Was my wrong really so shameful?]" therefore compels our deepest sympathy; for the severity of the punishment Wotan has prescribed for her seems wildly excessive, heartless, and unworthy of him. Yet even here, as in Fricka's earlier myopic perspective on the course of events, there is a danger that we shall take too limited a view, resenting Wotan's harshness without appreciating the disastrous character of his only apparent alternatives. There is another way to interpret what is going on here—or perhaps there is another dimension to it. At this juncture he may no longer actually still hope to solve the problem of stable order (since he presumably is still gripped by the despair of Act II, Scene 2); but even so, he evidently believes that the only possible course for him is to remain true to the laws and contracts he has instituted, notwithstanding the parts of him to which Brünnhilde is appealing. At some level, he surely understands that his "great idea" has come to naught because he allowed himself to step out of his role as Guardian of Law—but that very thought may impel him to play the role with grim rigor. Despite his love for Brünnhilde (manifest in their earlier exchange and to be even more evident in his valediction), he feels that he simply must honor his commitment to what he takes to be the higher, larger good—and has to work himself up into a rage to be able to do so.

The situation is intensified because as Wotan makes clear to the other Valkyries, Brünnhilde was brought into being precisely with the aim of contributing to his project of creating a stable order, out of his determination to shore up and extend the rule of law; and she has been his intimate and stalwart throughout his struggles to this end. Moreover, knowing himself to have been swayed culpably by his affections (he has protected Siegmund as a subverter of law), he must punish himself in condemning Brünnhilde. His dedication to the law comes at the cost of excising part of himself: out of love for the world, he must suppress his own personal love for her—as he had been earlier persuaded by Fricka that he must do in the case of Siegmund. From his entry, through most of the two scenes that follow, he succeeds in adopting the role of the guardian of justice, unmoved by love or mercy. We only understand the difficulties of the achievement, however, and its terrible costs, when at the very end of *Walküre*, he transcends the role he has assigned himself.

The extraordinarily moving outpouring of Wotan's love for Brünnhilde, as his valediction surges from the depths of his being ("*Leb' wohl* . . . [Fare well . . .]"), is made possible by the development of his judgment of what she has done, expressed in successive characterizations of what is initially viewed as an act of betrayal. Scene 3 opens with the god's anger dissipated, replaced by a solemn commitment to the judgment he has issued. Brünnhilde's touching questions elicit a recapitulation of his original verdict that she stands condemned by her own actions, delivered now with the anger drained away. She replies that what she did was meant to respond to the god's own intentions, not to the instructions he gave when he was "an enemy to himself." This prompts an initial change in his understanding of her conduct, moving him to see it instead as a form of blundering in matters far beyond her comprehension; who is she, this dependent being, to suppose that his godlike will can be distorted by pressures from Fricka, to presume that he might be weakly diverted from the most important things? His first shift in attitude is to dismiss her as lamentably foolish.

Brünnhilde humbly acknowledges her own limitations—she is not wise—but, with a quiet firmness in tender vocal lines, she explains her recognition of love, in Wotan, in herself, and in Siegmund (we shall have much more to say about this moving confession in Chapter 16). As he listens, Wotan's verdict alters again, although his response to her continues to be framed by a sense that his own perspective is far more encompassing than anything she can envisage. If, as he now believes, she was moved by love and a sense of his loves, it remains true (he supposes) that her emotional understanding is relatively shallow—"*So leicht wähnest du/ Wonne des Herzens erworben* [So lightly you thought that heartfelt delight might be won]"—and that she fails to appreciate the many-sidedness of his own love and the pains that its frustration brings to him. He answers her melting phrases with a passage of great beauty, conveying to us—and to her—the god's own comprehension of love and its temptations. So, after we hear him mourn the ruins of his world, the musical texture and tempo change, and the god sings of her "blissful abandon [*selige Lust*]" in lines that both express its sweetness and its inadequacy as a response to the grief that attends his shattered designs. She has chosen to follow love; and a life of love—but of mortal human love, with all of its liabilities and vulnerabilities—is to be her sentence.

Brünnhilde's last explanation is to bring home to Wotan an aspect of her love that he has not yet appreciated and that shows the predicament he assigns to her to be unjust, prompting him to modify his judgment yet again. Her emphatic repudiation of dishonor culminates in the impassioned plea that Wotan surround the rock with fire, making it impossible for anyone other than a true hero to take possession of her. And the god accedes. He does so, we think, because he becomes aware that she has not completely denied her nature after all, and that what he took originally to be a repudiation of both him and herself was a response to elements in his and her own character that are far from blameworthy—and more specifically to a capacity for love that is not merely (as he had previously charged) a hankering for sweet solace, but rather a deep response to what is noble and honorable. His recognition unfolds in the magnificent farewell, calling from him his own love and his own appreciation of her nobility. The separation between them can no longer be foretold in the stern tones of justice. Instead, we hear the heartrending expression of Wotan's love, suffused with the bittersweet rapture of their reconciliation and their parting, in music of unsurpassable beauty that leaves no doubt whatever about the truth and depth of that love. We have never heard Wotan sing anything like this before; and we never will again. Nor will we again be given any reason to believe that he remains capable of such a love, once he has left Brünnhilde to her human fate and sundered the tie that had seemed to bind them irrevocably.

Brünnhilde's last explanation makes possible the extraordinary valediction and the mitigation of her sentence. In the course of convincing Wotan that her love is not light but noble, a response to the honorable goals that he has struggled so hard to attain, she makes a crucial pronouncement, reporting on Sieglinde's survival and her pregnancy. The god's initial response is to misconceive the point of her news: dedicated to his role as the instrument of justice, he angrily dismisses any idea that he should give aid to Sieglinde (or to her unborn child) and warns Brünnhilde against further meddling. Once again, we sense the deep and bitter residues of Fricka's denial that he can manage by proxy what he is forbidden to do himself. Yet the information about Sieglinde begins to give Wotan ideas, even though he cannot yet give them conscious expression. He gains new hope, envisioning that the hero who will awake Brünnhilde will be one freer than himself; but he recognizes that the realization of that hope requires his clear commitment not to interfere. The hero must truly act independently of Wotan's designs. His new focus leads him to pursue (with increasing clarity of intent) an aim that has been dimly present since the end of *Rheingold* and that will become fully explicit in Act III, Scene 1, of *Siegfried*. The free being is no longer a mere means to securing the order of laws and contracts, and is instead emerging as the key to its transcendence.

But in the matter at hand, Wotan is paying a high price, and he realizes it. We take his self-description seriously: "*einer Welt zu Liebe/ der Liebe Quell/ im gequälten Herzen zu hemmen* [out of my love for the world, I was forced to staunch the well-spring of love in this tormented heart of mine]." He has indeed suppressed personal love in himself, and we witness his anguished mortification of it—accompanied by a version of the motif with which Alberich originally renounced love. But a personal love that one is willing and able to subordinate to any other purpose, however grand, is no longer the real thing. One may have good and sufficient reasons for making the choice, but it is a choice with fatal consequences for that love. Something fundamental in him dies with it, even if his care for Brünnhilde remains intense; and his very capacity for personal love survives only in transmuted form, as a profound yearning for a world in which such love might flourish, unthreatened either by the need for its sacrifice or by the results of not making the sacrifice.

As the Wanderer he now becomes, the ironist of *Siegfried*, Wotan is thus doubly diminished; for he has resigned himself to the need for his own passing, accepting the idea that the emergence of a new order of free and noble human heroes provides the best chance of satisfying his old yearning for an order that would enable life to attain genuine significance; and he has stifled his own capacity for love. (If we look forward to his subsequent state of mind reported in Waltraute's narration in *Götterdämmerung* and see him as moving beyond the hope for the triumph of heroism to the successor idea that love must be the new world-ordering value, its vulnerabilities notwithstanding, we may expect the sadness to be further deepened; for he knows all too well by then that he has sacrificed the loves he cherished most, and also knows that he is powerless to do anything to improve the chances of the rule of love being realized in any enduring way in the kind of world this is.) The rigor of the judgment of Brünnhilde remains, but it is no longer wrathful. Wotan is committed to playing by the rules—observing, but not interfering in an attempt to control the course of events.

Yet he is still there—and what he does could well have an impact. How, then, does Wotan avoid compromising the integrity of Siegfried's freedom? How does he solve the problem that seemed so intractable to the Wotan of *Walküre*—that of creating a being who would be no mere extension of himself, but rather, despite the effects of his continued presence, a genuinely autonomous agent?

During the course of *Siegfried*, Wotan does a number of things. To begin with, he engages in a riddle duel with Mime, at the end of which he provides the dwarf with a crucial item of information: only one who does not know fear can forge Siegmund's sword Nothung anew. He converses with Alberich, offering to warn Fafner that the hero is on his way and allowing Alberich to volunteer to take the Ring (thereby saving the dragon from Siegfried's sword). He summons Erda, and then delays Siegfried on his way to awaken Brünnhilde. These actions have causal consequences that seem to bear on the outcome for which Wotan hopes: Siegfried's forging Nothung, killing the dragon, and awakening Brünnhilde. Without Wotan's divulging to Mime the special attributes of the sword-repairer, would Nothung have been reforged? If Wotan had tried a bit harder to convince Fafner, could the dragon have been persuaded to give up the Ring to Alberich? And if Wotan had exercised his full godlike powers, could he have stopped Siegfried? If the answers to these questions are the wrong ones (No, Yes, and Yes, respectively), it would seem to follow that the Wanderer, for all his hands-off pretense, would still be manipulating and guiding the action; and like his father before him, Siegfried would turn out to be merely a Ring-retrieving, dragon-slaying puppet.

Within the Christian tradition, there is a long history of discussions of the compatibility of human freedom with divine providence. Typically, the questions begin from the supposed omniscience of the deity: since God knows everything, he knows how human actions are going to unfold, and that advance knowledge is often taken to preclude our freedom. Wagner's Wotan is a more limited god and is far from omniscient; for example, he often clearly does not know in advance how things will turn out. So there is no problem in the *Ring* about the possibility of human freedom on this score. If there is a problem, it relates to the question of the reconcilability of autonomy with external intervention. Wotan also is far from omnipotent. Yet he has a long history of actions that either modify the consequences of what agents do (so that they accord with what he wants), or else direct the allegedly free agents to want to do something that will issue in outcomes he seeks. Even with Wotan's limited powers, therefore, one might discern a problem for the possibility of human freedom—as Fricka did previously in the case of Siegmund. Do Wotan's actions render the idea of Siegfried's autonomy an illusion too?

Consider Siegmund. Wotan planted a sword with magic powers in Hunding's hut; and he also raised the young hero to behave in particular ways, so that he would be led into quarrels that ultimately left him in need of a weapon, and in the right place to find it. He both shaped Siegmund's will and altered what would have been the normal consequences of Siegmund's exercise of his will had he been left to himself from the outset. Are things any different with Siegfried? Wotan is plainly not responsible for the preservation of the sword for Siegfried's eventual use. That is Brünnhilde's work, undertaken while she is opposing his explicit commands. Nor can Sieglinde's escape (and thus the preservation of the embryonic Siegfried) be traced to any cunning plan on Wotan's part. For Wotan does not know either that Sieglinde has survived or that she is pregnant until it is too late for him to do much about it. But he would have interfered in a manner analogous to his shaping of Siegmund's life if he had given Siegfried instructions about how to refashion the sword. Nor would things have been better if he had told Mime, and the dwarf had passed on the instructions. From the beginning of *Siegfried*, the young hero wants a proper sword and, in his childish way, he rails at Mime for not providing him with one. Wotan would have played a role in shaping the outcomes if he had made it possible for Siegfried to obtain what he wants.

But this is not the way the forging of Nothung goes. When Siegfried returns, Mime does not hand him the pieces and tell him that to have the sword he wants, he, the unskilled youth, will have to do the job. Instead, after Mime's apparently evasive remarks about learning fear, Siegfried finally becomes impatient and decides to forge the sword himself. The consequence is achieved without the hero being *taught* anything; his emotional response to the dwarf's stalling simply leads him to grab the fragments and go to work. Wotan has taught Mime, but the chain of instruction stops there; so the god's intervention plays no real role in the actual manufacture.

Consider next the meeting with Alberich outside the dragon's lair. In the early phases of their conversation, Wotan informs the Nibelung that he is standing back and observing the attempts to regain the Ring, and that he himself will not play an active part. In what appears to be an act of bravado to prove his good faith, after explaining that the candidates for winning back the Ring are the hero and the two dwarves who covet it, he then offers to wake Fafner so that Alberich can try to persuade the dragon to let the Ring go. Wotan even acts as an impresario for Alberich's attempt, shouting to rouse the dragon, and then introducing the dwarf as someone who has come to issue a warning. The important point here, however, is that Alberich is allowed to try the ploy for himself. Perhaps Wotan could have done more to help; but what is crucial is that the god does nothing to hinder. Hence his action cannot be accused of slanting the outcomes toward what he prefers. On the contrary, tempting fate, he provides an opportunity for his own plans to go awry—an opportunity that comes to nothing.

The most challenging issue concerns what does and does not happen during Wotan's final active moments onstage. For Siegfried to supplant Wotan and his brand of admirable order, there must be a confrontation, in which the hero must be victorious. But in the scene immediately preceding their meeting, Wotan tells Erda that he wills his end. How then can there be a genuine struggle? If Wotan wills his own passing, then he must be determined to lose—but if that is so, how can the hero genuinely win? The fight is fixed, even if Siegfried has no inkling of it, or even of what is going on.

Interestingly, the Wanderer does nothing obvious to provoke a conflict with the youth. He poses a few questions, asks for respect, and responds "very calmly" (stage direction) when Siegfried exhibits some of his standard impatience. Even the hero's derisive laughter fails to arouse Wotan, who expresses both sorrow at the insults Siegfried has just flung at him and concern for the young man. Bent on climbing the slope, the uncomprehending Siegfried brusquely orders the god out of his way. And, at this point, Wotan's calm vanishes. Gentle admonishment ("*Kenntest du mich,/ kühner Spross* [If you but knew me, brave-hearted youth]") gives way to anger, when Siegfried's arrogance finally becomes intolerable to him; and out of what is clearly an emotional response, he brandishes his spear, thereby picking the fight that Siegfried quickly and easily wins.

We do not think that Wotan is play-acting here. The anger and passion are genuine. However strongly he may have resolved to remain in the mode of onlooker, and however genuinely he may have intended to let the hero surpass him, when the moment comes he cannot help asserting himself. Siegfried's brashness is so intolerable that we can well imagine the god wondering whether he should stand aside and relinquish the world *to this*. Among other things, the boy is totally devoid of any curiosity about the history that might stand behind this relationship, caring neither where the fragments of the sword came from nor why this old man professes love for him and his kind. So Wotan has grounds for doubt about the stability of the rule of the heroic. But "wondering" and "doubt" are probably the wrong words. Wotan does not reflect or calculate; rather, he is impelled by strong emotions. Yet, instead of preventing the outcome he had intended, his unintended emotional reaction is just what is needed to secure it. If Wotan had remained calm, things would not have transpired as his ending requires; for there would either have been no struggle at all, or any show of resistance on his part would have been a charade. At the last moment, however, the hero's extraordinary boorishness gets under Wotan's skin, generating a *real* contest and a *real* loss.

It is hard to tell, from the way Wotan "quietly" picks up the pieces of his spear, "falls back," says "*Zieh hin! Ich kann dich nicht halten!* [Go ahead! I can't stop you!]," and "suddenly disappears" (as the stage directions specify), whether he is acquiescing in what has just occurred or is a broken god with nothing left but his dignity. What has happened, however, is nothing less than he had envisioned with great fanfare in his final promise to the sleeping Brünnhilde at the conclusion of *Walküre*: "*Wer meines Speeres Spitze fürchtet, durchschreite das Feuer nie!* [Whoever fears the point of my spear will never pass through the fire!]." But it is one thing to put the matter that way, in the negative (which some translations obscure), and another to accept the reality of someone actually rising to the challenge and decisively succeeding. And what we subsequently learn of Wotan thereafter from Waltraute certainly would seem to support the conclusion that he is indeed broken by the encounter, left with little hope of any fitting ending to his strivings.

In any event, the upshot would seem to be the vindication of the idea of Siegfried's autonomy, despite the validity of Fricka's critique in a case like that of Siegmund. When someone other than the agent is in control of all of the critical variables, as in the instance of Siegmund, there is only the semblance of autonomy. But when at least some such variables are under the agent's control, then however witless the agent may be (and Siegfried is) with respect to the complexities of the situation, the ability of someone other than the agent (like Wotan) to intervene in certain ways does not suffice to preclude the possibility of action that may be considered genuinely (even if not unqualifiedly) autonomous—despite the fact that the outcome may be an action that happens to accord precisely with the desire prompting the intervention (as happens in the case of Wotan and Siegfried). The irony of the way the encounter between them unfolds only serves to underscore this point. For better or for worse, Siegfried acts independently of Wotan's will, even if he does realize Wotan's basic intention in doing so.

Armed with this account, we can return to the creation of Brünnhilde as a free being. After the god's revelation to her in Act II, Scene 2, of *Walküre*, she stages a minor attempt at rebellion, telling her father that she cannot kill a hero whom he loves. This provokes the curt and harsh rejoinder that she is nothing but the tool of his will; and as he storms off, she remains "shocked and stunned" (stage direction) by his torment and anger. The impact of that emotional response is then part of what prepares the way for the more serious revolt that soon follows. Wotan's jolt to her is thus a factor in her decision to aid Siegmund, without which she might well not have done so—although Wotan certainly does not plan it that way but rather intends precisely the opposite. As in the cases of Siegfried's forging of the sword and of the Wanderer's subsequent confrontation with him, the chain of causation runs through *emotional* states rather than through deliberate acts of planning, and indeed runs contrary to Wotan's settled intentions.

So also the decision to defend Siegmund itself produces new anger, and the wrath is expressed in a scheme of punishment, at first harsh and later ameliorated. The punishment, which strips Brünnhilde of her divinity and makes her fully human, is not intended to turn her into a free being—but that is its result. If Wotan had been serene and reflective, dreaming up a very similar plot, in which Brünnhilde was duped into "opposing" him with the goal of making her a free being, then he would not have achieved his end. The product would still have been a creature bearing the stamp of his will. Precisely because his anger overwhelms him, however, and because he is not deliberately attempting to transform her into a free being but simply to express what he feels to be the appropriate response to her betrayal, he does manage to produce an outcome he had thought to be impossible, even if in a very unexpected way and quarter—and even if that outcome is far from realizing the hopes he had had in seeking it, at least as he had envisioned them.

Wotan's lament that "servants are all I can produce!" is therefore wrong and yet well warranted; for free beings can only be generated from those of his actions in which planning does not play the central role—paradigmatically when his deliberations are overridden by the surges of his feelings, and when his conception of what he is doing overlooks important consequences that will result. In a very deep sense, the freedom of Brünnhilde and Siegfried is generated in spite of himself. There are times at which Wotan is dangerously close to his old self-defeating predicament of pulling the strings in the attempt to engineer autonomy, the most notable of which is the confrontation with Siegfried that ushers in his own passing and leaves him permanently out of control; and what saves him from that predicament is ironically not his intelligence or even his best intentions but rather his emotions—and unlovely ones at that.

We are given one last detailed vision of the god and of his judgment. In *Götterdämmerung*, Waltraute comes to Brünnhilde to ask her to return the Ring to the Rhinemaidens, and she quotes Wotan's whispered wish: "*des Tiefen Rheines Töchtern/ gäbe den Ring sie wieder zurück,/ von des Fluches Last/ erlös't wär' Gott und Welt!* [If she gave back the Ring to the deep Rhine's daughters, the weight of the curse would be lifted from both god and world!]." Waltraute has described Wotan as sighing, with a softer glance, as he thinks of Brünnhilde. His despair should not be understood as an expression of a residual longing for his system of laws and contracts. By this time his commitment to that order is long gone, and the order itself has passed with the shattering of the spear. Nor is Wotan simply coming to grasp the point that Loge insisted on many operatic hours ago—that the rule of law required and depended upon the return of the gold. Instead, we take Wotan to have become profoundly dubious about the possibility of any stable order that might succeed his own and fare any better.

The Wanderer ironist of *Siegfried* was reconciled to the prospect of his end because he supposed that it would usher in a new age of heroic virtue, with vileness vanquished and baseness banished under Siegfried's banner. In the confrontation scene, however, Wotan has surely observed the downside of naïve heroism—and felt it too, in the anger that flared up and led to conflict. Back in Valhalla, he broods on the world he has loved, left in the hands of a foolish boy. But it has not been left in Siegfried's hands alone. For there is also Brünnhilde, the recollection of whom can at least lighten the god's despair. So Wotan may at least be capable of entertaining the idea of love as a kind of consolation that might even be a last great hope—if only it were attainable and sustainable. Yet he quite certainly knows that the world still contains the enemies of love, Alberich and his kin, bent on instituting a very different order of their own, demonic and grim; and he already foresees what the action of *Götterdämmerung* will make devastatingly clear: that the rule of love has very poor prospects. The gray god therefore can only envision a bleak ending, a blank defeat. He is at a complete loss. All that remains for him is to arrange the conditions for the consummation of the gods, leaving the world to its own sad devices and sorry fate, and to await those ends, without hope, in infinite sadness.

14

Wotan's Authority

Despite the richness of the development of Wotan's judgments throughout the *Ring*, they — like Wotan himself — must be transcended. Even the final judgments we have ascribed to him are not the last word. For his exploration of the possibilities does not exhaust them. In particular, bound as he is to the thought that the endowment of life with point and meaning requires a stable order, he fails to appreciate a way in which his world can be brought to a different kind of meaningful end (as we have already intimated and soon will elaborate more fully). Before we leave Wotan, however, we should consider the scope and sources of his authority.

We have already drawn the distinction between *cognitive* or *epistemic* knowledge-based authority (focusing on what a character knows or is in a privileged position to know) and *directive* or action-related and power-based authority (concentrating on the areas in which a character's claims are translated into action and on why this character has the ability to affect events). With respect to the figures we considered earlier —Loge and Erda in particular — directive authority is always bound up with their influence on Wotan. To the extent that their judgments direct the course of the action, that is because Wotan cedes cognitive authority to them. For the most part, Wotan is good at identifying cognitive authority; he sees that Loge and Erda are in privileged positions to know certain kinds of things (although, as we have seen, he has blind spots), and he takes advantage of their abilities, modifying his behavior in response to what they tell him.

What is the source of Wotan's directive authority? It is easy to take for granted his ability to translate what he thinks he knows into action. Wotan himself is very clear what the source is supposed to be, as are Fricka, Alberich, and others: his power rests on the system of laws and contracts he has instituted. Once he has established it, however, it ties his hands. His difficulty for much of the *Ring* is that the judgments he wants to be effective in action are hard to reconcile with the system, and the struggles we have traced above can be seen as attempts to render the things he wants to do or accomplish consistent with it.

Compatibility with the system of laws and contracts, of course, does not guarantee that Wotan's actions will be effective. The power he has gained by fashioning the branch of the World-Ash into a spear is, like Erda's knowledge, extensive but not boundless. Moreover, it is compromised in several important respects that raise larger questions about both its legitimacy and its viability. We eventually learn that the branch from which the spear was fashioned was torn from the World-Ash, severely wounding it, and thus that the acquisition of power came at great cost to a source on which everything ultimately depends. As was noted above, Wotan's unnatural rending of the primordial state is not unlike the violence Alberich inflicts on the rock that bears the Rhinegold, even though Wotan aims at a positive improvement of the primal order. His dealings with the giants and many other previous attempts to achieve his high ends have involved Wotan in tricks, deceit, and naked exercise of power. As he admits to Brünnhilde, in his quest to win the world "*Untreue übt' ich* [I had no scruples]" (*Walküre*, Act II, Scene 2).

Thus the purportedly meaning-constituting order of laws and contracts was instituted and is being maintained by decidedly shady means, generating serious worries about the legitimacy of the entire arrangement. An order built and maintained in this way may be divine in inspiration and appearance, and even in substance; but an end achieved by such means is far from unproblematic, however immaculate its conception. The flawed basis for Wotan's authority, moreover, is reflected in the evident limits to its scope and sway. He therefore discovers, to his chagrin, that his ability to achieve his ends is also limited, even when they are consistent with his legal system. When his judgments are irreconcilable with the system, his ability to effect them is diminished further, even below the level of those on whom he tries to impose his will.

Götterdämmerung offers a narrative explanation of how this has come about: the story of the breaking of the branch from the World-Ash. Wotan paid a price for his gain. He sacrificed an eye to obtain (simultaneously) directive authority and a capacity for knowledge that transcended that of his companions. His cognitive authority derives, we suggest, from the fact that he was driven to make this sacrifice by his prior awareness of a question that other denizens of the world in which he found himself had never posed—the question of how to create a stable order that would make meaningful life possible. He alone saw (or perhaps he saw with greater clarity and focus) the vision of a world order that would at once supersede its primordial condition, establishing a context for nobler and grander life, and also subdue the countervailing and corrupting tendencies that are exemplified in various forms throughout the *Ring*, checking both their ugly assertiveness when unrestrained and their resentful vindictiveness when thwarted. An order based on the rule of law would realize that vision.

From the start of his quest, then, we suppose that Wotan linked two things together: the idea of the possibility and desirability of greater meaningfulness, and the idea of a system that would establish and secure the conditions of its real-world realization, while keeping the forces of darkness in check. His cognitive authority, large as it becomes, is always bounded by these guiding ideas. And whether he was right or mistaken to connect the possibility of greater meaningfulness with the attainability and sustainability of an admirable order by way of an enforceable system of laws and contracts, he achieved a genuine insight by seeing and posing the right fundamental questions. In the primordial land of the blind, that insight earned him the right to become the one-eyed king.

Yet Wotan saw more. Another part of what he recognized was that he needed to *learn* more and a further part of it was to grasp how he should do so. He did not stride away from the World-Ash with all the intelligence and acuity we see him applying in the *Ring*. Before the opening of *Rheingold*, he was able to appreciate Loge's aptitudes and to acquire his service. With the appearance of Erda, he saw a new opportunity for extending his intellectual grasp. He synthesized cognitive gifts that are distributed between these two, his principal sources, with the intelligence and vision he had already acquired. Throughout the *Ring* all are put to work as he wrestles with the problem that obsesses him. His knowledge becomes vast because he continues to understand what he still needs to learn and who might help him to learn it. (Thus there is a special edge to the exchange with Mime in Act I of *Siegfried* since, cunning though he is, Mime is not an intelligent learner.)

Long ago, at the World-Ash, Wotan's knowledge grew with the sacrifice of a part of himself. And the sacrifices continue. In tapping Erda's intuitive wisdom, he diminishes it, weakening and eventually losing her and her guidance. In exhausting Loge's instrumental rationality, he reduces Loge to a more primitive state, and so deprives himself of valuable counsel. In fathoming the intricacies of the relations among his goals and strategies, he must give up first Siegmund and then Brünnhilde. In finding his way to a new goal, the goal of achieving his own ending in a meaningful manner, he must forsake the active role he has played in the world. At each stage, Wotan mutilates himself; parts of him drop away, leaving a god ever more crippled and forlorn. Yet even at the end of his quest, even after all the struggles and sacrifices, he does not know enough. He cannot resolve the question of how his world is to end. A part of his tragedy is that he has abandoned love in the service of law; another is that along the way to the end of *Walküre*, he relinquishes everything that is most precious to him. At its center is his commitment to a grand task, which he pursues with ferocious determination—and yet he ultimately realizes that not only has he failed to achieve it, but he has also contributed to the failure by the ways in which he has attempted it.

But Wotan's failure is not complete. He makes possible one whose judgments and authority come to transcend his. And that is not Siegfried. It is Brünnhilde.

15

Siegmund and Sieglinde

Before we focus in detail on Brünnhilde, however, we need to consider two others, whom Wotan also makes possible, and by whom (in a significant sense) the Brünnhilde who transcends Wotan is made possible as well: Siegmund and Sieglinde. Their importance is greater than their presence; for, in a way that Wotan never imagined, they far overshoot the mark he set for them, attaining authority and making judgments that affect the entire course and meaning of the *Ring*. They herald and catalyze its metamorphosis from the saga of Wotan's great but doomed campaign into Brünnhilde's transcendent drama, anticipating not only Siegfried's heroic alternative to Wotan's divine way but also its Brünnhildean supersession. The kind of love Siegmund and Sieglinde discover and share changes everything.

Siegmund and Sieglinde are often regarded as little more than a warm-up act for Siegfried and Brünnhilde, foreshadowing in lower case what their successors display in capital letters, hero and HERO, love and LOVE. But this does not do them justice. Siegmund compares favorably in many respects with his son; and while Brünnhilde does surpass Sieglinde (along with everyone else) in the end, she never would have been able to do so without the lesson in love that she learned thanks to them. It is Siegmund whose love for Sieglinde makes such an impression upon Brünnhilde; but it is Sieglinde who introduces him to its possibility and inspires it in him, even as she is also the inspiration of his transformation from the sorry figure who turns up at Hunding's hearth—a man for whom nothing ever goes right—into the hero he had the potential to become.

Sieglinde's authority is nowhere more evident than in her bestowal of a name befitting a hero upon the stranger who calls himself Wehwalt, "woeful one." Her authority is grounded in part in her discernment of his true but latent heroic qualities. But that knowledge by itself is only one element of it. Another is the powerful attraction that she feels for him, not merely as her hero and deliverer but as her heart's dream come true, which is in the process of turning into an all-consuming love that knows no bounds. And she is no mere ordinary mortal, but rather the god's human daughter, in whom a spark of the divine lives; when fanned it will burst into a flame, endowing her humanity with its own version of divinity.

Sieglinde's warmth, compassion, and tenderness—along with her sorrow—are made evident from her first entrance, not only by the melting phrases Wagner gives her but also by the yearning expressed in the orchestral accompaniment. Her gentle concern for the unknown guest is quickly charged with sexual ardor, and it is no surprise that Siegmund revives, his downcast weariness giving way to the sweeping sense of new beginnings ("*die Sonne lacht mir nun neu* [the sun smiles upon me anew]"). Their swelling emotions are expressed in the intense sweetness of the musical phrases that follow (particularly in the strings, clarinets, and horns), as if the immediate consummation of their love were inevitable—until Siegmund abruptly breaks the mood, hesitantly confessing his ill-fortune and declaring his intention to leave. Only when her declaration of sorrow answers his—"You can't bring ill-luck into a house where ill-luck already lives! [*Nicht bringst du Unheil dahin,/ wo Unheil im Hause wohnt!*]"—does Siegmund give up his plan to leave; and then once again the orchestra gives voice to their mutual sympathy and sexual longing.

The sympathy is deepened by Siegmund's three-part narrative, the fatal confession of the outcast role he has played and of his recent violence against Hunding's kin. Sieglinde clearly hears the tale of his intervention not as an outburst of hideously misguided gallantry, but rather in terms of the oppression she has known and the deliverance for which she has waited. She sees the nobility of this luckless wanderer, this apparently lawless and blundering rebel, knowing him better than he knows himself. Responding to the heroic daring she senses in him, she prepares the drugged drink for Hunding and returns to reply to his autobiographical fragments with the account of her own forced marriage—a narrative in which past sorrows and past promises unfulfilled surge into a new confidence. In the wonderful climax (from "*O fänd' ich ihn hier* [Might I find him here]" to the end of her long monologue) she holds out to him the promise not only of his deliverance but also of the exquisite gift of herself.

The sexuality of Sieglinde's attraction to Siegmund could not be more overwhelming, or more evident. (Indeed, Wagner risks rendering the palpability of her desire almost comical in the way he has her react—"gripped by astonishment and rapture" and then "in greatest intoxication [*in höchster Trunkenheit*]"—as Siegmund draws out and brandishes his mighty new sword.) And it is made no less clear that Siegmund's desire is the full equal of hers, in both kind and intensity. But Siegmund's passion reaches its white heat in response to hers; she leads the way, opening the doors to it, and then releasing the floodgates for it. Her yearning to enfold the hero in her arms inspires his ardent embrace, transforming him from the luckless outcast to the sublime embodiment of her deepest longings, as "she sinks with a cry onto his breast" and "the curtain falls quickly" on the stage flooded with the light of the full spring moon.

It is important, however, that their attraction to and love for each other is not merely sexual. They are soul-mates as well, as their twin-relationship is also meant to convey and make plausible, their long separation notwithstanding. And they are as close to being equals as Wagner could imagine them and make them.

Moreover, even if Sieglinde's love of Siegmund is born of desperation as well as of attunement and desire, it clearly soars beyond these all-too-human origins and limitations, her subsequent post-coital trauma notwithstanding. She may lack the strength not to falter; but while her newfound love is at full sail, it carries her well beyond any concern with "good and evil" as they are ordinarily reckoned, not to mention prudence. For the sake of love she is ready, willing, and able to stand up to her dangerous husband, drug him, leave him, and forsake him for another—and for another who happens to be her brother at that. Borne along by the torrent of her love, the incest taboo means no more to her than do any of the norms she disregards where her husband is concerned. Nor does she do so out of mere susceptibility. On the contrary: she does so out of a strength and conviction born of her love, which itself endows her with the authority to make the judgments that these seeming wrongs are in this instance absolutely right. Everything she expresses in the third scene of Act I of *Walküre* (and thereafter) must be understood as a natural outgrowth of the warm tenderness with which she was introduced at the beginning of the act. Like Siegmund, we have watched the beauty of that growth, and this musical and emotional efflorescence is intended to leave no doubt about the goodness and truth (not to mention the beauty) of what they sing and do. (Only Fricka and her kindred spirits will want to carp.)

Sieglinde is thus endowed, by the power and essential purity of her love (its sexuality included), not only with the authority to summon Siegmund both to heroism and to join her on the heights of that love, but also to break conventions of all sorts for its sake. She ventures unhesitatingly beyond good and evil, suspending ethical considerations. Her actions reflect implicit judgments sanctioned by that authority that in turn inspire Siegmund to join her with an equally clear conscience. She falters, however, as the whirlwind of her passion subsides, veering close to madness—thereby making clear the dangers of the course she has taken. Even at this point, however, it is not the defiance of conventional rules of conduct that troubles her but rather the stain of the loveless marriage into which she was forced (as her first long monologue of Act II, Scene 3, makes clear, with its intertwining of the bliss of love and her anguished sense of her own unworthiness). That misshapen marriage has put her—and, what is more important to her, has put Siegmund—in peril.

When we encounter Sieglinde again in Act III, after Siegmund's death has deprived her of the relationship that has come to be the meaning of her life, she can only long for her own death. In effective counterpoint to Siegmund's earlier declaration that life without his sister-bride was unthinkable, she chides Brünnhilde for having rescued her. Her strength returns immediately, however, when Brünnhilde's revelation of her pregnancy provides her with a new focus and way of salvaging at least something of the meaning that her relationship with Siegmund had held for her. The longing for death gives way to urgent pleas for help, aid for the unborn child, designated by Brünnhilde as a great hero-to-be; and, although she is warned of the pain and burdens to come, her transmuted love can soar in the ecstatic theme that expresses the hope that has suddenly illuminated the depths of her darkness and despair. (Of this theme, and its significance, we shall have more to say in due course.)

It is not Sieglinde's newly burgeoning maternal love, however, that serves as such a powerful inspiration to Brünnhilde—nor is it even Sieglinde's love for Siegmund. It is rather Siegmund's love for Sieglinde. And it is the wonder of that love—for the sake of which Siegmund is prepared to renounce and relinquish everything else, even including the best of fates beyond death possible for a mortal—that so moves her, and ultimately so commands her. It is the key to her discovery that there is an authority even higher than that of Wotan himself. Moreover, it is Siegmund as lover, rather than Siegmund as hero—or rather, it is Siegmund-the-hero who shows his truer, higher identity to be that of Siegmund-the-lover—who has this impact upon Brünnhilde. One might regard his unwillingness to abandon Sieglinde, even when he can do no more for her, and even when what is at stake is a place in Valhalla as opposed to the sort of fate for which ordinary mortals are destined, as a kind of ultimate heroism. But his readiness to go so far as to slay Sieglinde rather than abandon her, out of a kind of love that knows no bounds, tells against that understanding of the situation. He now sees all things through the eyes of love—and of an extraordinary kind of love that is worlds removed both from common sense and from a purely heroic sensibility.

Wagner took an enormous risk in his setting of the scene in which Brünnhilde announces to Siegmund his imminent death (the so-called *Todesverkündigung*, Act II, Scene 4, of *Walküre*). The tone set by the opening orchestral music is solemn—almost religious; it would be easy for the orchestra to sound as if it were accompanying a hymn and for the simple melodic lines of the singers to ooze sentimentality. Yet the portents of a world beyond are clearly intended to expose the magnitude of the sacrifice that Siegmund is prepared to make. In his first refusal ("*So grüsse mir Walhall* [Then give my greeting to Valhalla]"), he rejects not only the obvious delights, the company of heroes and the daughters of Wotan, but even the god himself and his beloved lost father as well (not realizing them to be one and the same). The quasi-religious solemnity of his expressions of greeting make even more striking the change of musical tone with the bitter rejection—"*zu ihnen folg' ich dir nicht* [to them I follow you—not!]."

What is so interesting and so significant about Siegmund, to Brünnhilde as well as to us, is that the *heroic* nature Sieglinde helps him to discover in himself is subordinated to the *loving* nature she *further* inspires in him, answering to her own. For him as for her, the kind of love they have found and realized with each other is all that matters; and his heroism is absorbed into his commitment to his love-relationship, subordinated to love's values and guided by love's commands. As he learns the terrible news that the power of the sword has been withdrawn, his immediate reaction is to protect the sleeping Sieglinde: this dreadful betrayal must not frighten her. Undaunted, he resolves to fight on—and if death is to be his fate, then so be it, though he will resist it. He will not be induced to resign himself to his fate and to accept the summons to Valhalla with its honors and delights. With angular lines that leave no doubt, sung against the agitated repeated notes of the strings, he proclaims his defiance and preference for Hell: "*Muss ich denn fallen,/ nicht fahr ich nach Walhall—Hella halte mich fest!* [If I must fall, I'll not go to Valhalla—Hella shall hold me fast!]."

Brünnhilde is astounded by the vehemence and determination Siegmund exhibits. He is prepared to sacrifice everything for the "pitiful woman" who sleeps in his arms. She is further pierced by his charge that she (whose emotions have resonated in anguish to her father's pain) is cold and hard. Explicitly recognizing his agony and his need, she vows to care for Sieglinde, if he will entrust his sister-wife to her care. But Siegmund will have none of it. With the wild resolve we have heard about in Act I, he declares that death together is preferable to any parting, that the sword bequeathed to him by a traitor shall end both lives with a single stroke. The turbulent passion erupts in voice and in orchestra, prompting Brünnhilde to her own passionate response and to her fateful change of plan.

Brünnhilde sees that the love between Siegmund and Sieglinde may be heroically true unto death and beyond, but that it is love's values rather than those of valiant heroism that rule this ill-fated pair. The truth and ultimacy of their love, vouchsafed by the unconditionality of their commitment to it, is precisely what becomes so profoundly authoritative in Brünnhilde's eyes. The sequence of judgments Siegmund delivers with respect to her summons to Valhalla and her clear recognition that he really means what he says, move her powerfully, in a way and direction making possible both her own immanent rebellion and her eventual utter commitment to Siegfried. Siegmund is slain moments later; but even though he disappears in person from the *Ring* at that point, his spirit lives on in it to its end—not in the son born of his and Sieglinde's love, nor even in Sieglinde herself, who disappears and perishes, but rather in his other (half-)sister, Brünnhilde.

16

Varieties of Love

Brünnhilde does not formulate issues as Wotan does. She is her mother's daughter. In response to Wotan's tortured explanations in the pivotal second scene of Act II of *Walküre*, her reactions are intuitive, sympathetic, in tune with the emotions he expresses rather than with the detailed content of his account. Her first small rebellion is to try to persuade him to acknowledge his real wishes: "*Du lieb'st Siegmund:/ dir zu Lieb'—/ ich weiss es—schütz' ich den Wälsung* [You love Siegmund: out of love for you—I know it—I'll shield the Wälsung]." That initiative is quashed by Wotan's stern rebuke to her, as he provides her with a foretaste of his immense anger when crossed, particularly by someone who owes obedience to him. Subdued, she leaves to do his bidding. But she has already considered the possibility of disobedience. That possibility is revived two scenes later in the emotional confrontation with Siegmund. In the course of this encounter she is moved to full defiance of Wotan—and not merely to attempt to argue with him in the way that provoked his wrath two scenes back—by her own emotional response to the love, manifested in Siegmund's courageous determination. Her world has never contained anyone who would be prepared to do what he is on the verge of doing. But to understand what is happening here, we should set it in the frame both of her earlier resistance to Wotan and the explanation she will later give for her defiance.

After the Valkyries make their clucking retreat from Wotan's threat to strip them of their status, and after the agitated orchestral music that follows, the tempo slows, and eventually dies away, leaving Brünnhilde to begin her apologia unaccompanied, with a phrase of simple poignancy, set in low register. She begins in an unexpected place—not with the power of Siegmund's love that had so moved her, but with the protest that she has kept faith with Wotan. He drily dismisses her initial claims to have carried out his orders (they were, after all, countermanded). She responds that she has felt and acted on his genuine will, not on the contorted version of it that he had proclaimed following his confrontation with Fricka. Quite understandably, this provokes a bitter reply from Wotan: who is she to say what he really wants? (Wotan can be excused for thinking that, Loge and Erda aside, the others with whom he deals have nothing like the depth of understanding of the issues that concern him; but it should have occurred to him that his daughter just might have inherited something not only of her father's intelligence but also of her mother's power of insight.)

At this point we finally start to understand where Brünnhilde's oblique narrative is heading. She prefaces her explanation of her action by connecting her deed to love—and to Wotan's own love of Siegmund in particular. The music slows for emphasis as, after confessing that she is "not wise," she tells Wotan that that is one thing of which she was certain: "*Nicht weise bin ich;/ doch wusst' ich das Eine –/ dass den Wälsung du liebtest* [I am not wise, but one thing I know—you loved the Walsung]." As she proceeds, she makes it apparent that her response involved her awakening to the reality and power of love. This awakening undoubtedly was primarily generated by the effect on her of Siegmund's unbounded love for Sieglinde; but it was reinforced by that of Wotan for Siegmund, together with her own love for Siegmund (which she tells Wotan he had taught her, but which was certainly intensified by his impassioned stand), and indeed with her love for Wotan (although she might well be wondering whatever happened to his for her, a love she had always been able to take for granted). All these latter loves are surely ingredients in her emotional state as Siegmund overwhelms her with his extraordinary commitment to love at any cost.

So Brünnhilde arrives at her decision to protect Siegmund, despite Wotan's instructions and his warning to her not to defy him. She does not present this to herself as asserting the priority of love—either in general or in these particular forms—over the acknowledgment of laws, contracts, orders, and formal obligations. Like Erda, she makes a judgment without articulating its basis. Even in retrospect, her account of what occurred is that she was moved, that her senses resonated to the terrible pain that Siegmund expressed, that her heart was caused "to tremble in holy awe," that she felt shame for what she was doing, and that her flouting of Wotan's command was true to the will—his true will—that had taught her whom and how to love. She does not know how to explain it; she lacks the words. But she undoubtedly senses that her love and sympathy for Siegmund derive in part both from her love for Wotan and from her knowledge of his love for Siegmund, denied in his explicit instructions to her.

Even if Brünnhilde herself cannot sort this all out—at least not at this stage—it will help to distinguish three different forms of love that are pertinent to this scene. (There are of course many others; but the human possibility of these three is of particular importance for present purposes.) The first is what we shall call *benevolent* love. Those who love in this way are concerned about the well-being and sufferings of others and may be prepared to make efforts and even sacrifices to promote their well-being and to alleviate their sufferings. Yet their caring is more a matter of conviction than of emotion (or perhaps it is a matter of emotion led by conviction), and it is the general character and quality of life of humankind, contemplated as a god or sage or saint might view it, that is their primary concern. Their focus is on humanity generally rather than particular individuals as such—or rather, their concern with the former will be felt to take precedence over their attachment to particular others. This sort of love is mediated by commitment to general principles of one sort or another—to a concern for justice, for example, or human happiness, or the enrichment of human lives. Wotan loves after this fashion, even if he has felt and still feels the pull of more fundamental but (by his lights) less godly sorts of love. So we take him at his word when he declares that he has had to "staunch the well-spring of love" (in such other senses) out of his "love of the world," which we suppose to be of this first sort.

A second type of love, which might be called *empathic* or *compassionate* love, is more a matter of feelings for others (either specifically or under some more general description) than of principles and convictions. It may be inspired by interactions with particular individuals to whom one thereby becomes closely attached, as well as by encounters of a less personal nature. Those who love in this way respond emotionally to others whose qualities or circumstances come to their attention and move them in one way or another. So, for example, they may be affected by someone's sufferings, or (quite differently) stirred by someone's virtues. They are drawn by the feelings thereby aroused to protect and support things that they take to be truly worthy wherever and whenever they encounter them, even at significant cost to themselves.

Love of this sort springs from the heart rather than from the mind and will; it has nothing forced or strained about it, for it is not dependent on commitment to abstract ideals or principles—for which reason it may both wax and wane quite unpredictably and may pull one in quite different directions. It may focus on particular individuals who arouse admiration or compassion; but it may also flow out more comprehensively, to any whose needs or attributes are of some sort to which one has come to be sensitive. At this stage of her development, Brünnhilde loves after this fashion. Her heart goes out to a number of other characters, for reasons relating both to their admirable qualities and to their distresses. For one whose heart is as large as hers, this may move her in contrary ways; but this multiplicity does not violate the demands of such love, which can be felt for many without compromise.

There is also a third and very different type of love; and if it too is associated with the heart, metaphorically speaking, its seat is a very different chamber of that heart. It may be styled *erotic* love, to acknowledge its fundamental link to human sexuality; but it is to be understood in the broad sense of that term and is by no means a matter of sex pure and simple. Overtly sexual relationships may be its fundamental and paradigmatic forms of expression; but there is much more to it than sexual activity. Indeed, it may express itself in many other ways as well, even in relationships of an overtly sexual nature, and also in others that have no recognizably sexual dimension at all. On our understanding of it, however, it is sexually charged, even if the sexual impulses aroused are sublimated rather than directly expressed. (This of course is to say nothing against it, even though this dynamic can and often does lead to complications, as well as making it an enormously powerful sort of love.)

For related reasons, perhaps, erotic love is intensive rather than extensive, and indeed tends toward exclusiveness—and toward the expectation of exclusiveness in return, in marked contrast to both benevolent and empathic love. While it may wander, it characteristically focuses at any given time on a single special relationship to the exclusion of all others, which its intensity reduces to relative indifference. Several instances of it in variously sublimated forms may exist and be sustainable in the same breast, even alongside an overtly sexual attachment; but that often proves to be a very tricky business, since such love is not easily shared. The extreme form of erotic love consists in an absolute and exclusive attachment and commitment to a single person—a feeling that nobody (and nothing) really matters except that other person, and a readiness to place that person and one's relationship to that person ahead of everything else, one's own other interests included. General considerations of justice, the general good, and the attainment of richer possibilities for humanity pale in the face of that commitment; it sweeps all before it, including any other impulses of compassion and empathy that may happen to conflict. Siegmund's love for Sieglinde, expressed in his all-or-nothing rejection of Valhalla in favor of Hella, and of existence apart on any terms for either of them in favor of death together, is of this exclusive type—as is hers for him, expressed in her willingness to do whatever she can to promote his noble destiny. (Thus even in her distraught flight in Act II, Scene 3, of *Walküre* she is impelled by her resolve not to "stain" her beloved.)

Act I of *Walküre* shows us how swiftly impersonally benevolent principles of courtesy and generosity can be swamped by a wave of empathic love, and how quickly that in its turn can be overwhelmed by an upsurge of erotic attraction. Sieglinde observes a tired stranger who has collapsed at Hunding's hearth, and within a few measures, she has moved from expressing norms of hospitality (care for the weary who come in peace) to an empathetic response to the need and the worthiness of the person before her ("*mutig dünkt mich der Mann* [valiant seems this man]"). But already the orchestral lines have indicated the stirrings of something more intensely personal and emotionally focused, and this is reinforced by the cello solo after she gives the water to Siegmund. Erotic love has already begun to grow within her, and Act I shows its flowering into open expression.

The exclusivity of the passion does not trouble us (Fricka's response to it notwithstanding) because its power and essential innocence enable us to overlook both its heedlessness to social taboo and its reckless disregard for others—particularly since the person whose interests will be slighted is the brutish Hunding, Sieglinde's husband by force rather than by choice. The problems of celebrating erotic love are much greater when, as so often happens, that love causes pain to people who merit respect and sympathy (although Wagner rose to that challenge in *Tristan*, when he replaced Hunding by King Mark).

For all his dalliances and airy dismissals of Fricka's objections, Wotan is no champion of erotic love. He sees with perfect clarity that it provides no basis for stable order, which remains the focus of his concerns; and indeed he is not oblivious to Fricka's observation that erotic love is disruptive if unregulated. Erotic lovers tend toward single-mindedness; like Wotan, they see with just one eye. Such love is not blind—but it is tunnel-visioned and myopic. There can be no viable order based on it; for it is heedless—as heedless as Siegfried's brand of heroism will turn out to be—and Wotan knows full well that order and heedlessness do not combine. Indeed, it is hardly surprising that the "love that knows no bounds" figures prominently in tragedy; for where such love rules, tragedy reigns. This is by no means to condemn it (particularly for Wagner); but erotic love will be a threat to those who share Wotan's sensibility—even if those in whom it glows and burns are quite generally unmoved by any awareness they may have of disruptive tendencies.

Wotan is not immune to the pull of erotic love himself, of course. He has known it in the past and would seem not to have lost his taste for it even during the time of the *Ring*. His fathering of Siegmund and Sieglinde may not count, since that was a piece of business (although one presumably transacted in a very different spirit and manner than Alberich's somewhat similar siring); but his affair with Erda surely does. He is also no stranger to empathic love, as his strong and tender feelings for both Siegmund and Brünnhilde attest (even if in the latter case there is surely more than a trace of eros in the mix as well). In his dedication to benevolent love (undergirded and fueled, to be sure, by his self-regarding desire to be the author of the world's betterment), however, he is prepared, when he feels he must, to override these other feelings, thereby doing violence to a part of himself—or, as he says, staunching the well-spring of love in his heart.

Wotan chides Brünnhilde for what he takes to be her feckless acquiescence in an inferior, self-indulgent type of love when he has endured the pain of opting (as he believes a god must) for love of a higher, principled, and therefore more impersonal sort. Indeed, he goes so far as to construe her preferred type of love as basely sensual, appearing to suppose—at least at one stage of his progressive judgment of her—that that is what all nonbenevolent forms of love must fundamentally be: "*da labte süss/ dich selige Lust;/ wonniger Rührung/ üppigen Rausch/ enttrank'st du lachend/ der Liebe Trank* [you found sweet satisfaction in blissful lust; you drank gleefully of delightful emotion and voluptuous intoxication from love's cup]."

But this is to mistake the form of Brünnhilde's feeling. She is no Sieglinde (or Siegmund), nor is she a predominantly benevolent lover like Wotan. At this point in her development, she experiences and expresses a number of instances of empathic love, responding in an impulsive and unreflective emotional way to the needs, suffering, nobility, and worth of others. Her predicament exhibits the liabilities of compassionate love; and as Wotan recognizes, she demonstrates all too clearly that it is ill-suited to his purpose of achieving a stable order. In any world in which the distribution of distress and virtue can give rise to conflicting empathetic responses, those swayed by the vicissitudes of such loving will have no compass for directing their actions and will be incapable of maintaining a steady course. As in Brünnhilde's case, their attitudes and actions will be only too likely to fluctuate as the emotions of the moment may prompt them.

Unlike the benevolent lover, Brünnhilde cannot sort things out by adopting a more abstract general perspective; nor does she yet have the unwavering attachment and commitment of the erotic lover, which can and does bring at least a kind of order into one's emotional life by overriding everything else. Her empathic way of loving (to this point) has led her first to protest Wotan's decision to abandon Siegmund, then to acquiesce in his command, and then to revive her initial impulse in the presence of Siegmund's noble dedication. Even after the event, she does not have a clear view of what she has done, admitting that she "understood nothing."

Yet Brünnhilde understands one important thing that Wotan is initially unwilling to acknowledge—perhaps because he cannot bear to do so, owing to his own quandary (since, as she points out to him, she does not love anything that he himself does not love as well). She grasps, even if only intuitively, that there is more than one alternative to the kind of (benevolent) love he bears toward the world and is attempting to implement—and not just the erotic kind, in which (at this point) she has no interest whatsoever. Between the more detached commitment to benevolence and the tunnel-visioned exclusiveness of erotic love, there is the empathic love that responds to nobility and virtue—the kind of love that Wotan is rejecting in his turn away from Siegmund. Wotan's explicit conception of the forms of love is starker and simpler (although we suspect that he has some tacit awareness of the kind of love that he has denied and betrayed). Those who defy duty in the name of (nonbenevolent) love, he tells her, should live by (nonbenevolent) love in whatever form it comes—which obviously is most likely to be the sort of grim sexual and personal domination that had been Sieglinde's lot before Siegmund came along. To his decree that she should follow the man whom she is forced to "love" in the lowest sense of the term ("*folge nun dem,/ den du lieben musst!*"), she counters with an emphasis on the character of her sort of love. As one given to empathic loving, she has responded only to what is worthy and noble. It is therefore wrong, she insists, for him to condemn her to the nightmare life of an exclusive bond and submission that is a travesty of love, having nothing whatsoever to do with her own manner of loving (which had had nothing erotic or exclusive about it). Even if what she did was a crime, the punishment does not fit it.

Brünnhilde can only convey this to Wotan by way of the violence of her abhorrence of the possible fate that awaits her, but she stands before him with the blazing eyes of the misunderstood empathic lover—and he is touched. His own (fundamentally empathic) love for her reasserts itself. The peace that both she and Wotan attain, in their exquisitely painful farewell, is made possible by his recognition of the purity of her loving heart and nobility of the qualities to which it is attuned, even if he cannot allow himself to concur in or forgive her subordination of the strategic dictates of his version of benevolent loving to it. But what he sings to her is at once a wondrous song of love and a heartbreaking song of farewell to that love, as well as to her. For he cannot allow himself that relationship with her, or (for that matter) that sort of relationship with anyone, in view of what he feels he must do. His official conception of the varieties of love must be kept stark and simple.

Brünnhilde can be protected, because this protection is consistent with the law and also because Wotan recognizes that there is a part of her nature that she has expressed—not denied—in what she has done. This makes it legitimate and even fitting for him to set particular conditions on her fate, and more specifically to require that she come under the sway only of a man who might have the qualities to arouse in her the kind of empathically loving response of which she is presently capable. So he can give her both punishment and blessing, hailing her as valiant and glorious while, with infinite sadness, he eradicates his own last—and perhaps greatest—impulse to love beyond the bounds of benevolence.

17

Brünnhilde's Progress

When Brünnhilde awakens in the closing scene of *Siegfried*, she repeatedly expresses her dedication to love. Her earlier feelings, expressed in the defiance of Wotan, are now articulated (with the admission that she could not previously name the thought) as her having "always loved" Siegfried. But who or what is Siegfried to her? The judgment ought to strike us as unconvincing, as a falsification of what she was feeling and doing in *Walküre*. There her love was directed toward Wotan, and through him to Siegmund, and then, when the die is cast in the final scene, to her conception at that point of the highest and noblest form of life that humanity has to offer: "*ein furchtlos freiester Held* [a fearless, freest hero]." But she went to sleep an empathic lover, and it should not occasion surprise that she re-awakens as one. She was in love, at the end of *Walküre*, not with Siegfried himself before the fact, but with The Hero as an ideal human type, for which Siegmund's free-spirited, fearless resolution served as her exemplar. Give her such a hero, and her love will have a proper object. Siegfried is to be the former, and therefore the latter.

The love Brünnhilde "always" had was already revealed in her actions prior to and independent of the plan to protect Sieglinde and her unborn son. It was an empathic love rooted in part in her strong emotional responsiveness to high worth, which she certainly recognizes in her father and which she had also sensed in Siegmund. In Siegmund's case, her responsiveness was raised to a level of particular intensity because it was combined with another of the roots of her capacity for empathic love: her protectively caring nature. One can even see her as having long had such feelings for the many heroes she had previously gone out to call to Valhalla, even if on a lesser level of intensity—perhaps owing to the absence in their cases of anything like Siegmund's distinguishing kinship with Wotan.

Brünnhilde's initial declaration to Siegfried, "*Du war'st mein Sinnen,/ mein Sorgen du!* [You were my thoughts, you my care!]," is continuous with this history. It is easily read by making the sense exclusive, and thus representing her love as exclusive—"You yourself were all I thought of, all I ever cared for!" (as the generally excellent standard translation by Stewart Spencer renders it). But this is to introduce particles not present in the German, thus conjuring a Brünnhilde who is plainly self-deceived. Rather, we read and understand her to be identifying the man standing before her as one who has passed the Fire Test, and so has shown himself (*Gott sei dank!*) to be a paradigmatic embodiment of her old ideal, whose earlier manifestations she has also (even with less at stake personally) empathically loved.

That, at least, is where Brünnhilde begins. A transition is already under way, however; for upon her awakening she feels, for the first time, the confusing stirrings of her human sexuality. Like Sieglinde before her, under somewhat similar circumstances, Brünnhilde will move to an erotic love—and one that is committed to its object in a way and with an exclusiveness that she has never known. Her transition is not as smooth as Sieglinde's was, for it is fraught with her memories of different possibilities of love; but when Brünnhilde makes the transition, she does it in a way that leaves her no longer vulnerable to the turmoil that overwhelms Sieglinde when her passion subsides (although it certainly leaves her vulnerable to distress of other sorts). Sexuality floods her with a kind of desire that is new to her; and it mingles with her still-vivid recollections of her previous, virginal, loves. This has an impact for which she is completely unprepared, the meaning of which for her new encounter is beyond her powers of comprehension. In the beginning, she only knows that she is profoundly moved and shaken. The uncertainties of her judgment are indicated by the shifting mood throughout the scene: first elation, then fear and confusion, and finally joyful acceptance as she comes to view herself as having been saved for this new and wonderful event, in which the greatest of passions and the highest of admirations are blended and focused on a particular seemingly godlike human being.

Before Brünnhilde awakens, Siegfried has been alone on stage, attempting to work out what she is and what he should do with her. Even before that, Wagner has begun the scene with an extraordinary orchestral introduction, whose spare textures and unusual instrumental combinations really do seem to usher in a new world. (It is as if we "breathe the air of a new planet," in the phrase of Stefan Georg that Schoenberg employed to make the decisive break with tonality in his second string quartet.) But for all the musical richness and brilliance with which the scene begins and continues, Wagner faced at this point a formidable dramatic problem. Naïvete is part of Siegfried's nature; and this entails an ignorance that must somehow be dealt with. Wagner's solution was to have him express it in lines that at least appear to be among the worst pieces of libretto he ever wrote (and must be awful to have to deliver, with a straight face), from blurting "*Das ist kein Mann!* [Better left untranslated!]" to crying out to his mother's memory for help. Such lines are at odds with the exceptional tenderness and emotional depth of the orchestration and would seem to represent a tremendous lapse on Wagner's part at a crucial moment. But upon reflection, we suspect that this scripting is quite deliberate and has a point. For as we see him, Siegfried is meant to be a hero whom it will be difficult to respect, however admirable and appealing he may be in some ways, and to some eyes.

The ludicrous character of this moment infects the scene that follows. For all its psychological fascination, it has to fail as a depiction of true—and therefore necessarily mutual—love. We simply cannot believe in the relationship between Brünnhilde and Siegfried as we can believe in that between Siegmund and Sieglinde, or that between Tristan and Isolde. (In some ways, the psychological atmosphere induced is closer to that of the Parsifal-Kundry encounter in Act II of *Parsifal*.) The difficulty stems from the inequality of the participants. It is not simply that Brünnhilde is Siegfried's aunt (although Anna Russell's sardonic comment on this point, as so often, is quite apt). She is a figure whose emotional depth has already been sounded—and the echoes of Wotan's farewell to her periodically remind us of the kinds of love she has known and has expressed. Siegfried, by contrast, is at best a naïve and insensitive youth, with an astounding (if readily understandable) ignorance of women. (It is an ignorance, moreover, that is not much alleviated subsequently.) The scene is best heard not as a duet but as a pair of monologues, which interrupt one another before culminating in a rather contrived union. In the course of these monologues both characters undergo important transformations. Siegfried's strikes us as incredible (of which more below); but Brünnhilde's is a different matter and is of great importance.

Brünnhilde's empathic love has a new and (by her lights) eminently worthy object; the hero who stands before her is as splendid as the sun. Her ardent sympathy pours out in expressions of her love for him—the kind of love she understands, a passionate response to what is noble, but with an intensity she has not previously felt. Part of the intensity derives from his apparently special worth, demonstrated by his evident fearless valor. But another part reflects her new sexuality. Initially she addresses him with a freedom and joy that is untouched by any sense that her love for Siegfried will turn out to have a sexual and exclusive character. She takes him to be supremely noble and therefore to be loved and cherished—as are all noble things, but beyond all others. So she articulates what she takes to be "Wotan's thought"—a thought she was previously unable to express but is now seen as asserting the priority of the heroic and worthy, whose epitome she takes to be the youth before her. Something—perhaps her mention of her father, perhaps Siegfried's (understandably) uncomprehending reaction to her declarations—drives her thoughts back to her past. She considers the relics of her life as a Valkyrie that are around her on the rock—her armor, her horse Grane; and then, just as nostalgic regret overcomes her, Siegfried's sheer desire surges, and he "embraces her violently" (stage direction).

The overt advance prompts a startled and unreceptive Brünnhilde to reflect on love present and love past, and to confront the choice between open-ended empathic love and exclusive erotic love, whose nature and power she is now beginning to learn. Her initial fear and shame give way to confusion. We take her to be torn between an ideal of empathic love that has permeated her life up to this moment and the sexual impulses that urge her to an erotic love. To a phrase of melting tenderness, Siegfried reminds her that the wisdom she seems to have lost was supposed to derive from her love for him; but this misses the point, for what is at issue is the form that love is to take, and Brünnhilde has tacitly assumed that wisdom reveals empathic love to be its highest form. Her first intimations of sexuality seem to her to bespeak a frightening and dark world, to be contrasted with the lucid image that emerges with the introduction of the "Idyll" theme. (It seems to us that Wagner's introduction of this theme is a piece of technical brilliance, for he was committed to using music that fits poorly with the superficial mood of the scene, the celebration and expression of erotic love. He solves the problem by using the theme to elicit Brünnhilde's continuing commitment to a very different type of love—the empathic love that was so vividly displayed in *Walküre*.)

Returning to the tone of her earlier expressions of her love for her newfound hero, therefore, Brünnhilde tells him that she has always been working for his good. "Ardently, but tenderly" (stage direction), she pleads with him to leave the old—empathic—form of her love undisturbed. Her love, she suggests, is a "limpid brook," not to be stirred into a roiling torrent. Her plea culminates in an alternative to the sexual intimacy he is urging upon her: "*Liebe—dich,/ und lasse von mir:/ vernichte dein Eigen nicht!* [Love—yourself, and let me be: do not destroy what is your own!]." He is pressing for a form of love that will make demands of exclusivity and risk unlike any love she has ever known—and there is a poignant reminder of the forms of love she knows so well, as she sings "*dein Eigen,*" where we hear the lovely descending motif that pervaded Wotan's leave-taking of her. She resists, in appreciation of the love she has experienced in her earlier life, and protests—no doubt against her own surging desires as well as against Siegfried's advances—that love should not be exclusive, and that sexual love must not be allowed to eclipse and supplant the forms she has previously expressed, including her own love for the unborn Siegfried. (There is, we think, some excuse for his earlier confusion about whether the love she has originally declared for him is sexual or maternal.)

But the apparent triumph of Brünnhilde's commitment to empathic love is unstable and is only momentary. Siegfried does not immediately win her over by the effusions of his surging sexual desire; she can feel this surge in herself and strives to check it. But his doubts about her love for him, building to the anxious uncertainty of "*ob jetzt Brünnhilde mein?* [if Brünnhilde were now mine?]," first unsettle her deeply ("*Ob jetzt ich dein?* [If I were yours?]"—with its implied "How can you doubt it?"), and then her recognition of his doubts releases a flood of erotic passion in her that sweeps all before it. Now she responds to him in kind, ecstatically dismissing the world she has previously served, and proclaiming the end of the gods and of their order in the frenzy of this new love. Erotic love in all of its exclusiveness and danger is at last joyously embraced. Nothing else except the beloved matters, come what may: for all she cares, in her rapture, the world can end, darkness can triumph, the gods can perish.

Brünnhilde's last two words (and Siegfried's as well), "*lachender Tod!* [laughing death!]," recall the direct association of intense sexual love with death that *Tristan* has made famous. But the idea that death is some supreme expression of love is not their thought here. Their gloriously set and sung final words reflect the enraptured conviction that though living may mean dying, it can also mean loving, and that this miracle makes it all worthwhile. If Brünnhilde has had any regrets about losing her divinity or about subordinating all empathic love to her new and overwhelming impassioned affirmation of this deep and disturbing form of loving, she has none now. Her initial taste of erotic love, powered by the upsurge of her sexuality that Siegfried has awakened and enflamed, convinces her that nothing could matter more; and she is prepared to give it (and Siegfried) her all. Death would not matter as it does without love; but love would not matter as it does without death—and life would not matter as it does without both.

Brünnhilde does not have this worked out with any clarity; but she does grasp it intuitively. (In this she greatly surpasses Siegfried, who, while equally impassioned, is constitutionally incapable of comprehending very much at all, and whose closing counterpart to her repudiation of the importance of anything except love consists of Happy Lover boilerplate.) And she is no Isolde in other respects as well. Suppose that the *Ring* were to end here, on this note of terminal hilarity. (Imagine Siegfried and Brünnhilde deliriously laughing themselves to *Liebestod* as the final curtain falls.) This would not only leave Wotan's problems and concerns dangling but would also be inapt as a resolution of Brünnhilde's predicament. For the judgments she has expressed in this scene, conflicting though they may be, both have a claim on her. Dominant though erotic love may now be for her, it has not obliterated her empathically loving nature—the triumph of the erotic comes relatively late, and we may reasonably wonder how enduring it will be. She must now judge *both* that love should be erotically intense and exclusive, divorced from the world and consummated in the denial of the world, with life purified of anything other than its essentials of love and death, *and also* that love should do its work *in* the world, that it should be open-endedly empathic in its encouraging and sustaining whatever is noble and worthy (as was Brünnhilde's love in caring for Wotan, Siegmund, Sieglinde, and the unborn Siegfried).

The oscillation between these two judgments that occurs in Brünnhilde's mind and heart in the final scene of *Siegfried* cannot be ended simply by affirming one and rejecting the other. To be true to what she is discovering to be the whole of herself, she must find a way to embrace them both, their seeming irreconcilability as ultimate concerns notwithstanding. That is her dilemma, and her great challenge.

18

Brünnhilde's Transformation

Not all the authority and judgments to be encountered and reckoned with in the *Ring* are those of the individual characters. So, for example, and perhaps most importantly, *Götterdämmerung* itself may be thought of as expressing judgments—both dramatically and musically—from a standpoint transcending that of any of the participants in the drama, and in doing so, as laying claim to higher and greater authority than that of any character. Brünnhilde might be regarded as an exception to this generalization; but it is precisely by virtue of the greater authority of the work itself that she is endowed with the enormous authority she ultimately comes to have within it, and beyond it as well. We suggest that the ultimate task of *Götterdämmerung* (and the many-sided judgment of the entire work) is to reveal how a solution to Wotan's apparently insuperable problem is achieved in Brünnhilde's resolution of her own dilemma within this larger context that enables its meaning and significance to be grasped, after eliminating Siegfried and the rule of the heroic as competition.

On the face of it, the mechanics of the plot in this fourth and final part of the *Ring* are of little interest, introducing us to a different—and diminished—dramatic world. The central parts of the drama appear to have a contrived complexity more readily associated with Verdi than with Wagner (think of *Simon Boccanegra*), and we seem to have lost the powerful mythological narrative that dominated the earlier segments of the *Ring*. Action is not necessarily uninteresting, but by this stage we have such an extraordinary sense of the depth of characters, intricacy of thoughts, emotions and intentions, problem and menace that the intrigues of the social-climbing Gibichungs look trivial. Yet to find *Götterdämmerung* wanting on these grounds would be to sell it very short. We can achieve a more adequate perspective on it by focusing on Brünnhilde, the progression of her judgment, and the growth of her authority.

After the Norns' rope snaps and they descend to Erda, a new day dawns. Brünnhilde emerges to bid Siegfried farewell. As befits a hero, he is to set forth in search of new adventures, and in her love for him, she desires that he be true to his own heroic self. It is far from her mind to keep him to herself on the mountaintop (as Fricka would have liked to confine Wotan). Yet for all her radiant trust in him, she has some concerns. Knowing that innocence is part of his heroic constitution, she wonders whether she has taught him enough. As in the case of her mother before her, sexual love has apparently diminished her wisdom; and although she has passed on what she can, there are hints of concern that the traveling hero may need more. His declaration that he is her arm is met with her wish to be his soul—as though she understands already that his brain (or even his character) may not be up to his brawn.

Yet Brünnhilde plainly continues to acquiesce in the transition in her manner of loving that occurs at the end of *Siegfried*. Her love is now erotically exclusive, and she rejoices in it. So, for her, nothing matters except what is good for Siegfried—and that is seen by both of them in terms of his returning to his career as hero. But what of his dedication to her? Should that not equally be expressed in his giving supreme importance to her realization of her own self, her own destiny? Perhaps it is. In following his own ends, he does what she in her love for him would have him do. To share a love with another may be in part to understand and accept this from the other with loving gratitude and to feel liberated thereby, so that an action that may even seem selfish and heedless of the other can actually be undertaken in the confidence that it accords with the other's deepest desire. It is doubtful that Siegfried would be able to articulate this thought, but he may have an intuitive sense or confidence that their desires are in harmony in this way. While this idea can all too easily be or become self-serving, it can also be genuine, and warranted. The situation may thus be more symmetrical than it at first appears to be.

Indeed, musically and vocally, there is more equality between the lovers in this scene than when we last saw them at the end of *Siegfried*. Brünnhilde remains wiser than her callow lover, even as she laments the diminution of her own powers, but he does at least appreciate the extent of her gifts to him. Moreover, their closing exchange, in which they hail each other in parallel lines of great power ("*Heil dir, Brünnhilde*," "*Heil dir, Siegfried*"), expresses more unity of love and mutual dedication than anything we have yet heard from them—or will hear from them again. (It may be worth noting, however, that they do not hail each other on identical terms. He hails her as "*prangender Stern* [glorious star]" and "*strahlende Liebe* [radiant love]," while she hails him as "*siegendes Licht* [victorious light]" and "*strahlendes Leben* [radiant life]." These are no mean differences, even if they are readily comprehensible stereotypically; and they do reveal something fundamental about the difference between values each of them incarnates, concerning which we shall have much to say below.)

But their ardent vows are of little avail; and their love is all too quickly and easily undone. Before Siegfried has arrived at the home of the Gibichungs, Hagen has persuaded Gunther and Gutrune that they can gain the honor they crave (or, to put it more cynically, that they can make a splash in Rhineside society) by marrying Brünnhilde and Siegfried, respectively. Everything turns on giving the hero a magic potion that will blot out Siegfried's memories of previous women and so lead him to fall for Gutrune. And that is exactly what occurs. Siegfried shows up, has his drink, and in short order is planning to disguise himself as

Gunther, climb the rock, win Brünnhilde for his new blood-brother, and obtain Gutrune as his reward.

What has happened? It is clear enough that love, even at its most intense, is no match for the tricks and treachery of the world. Wotan would be right to judge that the sway of love in its erotic form is doomed to defeat. Yet it is worth reflecting on the device of the drink, strikingly similar to the love potion that figures in the first act of *Tristan*. Interpreters have often claimed that a placebo would have done just as much for Tristan and Isolde: thinking that they are about to die is enough to liberate them from constraint and to express (and be prepared to consummate) their previously unacknowledged love for one another. We would raise an analogous question about Siegfried: to what extent do his loss of his memory of Brünnhilde and his sudden ardor for Gutrune correspond to something in his own character?

The Siegfried who strides up from the banks of the Rhine is already something of a regression from the figure who bade farewell to Brünnhilde. On the mountaintop, raw youth though he may have been, he nonetheless seemed—under the influence of Brünnhilde's more mature loving nature—to have gained glimmerings of sensitivity. (They shine through the music of the Prelude, even though there is evidently still much that he does not comprehend.) In her absence, that influence fades. As Siegfried greets the Gibichungs, we see the same brainless youth who encountered the Wanderer in Act III of *Siegfried* with such adolescent boorishness and obliviousness to his own ignorance. He issues an immediate challenge: "*Dich hört' ich rühmen/ weit am Rhein/ nun ficht mit mir/ oder sei mein Freund!* [I've heard you praised up and down the Rhine: now fight with me, or be my friend!]." This puerile swaggering seems a poor way of pursuing the venture to which Brünnhilde committed him. (When we heard her commit him to his heroic calling, she and we certainly expected better of him than muscling his way up and down the Rhine, in search of pals or sparring partners.) Indeed, there are plenty of later hints that the young hero has been coarsened by his brief sojourn through the world. So, for example, he has been quick to pick up mead-hall stereotypes, casually talking of men's disdain for "women's wrangling," making light of the quick passing of "women's resentment" (Act II, Scene 4), and attributing Gunther's gloom to Brünnhilde's henpecking (Act III, Scene 2).

The drink, we suggest, should be understood as a distillation of the debasement to which desire is susceptible in the absence of true inner strength and quality. Exclusive erotic love is hard to sustain, requiring greater wisdom than Siegfried can muster. (Brünnhilde was prophetic in worrying that she had taught him too little, although, characteristically, she blamed her own gift rather than the extent to which the hero needed an education.) Moreover, there are elements of his character—rashness, pride, crassness, insensitivity—that do not require magic to cause trouble for him, easily leading to different ways of demeaning and even forgetting his love in many readily imaginable contexts. Perhaps we should see the magic drink as simply a way of *accelerating* a process of love's decline that would have happened anyway. Give Siegfried enough time and enough exposure to a base and corrupt world—a world in which love is seen, as Gunther plainly sees it, as a mere means of social climbing—and he would be all too likely to lapse from his love soon enough of his own accord.

Brünnhilde knows nothing of this. We see her again after a rich orchestral interlude has woven themes we associate with their erotic love into others that portend doom and loss. Melancholy clouds seem to hang over the rock; but her own music conveys the strength of her confidence in her love (and in her beloved), which holds them at bay. When Waltraute arrives, Brünnhilde's older forms of love stir once again, first in her affection for her sister and then in the hope that Wotan may have relented. The reflection that her love for Siegfried (and his for her) was made possible by Wotan's accession to her wish, in protecting her with a ring of fire that only a hero would brave, prompts the wonderful thought that this is all somehow in accord with the god's deepest wishes and true designs. The glorious celebration of her newfound love (in the lines beginning "*So zur Seligsten schuf mich die Strafe* [So his punishment made me most blessed]") echoes her impassioned declaration in the Prelude ("*O heilige Götter* . . . [O holy gods]) in suggesting a wonderful harmony between the union of Siegfried and Brünnhilde and Wotan's striving.

There is thus a change in Brünnhilde from the closing of *Siegfried*; for in her heart the claims of empathic love are being heard and felt once again. It is no longer the case that *nothing* whatsoever matters to her other than Siegfried's good; Brünnhilde is alarmed by the suggestion that something "ails the immortal gods" (compare this with her blithe acceptance of the passing of the gods at the end of *Siegfried*). Yet when she learns what the condition of avoiding the gods' predicament is supposed to be, her choice is completely clear. Nothing else matters *enough* to her to override the demands and expression of her love for Siegfried: she will not return the Ring, though the heavens should fall. Just as Siegmund once (to her amazement) held the "poor, tired, fearful woman" with him dearer than the prospect of bliss in Valhalla, so now she sings "*Mehr als Walhalls Wonne,/ mehr als der Ewigen Ruhm –/ ist mir der Ring* [More than Valhalla's bliss, more than the glory of the immortals is the Ring to me]." Just as Siegmund once accused her of coldness, in her failure to understand what his love for Sieglinde meant, she rebukes Waltraute with the same phrase: "*fühllose Maid* [unfeeling girl]." (Not only are the words the same, but the vocal lines echo one another—in each case a descending phrase in low register, Siegmund's going down by seconds, Brünnhilde's by minor thirds.) For to her the Ring betokens Siegfried's love and so is endowed with all of the significance that she attaches to that love, by virtue of her own for him.

The audience already knows (as Brünnhilde will soon learn) that Siegfried has been corrupted and his love for her subverted. But suppose she had been informed *now*—perhaps by Waltraute, who had learned of it en route—that Siegfried has forgotten her, that he is besotted with Gutrune, and that he is scheming to win her for Gunther. Would that have made it possible for her to accede to Waltraute's urgings? We think not. For the intensity and exclusivity of her love would undoubtedly impel her to continue to hold fast to it even in the teeth of whatever the news with respect to Siegfried's faithlessness, as long as there were any way at all to question the report. She would search desperately for an explanation that would enable her to save her love, or at least to find some way of reshaping and rededicating it. We should believe her when she sings, to music we associate with the fashioning of the Ring through the renunciation of love (originally sung by Woglinde in Scene 1 of *Rheingold*), that she will "never relinquish love"; and we should approach her later judgments and actions with this commitment in mind.

Waltraute leaves, and almost at once Brünnhilde experiences her human vulnerability. Siegfried returns, disguised as Gunther, and overwhelms her, wrenching the Ring from her finger and forcing her not only into the cave that had been their bedchamber but thereby also into a new role, as Gunther's wife. This scene is almost unbearably painful. Primarily, of course, that is because of what happens to Brünnhilde—because her resistance is overcome by superior force, because her defeat brings home to her the meaning of her punishment, because she is led to wonder (quite understandably) whether what is occurring is the working out of Wotan's punitive will, and because the reality and the symbol of her love cannot prevail against desecration and loss.

Yet we should also be pained by what has happened to Siegfried. Even if we imagine him as unaware of the vows he has sworn to this woman (owing to the drink), even if we suppose him to be fired by desire for Gutrune in a manner made possible by his forgetfulness, and even if we think of him as a boorish adolescent whose heroic capabilities greatly outstrip his intelligence and self-control, there still is a shock in what he shows himself to be capable of doing: he is, as he announces, quite prepared to "tame" a vehemently resisting woman by brute (and brutal) force. A capacity for rape—not to mention a readiness to use it as a tactic—is no part of the package of a true hero, even if one is naïve, foolish, arrogant, and confused. What Siegfried does here should make us mindful of differences we have already encountered—and in particular, of the contrast between his father, whose (impetuous) gallantry and tender treatment of Sieglinde were so moving, and the likes of Hunding, for whom women are goods to be owned, traded, and abused. Indeed, Siegfried's conduct as he sends ("drives") Brünnhilde to the rock-chamber (with a "domineering gesture") should remind us of nothing so much as Hunding's peremptory command that Sieglinde prepare the night drink—only it is yet more appalling, even if Siegfried is just putting on an act. For it is an act intended to break her spirit. The corruption has gone very deep.

The next morning, Brünnhilde is dragged from the mountaintop. We meet her as Gunther accurately but misleadingly introduces his trophy to the Gibichung clan: "*ein edleres Weib/ ward nie gewonnen!* [a nobler wife was never won!]." (The passive neatly avoids the question of who did the winning.) She is downcast, seemingly defeated and resigned to her plight, and at first does not raise her eyes. Then Gunther announces the two "blissful couples"—"*Brünnhild' und Gunther, Gutrun' und Siegfried*"—and Brünnhilde looks up to see the hero. But at this stage, she expresses confusion rather than rage; her vehement protest is directed against the suggestion that she is married to Gunther, as though she were warding off a charge that *she* has been the one to betray the love so rapturously sworn on the mountain. Realizing that Siegfried does not appear to be responding to their shared past, she guesses that something strange has occurred: "*Siegfried . . . kennt mich nicht?* [Siegfried—doesn't know me?]" There is no accusation against him—yet.

But then, as Siegfried "supports her" (stage direction), Brünnhilde notices the Ring on his finger, and draws upon that astonishing circumstance as a clue to try to unravel what has occurred. For the Ring was wrested from her by Gunther—or by someone who presented himself as Gunther. If therefore it was Gunther who abducted her, then Siegfried has obtained it from her alleged "husband." But both Siegfried and Gunther deny any such transaction. Brünnhilde immediately leaps to the correct conclusion: the man who recently braved the flames, as Siegfried earlier had, and who ripped the Ring from her was none other than Siegfried himself. He is the central actor in this hideous charade, forsaking their love completely and thoroughly, not only by becoming amorously entangled with and betrothed to Gutrune but also (even more insidiously) by procuring her for Gunther and by tearing from her the token he had previously given to her in expression of his love. By her lights, no greater profanation of her love can be imagined; and, first in rage and then in anguish, she accuses Siegfried not only of theft but of ultimate betrayal.

How does Brünnhilde reach her judgment so quickly? For one thing, she no doubt immediately recalls the fateful moment after Siegfried-as-Gunther tore the Ring from her finger, when her blankly despairing look had met his eyes. (Stage directions: "*streift ihr Blick bewußtlos die Augen Siegfrieds*.") For another, she undoubtedly has taken Gunther's measure by now and finds it hard to imagine him being capable of breaching the flames. Thus, when the mystery of the Ring on Siegfried's finger presents itself, Brünnhilde is already predisposed to consider the possibility that the man who took it was not Gunther, but one of more heroic quality.

But why does Siegfried still possess the Ring? After the successful abduction, he and Gunther have quickly exchanged clothes, and, courtesy of the Tarnhelm (the magic helmet that not only enables its wearer to assume any form but also to engage in teleportation), returned to the banks of the Rhine. Why was the Ring left out of the exchange? The Siegfried we have previously met has not been particularly interested in it. He originally takes it on the Woodbird's advice; and it seems to have been a mere minor memento (not even worth mentioning in his exchange with the Wanderer) until he gives it as a love token to Brünnhilde. (Then, of course, it acquires a new significance for them both, but Siegfried must forget that under the influence of the magic draught.) Later, in Act I, Scene 2, he tells Hagen of the items he took from the dragon's lair—and Hagen has to inform *him* about what the Tarnhelm will do. If we assume that Siegfried is similarly innocent about the power of the Ring, he ought to secure the plot by passing it on to Gunther, or failing that, to Gutrune.

Of course, it is entirely appropriate that the man whom Brünnhilde sees as thoroughly profaning their mutual love should be wearing the Ring that was forged through (Alberich's) renunciation of love. But there is more here than a merely symbolic connection. Siegfried's keenness to retain the Ring and to protest that it is his is another indication of the corruption of his character that we have been concerned to emphasize. Heroic exploits are no longer sufficient; perhaps infected by Gunther's concerns for status, Siegfried now also wants a symbol of those exploits so that he can advertise his heroism. In response to Brünnhilde's charge of theft, he changes the subject. He did not receive the Ring from a woman, he tells the onlookers, but from the dragon whom he killed at Neidhöhle. Of course, this is literally true, since he did win the Ring from the dragon in the first place; but it is deceptive in the present context, to say the least—as Siegfried must be aware, drug or no drug, and as naïve as he is. He knows that the Ring has indeed been taken from Brünnhilde, and, presumably to avoid shaming his blood brother, he is prepared to dissemble. Brünnhilde is quite right to make her accusation of deceit. So far has the hero fallen.

Confronted with the desecration of her love and disillusioned with the very idea of the kind of love she had thought she and Siegfried shared, Brünnhilde reverts to the idea that her predicament is Wotan's punishment, and she calls on the old order of justice to avenge her. In response to Siegfried's dishonesty, she will declare the truth: it is he, not Gunther, to whom she is married. But she elaborates her account in ways that are potentially misleading: he "forced delight and love [*zwängt Lust und Liebe ab*]" upon her, and Nothung rested in its scabbard as he did so. Of course, both claims are true enough with respect to what transpired upon his *original* arrival at the rock; (and are obviously pertinent to her central assertion that she is married to Siegfried). But are they true as well with respect to his return to it? She certainly conveys the idea to her audience (to Siegfried's serious detriment) that this is so—and emphasizes the point that it was not Gunther but *Siegfried* who in this manner made her his wife.

What exactly transpired in the cave on that second occasion is far from clear. It is also a matter of some awkwardness for Siegfried. So we find him claiming (with greater logical and rhetorical agility than one would have thought him capable of) both that the marriage really was in some sense consummated for Gunther, in "a complete nuptual night [*eine volle bräutliche Nacht*]," and that he nonetheless actually did not dishonor his new blood brother and his own bride-to-be—thanks to the presence of his sword Nothung between Brünnhilde and himself. Brünnhilde makes it clear, in her dramatic confrontation scene with Siegfried before the assembled Gibichungs, that she knows what ravishment is—and here of course she draws on her sexual initiation on the rock. If his claim of honorable innocence is indeed the truth, therefore, one has to wonder just how Siegfried-in-disguise managed to be as convincing as he quite obviously was to her that night, in view of her submissive comportment at the beginning of this scene.

We do not think that it is crucial to resolve the dispute about what happened after Siegfried-as-Gunther ruthlessly "tamed" Brünnhilde. Wagner uses their impassioned disagreement as a device to advance the plot and more specifically to set in motion the events that will lead to Siegfried's death. For us the important question is, does Brünnhilde too, in her fury, sink to mendacious deception? We think not, regardless of what Siegfried-in-disguise actually went on to do. She obviously does not intentionally deceive if, shattered and confused by the events we have witnessed, she has formed the belief that her assailant followed up the ripping of the Ring from her finger by forcing sexual relations. Yet, even if she knows that on that night, Siegfried-as-Gunther held back, her accusation that he has forsworn himself remains justified. She has heard Siegfried deny their love, speaking as though it had never been, as if to blot it out; and she takes the crucial point to be not just whether he no longer loves her (and is refusing to acknowledge having done so), but rather *whether he even loved her once*.

In light of the terrible possibility that *that* part of what he says is true, Brünnhilde must reconceive everything that has happened to her, including the original appearance of Siegfried on the rock: *perhaps from the beginning he never loved her*. After all, she now must realize that she has no clear view of the chronology; and, for all she now knows, the original awakening, the apparently tender wooing, the consummation of sexual love and the swearing of vows could all be part of the same hideous sham, with the veils partially ripped away on Siegfried's brutal return. Siegfried is either forswearing himself in denying that he ever loved her, or he has practiced upon her, from the moment he first appeared, the most cruel of deceptions. (If that were so, of course, any distinction between the two occasions would be irrelevant.)

Brünnhilde's account is an elaboration of the claim that for all his apparent denials and the falsity of his actions and his speech, she and Siegfried had in fact been wedded. If his account of the night on the mountain is to be believed, Siegfried can quite legitimately swear that he has kept faith with Gunther (and Gutrune). But even so, Brünnhilde can with equal justice declare that he has "broken every oath he swore"—for, from the perspective of erotic love and its presumed exclusiveness, the oaths that count are those they once exchanged. So there is an apparent return of the order of laws and contracts, with Hagen's spear appropriately serving as a perverted substitute for Wotan's. Siegfried takes an oath upon its point, swearing that his conduct has been honorable; Brünnhilde calls upon the same spear's point for his downfall for having sworn falsely and broken his oath to her. Once this is done, Siegfried just wants to get on with the party, telling Gunther not to worry about Brünnhilde's little tantrum because women do not stay upset for long, throwing an arm around Gutrune, and exiting "in exuberant high spirits" (stage direction).

Brünnhilde, who cannot believe her eyes and ears, senses that there has been trickery and tries to probe it. Although she suspects that her intuitive wisdom has been diminished by her commitment to love, she understands a great deal. There has been a plot to which Gunther has acceded because he has wanted "rewards of fame [*Preise des Ruhmes*]," in which Gutrune has been centrally involved, somehow casting a spell that "spirited away my husband [*der den Gatten mir entzückt*]." Brünnhilde suspects that they all are complicitous in her betrayal; but because Siegfried has been the central actor in this plot, and because he has profaned their love, his death will suffice to atone for it as far as she is concerned. But

Brünnhilde's discernment falls just short. She has failed to appreciate the prime mover in her betrayal, underestimating Hagen. When he suggests that he will avenge her, her (understandable) reply is "*An Siegfried?. . . du?* [On Siegfried? . . . You?]"—and we should hear this against the background of the chilling menace of the closing lines of Hagen's "Watch" (which ends Act I, Scene 2): "*Dünkt er euch niedrig,/ ihr dient ihm doch –/ des Niblungen Sohn* [Though you think him lowly, you'll serve him yet—the Nibelung's son]."

In the last two scenes of Act II, the trajectory of Brünnhilde's changing concerns intersects with Wotan's. Recognizing that the world is inhospitable to love and that Siegfried's love and heroism alike are corruptible, she seems at first to revert to the role Wotan originally assigned her: an instrument of his will in the service of his system of laws. The act closes with a trio in which both Brünnhilde and Gunther call on Wotan as guardian of vows. But that order has passed; what remains is a semblance, in the form of Hagen's perversion of it. Indeed, Hagen responds to their invocation of Wotan with his own (sotto voce) appeal to Alberich. (Once again *Licht-Alberich* and *Schwarz-Alberich* are counterposed.) Not content merely to invoke laws and contracts and to appeal for justice, Brünnhilde is moved to action, providing Hagen with the all-important secret to the killing of Siegfried. But, of course, her directive authority in this scene is merely apparent; and her judgments are accepted only insofar as they aid the plans of those who have tricked her.

Once the deed is done and Siegfried is dead, however, Brünnhilde is transformed further and reappears with a new authority. Although she announces herself as Siegfried's wife, in search of revenge, her underlying concerns are now far higher. She comes to fulfill Wotan's longing for a conclusion, and, at the same time to vindicate his quest for meaning. The forms of valor and love that he has encouraged are conjoined and transfigured into the new nobility she attains and of which she becomes the apotheosis. In her new state she is enabled to love Siegfried anew and differently; to love more wide-rangingly and compassionately, honoring some of the claims of her former comprehensive love; to rise to a new kind of heroism; and to accomplish a higher justice.

19

Brünnhilde's Authority

Brünnhilde, in the end, has an extraordinary measure of authority. That authority is at least in part epistemic. She has it because she knows. Her confident phrases make it apparent to those who hear her that she knows. She can explain what has occurred. She has learned wisdom. She poses a crucial question to the gods (stage directions: "looking upward"), after upbraiding them ("behold your eternal guilt [*erschaut eure ewige Schuld*]") and exhorting them to "look upon my surging suffering [*Lenkt euren Blick auf mein blühendes Leid*]" and "hear my lament [*Meine Klage hör*]"—and then more than answers it: "Do I now know what you require?—All, all, all I know, all is clear to me now! [*Weiß ich nun, was dir frommt? Alles, alles, alles weiß ich, alles ward mir nun frei!*]." But she does not elaborate—even though what she means is obviously of the utmost importance. What, then, does Brünnhilde now know?

First, we suppose, she now knows that the dominion of love is not a solution to Wotan's problem of order. Exclusive erotic love can neither turn away, renouncing the world for private ecstasy, nor can it prevail and triumph over the contagious corruption of the world. The first option was unthinkable for the happy pair at the very beginning of *Götterdämmerung*: they rightly saw that life on the mountaintop would only narrow them both and stultify their love, since it would stifle them (Siegfried in particular). But for erotic love to survive in interactions with others requires a combination of luck and wisdom. There are too many fair-seeming competing claims and attractions that can subvert or corrupt what was once pure and good; so, most notably, Siegfried falls not only to a magic potion and to the potent evil of Hagen but also to the superficial charms of camaraderie and reputation—and Brünnhilde's own blind (if understandable) rage at Siegfried is easily exploited by Hagen, thereby involving her—misguidedly but nonetheless willingly—in the killing. Deceit and profanation come quickly in *Götterdämmerung*, but we take it that we are being invited to think that debasement was almost inevitable, even without the apparent contrivances that drive the plot.

The other forms of love have previously been tried and found wanting. Wotan's impersonal benevolent love for the world was noble, but the system of laws and contracts, through which he tried to articulate it, failed despite all his striving. Brünnhilde has been an admirable empathic lover; but she has come to know all too vividly the confusion, uncertainty, and instability of an order based on this form of love. Their experiences are indicative of the hard truth that there simply is no viable solution to the problem of stable order that Wotan set for himself. By the end of *Götterdämmerung* Brünnhilde knows this. She does not actually say so; but she is not given to such pronouncements. Her knowledge is implicit in what she does.

Brünnhilde also knows that the claims of the different forms of love are often irreconcilable and that to opt for any one over all the others is to incur a genuine loss. The apparent resolution reached at the end of *Siegfried* was premature, not only because the commitment to exclusive erotic love turned out to be unsustainable, but also because of the pretense that nothing else mattered except the demands of that love. She has come to see that Wotan, and what is noble in his world, continue to have claims on her. And this creates a dilemma; for, as Brünnhilde recognizes, to honor those claims would be to slight the demand for exclusiveness of her very different sort of love for Siegfried, and thus to debase it—but to dismiss them would be to cheapen other forms of her commitment. Neither she nor *Götterdämmerung* offers us a way to resolve this predicament in general; indeed, both she and the drama itself suggest that the general problem is insoluble. But she sees—and the drama shows—that at least in certain special circumstances it is possible to take a specific action that can express, through great personal sacrifice, a profound conjoint commitment to the world's benevolent betterment, to a comprehensive empathic love, and yet also to exclusive erotic love.

Justice requires, as Loge saw long ago, that the gold be returned to the Rhinemaidens. In *Götterdämmerung*, returning the gold has taken on new meaning—as has the gold itself. For the Ring, into which it has been shaped, is now the symbol of the romantic love Brünnhilde has discovered with Siegfried. To relinquish it, signifying subordination of that love to something else, would now be to make a great sacrifice—and indeed a quite inconceivable one for her, however grand and compelling that "something else" might be. For looked at in a certain way (as she undoubtedly looks at it), relinquishing it would be almost tantamount to what Alberich did in the first place—that is, to renouncing love itself, as she now understands and embraces it.

Earlier, when Waltraute asked it of her, this sacrifice was unimaginable for Brünnhilde, even for Wotan's sake; for Siegfried was alive, the love between them was still perfect and unsullied (or so she confidently believed), and she saw all only with a lover's eyes. But by the time of the *Ring*'s final scene, Siegfried is dead, and that love too has died an awful death. Yet for Brünnhilde simply to cast the Ring away at this juncture, after she has retrieved it from Siegfried's (now unprotesting) dead hand, might be seen as acquiescing in those deaths, bleakly admitting the defeat of love. Indeed, that would surely be the significance of returning the Ring, if that were *all* Brünnhilde did. In the aftermath of Siegfried's death, however, she can declare her love anew, offering a quite different token—in the form of herself. She can do what Siegmund was prepared to do in their critical encounter, proclaiming that life without the beloved is unthinkable and expressing her unsurpassed love for him by joining him in death—not "laughingly," to be sure, but most certainly triumphantly.

Moreover, by making the form of her death one in which the vain splendor of the gods is also consumed, she can give voice to her love for Wotan and the things about him that inspired love. She can bring about the kind of ending for which he has yearned, purging the world over which he has presided of the corruption that has infected the noble things they struggled to foster. So she at once sacrifices and sanctifies both the token of her first love for Siegfried and herself. And in doing so she also affirms and consummates Wotan's strivings, thereby achieving for him (as well as for herself) the ending he had sought, in the only way possible. For although no stable order has been—or can be—found, her action simultaneously honors the justice that was informed by his benevolent love, her earlier empathic love, and the erotic love she has felt so intensely for Siegfried. Her joyful embrace of this end honors the conflicting demands that beset her at the close of *Siegfried* (and so she escapes her own dilemma) in a many-sided expression of her many-sided love, and provides a kind of resolution to Wotan's problem after all. Her new kind of loving, expressed rather than extinguished by her chosen death, transcends all three of these others, even as it negates and preserves them, in Hegelian *Aufhebung* or transformation beyond compare. One might call it *ecstatic* loving, for "ecstasy" denotes an exalted state of feeling, and there surely is none more exalted than that by which Brünnhilde is transported at *Götterdämmerung*'s conclusion. Indeed, it is the *Ring*'s version of the humanly divine, with its hallowing power.

Brünnhilde goes beyond Wotan. Because he can see no prospect of stable order, he comes to doubt the possibility of endowing this life in this world with meaning. She sees that there can be meaning without stable order of the mundane sort that Wotan unsuccessfully attempts to establish securely, and that there are or can be actions that are meaning-creating in ways that transcend their transience; she both sees and does. She vindicates the world that makes possible her own final action, affirming love, valor, and justice despite their instability and frequent corruption; and she thereby vindicates her own life—as well as Wotan's, and even Siegfried's—in ending it.

Brünnhilde ends the world—but she does not negate it. Fire and flood wipe the slate clean, reestablishing the primordial state of natural and human simplicity in which it all began (albeit with Alberich still around to mar and jar its rhythms). But we—*we*—are not simply returned to Square One. We now know something we did not at the beginning, or along the way. Love may not conquer all, or resolve all, or even preserve all; but the kind of love Brünnhilde comes to know and to express at the end can *vindicate* all, the inevitability of death and destruction notwithstanding. Love may not have the *Ring's* last word; but it has the final word. It is not Wotan's, or Erda's, or even Siegmund's, and certainly not Siegfried's. It belongs to that final Brünnhilde alone. But it is less a matter of what she says than of what she becomes and does.

A last comparison with *Lear* may help clarify our reading of this magnificent scene. It may appear fanciful to compare Brünnhilde with Cordelia; for after all, one could surely not describe Brünnhilde in the terms used by the grieving Lear: "Her voice was ever soft,/ Gentle, and low, an excellent thing in woman" (V-iii-270–1). But both characters are alike in their illumination, through love, of a world of cruelty and darkness. The world of *Lear* is one in which order passes with Lear's fading strength, and we know that it cannot be restored. Nevertheless, Cordelia shines with the vulnerable flame of her love, doomed though it is to be snuffed out. But when she is gone, the darkness that descends on the stage is complete and without hope.

And the *Ring*? It initially revolves around a struggle—first to establish a certain sort of order and then to achieve a meaningful ending to that endeavor—that appears doomed to failure, Wotan's persistent and increasingly desperate efforts notwithstanding. Then, just when failure is manifest—when Siegfried is dead and Hagen advances to claim the Ring—Brünnhilde's radiant presence transforms the scene. And while she too meets her end, it is one that she embraces, delivering the final *coup de grace* to Wotan's failed order as she does so, but in a manner denying victory to the looming darkness as well. She *acts*; and her act is (as we have said) a many-sided embodiment of her many-sided love.

Lear and the *Ring* are both studies in the power and expression of love. Cordelia and Brünnhilde are both beloved and then harshly rejected by their fathers (who themselves had felt betrayed by them). For both, the rejection brings severe costs. Both feel the competing demands of different forms of love. (Cordelia earns her banishment, after all, by declaring to her father "Haply when I shall wed,/ That lord whose hand must take my plight shall carry/ Half my love with him, half my care and duty" [I-i-100–102].) Yet both daughters not only sustain the loves they return but raise them to new heights, even while coming to love in other ways as well. Few lines in the world's drama are as simple as Cordelia's response to Lear's suggestion that she has reason to punish him—two monosyllables repeated ("No cause, no cause" [IV-vii-75])—but, in context, they are among the most powerful lines Shakespeare ever wrote. Similarly, in the entire emotional spectrum of opera, few passages are as simple as Brünnhilde's low-register benediction to her father ("*Ruhe, ruhe, du Gott!*" [Rest, rest, you god!]); but few can rival it for emotional impact.

The glorious theme that soars in the orchestra after Brünnhilde has sung her final lines has been heard just once before in the entire *Ring*, sung by Sieglinde at the moment she learns that she is carrying Siegmund's child, and that he will grow up to be a great hero. This motif is conventionally referred to as "Redemption through Love" (although Cosima Wagner reported that Wagner resisted giving it any name, but that, if he had, he would have chosen "Glorification of Brünnhilde"—in our judgment a more apt choice). Any shred of justification for the link to "redemption" must rest on Wotan's prophecy of a "redeeming world-deed [*erlösende Weltenthat*]" to be enacted by Brünnhilde. Yet nothing is "redeemed" in any standard sense of this term, either when Sieglinde introduces the theme or when it recurs at the end of *Götterdämmerung*. The importance of these moments, however, is great.

With *Lear* in mind as well, we would characterize it differently. This theme certainly has to do with love; but what it evokes is the possibility that despite all, love can achieve a form of triumph, giving meaning and value to what would otherwise be blank and bitter defeat.

At times of deepest darkness, when it seems that everything good and true has been defeated, acts of love can at least temporarily illuminate a collapsing world in a way that crucially alters its countenance, making possible an affirmation of life—and of death as well—in spite of the inevitable destruction of all that lives. (So a better title might be the "Phoenix theme.") Sieglinde's cry—"O *hehrstes Wunder!* [Sublimest wonder!]"—expresses her realization and joy that not everything has been lost, that Siegmund's love and her own live on in her womb, that this means something that matters far more than the stark facts of the situation would seem to indicate. This is not "redemption." The Christian term is out of place here. (Furthermore, even in other music dramas, where Wagner seems to veer closer to expressing the possibility of redemption— in *Der Fliegende Holländer*, for example, or in *Parsifal*—his idea is not entirely coincident with an orthodox Christian concept.) The end of *Götterdämmerung*—the apotheosis of the *Ring*—has a resonance that is Greek rather than Christian, tragic rather than salvific, and more profoundly affirmative precisely on that account. We prefer to call it "vindication."

At the end of the *Ring*, Wotan's struggle has failed, his order is gone, and he and the rest of the gods are gone as well. Siegfried is dead, Brünnhilde rides into the flames and is consumed, and the petty world of the Gibichungs is swept away, leaving only the Rhine flowing on, the Rhinemaidens back at mindless play in a world purged of all that had made it both troubled and interesting—and Alberich. Yet Brünnhilde's action stands, as Sieglinde's pregnancy did earlier, as a memorial and testament to something deeply valuable and enduringly true. Alberich's world, like the world Edgar is left to run, is "cheerless, dark, and deadly"; and even that of the Rhinemaidens is shallow, if innocent and beautiful. But the world Edgar inherits had been graced by Cordelia, and the world inherited by Alberich and the Rhinemaidens, by Brünnhilde, and that is of enormous importance. For their lives and actions have given point to their worlds, and to the lives of those who struggled against the worlds' darkness and mindlessness. That judgment is not theirs; indeed, were they to have made it, the significance of what they do would be undermined—they would not be Cordelia and Brünnhilde. The judgment belongs to the larger works in which we encounter them.

Brünnhilde's perspective on the world of the *Ring* surpasses those of her companions in it. She sees that Wotan's problem cannot be solved as he conceived it, and that what must be done is to end his order in a way that expresses its worth. Through her human awakening, suffering, and transformation, she gains both cognitive authority and the power to translate her judgment into action. As we observed earlier, she does not simply see the world end; she ends it. She also vindicates it, illuminating it anew and offering the possibility of renewal.

Wagner does not give the last line to her. He gives it instead to Hagen, oddly enough, in Hagen's last desperate and doomed lunge for the Ring—an expression of utter futility if ever there was one. But perhaps that is more fitting than it might at first appear, as a last word and judgment on those who cannot, or will not, learn Brünnhilde's lesson. And the real last lines are neither his nor hers but the wonderful final measures of Wagner's orchestral score, which speak with unsurpassable eloquence. They bespeak affirmation as well as ending. They do not mourn and salute the devastating conclusion of a long day's journey into night, as does Siegfried's Funeral Music (the "false" and merely penultimate finale of *Götterdämmerung*), which they transcend. Instead, they celebrate the wonder of Brünnhilde's transformation in the final scene, its value beyond all mere mundane reality, and the prospect of its perpetual possibility.

20

Siegfried and Other Problems

But what about Siegfried? Our excursion through the *Ring* has consistently downplayed his significance; and much of what we have said about him is dismissive, even harsh. Yet we are well aware that the entire *Ring* grew out of Wagner's original intention and effort to write and compose a single music drama that was to be entitled *Siegfrieds Tod* [Siegfried's Death]; and it is undeniable that large chunks of the *Ring* seem to be devoted to his anticipation, his youth, his adventures, his fearlessness, his ardor, and the events surrounding his demise. How, then, can we say so much about other characters and so little about the apparent star of the whole show?

In fact, we do assign Siegfried considerable significance—but in ways that have little to do with the complex of philosophical issues we have pursued through the *Ring*. We draw a distinction we take to be valuable in thinking about this drama (and others as well). There are characters who are important from a psychological or philosophical point of view, because their thoughts, feelings, and actions embody the subtle meaning of aspects of the work. Interesting questions arise about what they are doing and why they are doing it. Other figures perform actions that affect the development of the intrinsically interesting characters, even though their own thoughts and emotions are of no independent significance. These figures may even bulk large in the action, and they may sing glorious music; but they are important chiefly because of their impact on the ideas, feelings, and plans of the first set, and more for what they signify and what becomes of them (and what this means for what they signify) than for what they say or do. Siegfried, we suggest, is among the latter, even if by far the largest of them.

Consider Fricka and Wotan. We do not think we are unsympathetic in consigning Fricka to the second category. In essence, she is a device that turns Wotan's thoughts and aspirations in new directions. Heretical as it may seem, we believe that the same holds for Siegfried. He is immensely important to the action in the second half of the *Ring*, and he has a massive amount of air time. Yet it is a strain to analyze him psychologically, or even semiotically, at anything like the same level as Wotan or Brünnhilde (or Loge, or Erda, or Alberich, or Hagen, or even Siegmund or Sieglinde)—*except* in terms of the inadequacies and shortcomings of what he paradigmatically represents, and of what he fatally and devastatingly *lacks*. He is one striking version—approaching caricature—of The Hero; but we take it to be a major part of the burden of his portrayal to convince us that he is as lamentable as he is admirable, and that his heroic virtues are bound up with the serious limitations and liabilities he displays as a human being. These traits render his version of a higher sort of humanity not only hopeless for Wotan's purposes in solving the problem of order, but also self-destructive, and more harmful than helpful even to those he would assist—even if he is awe-inspiring in his own way, and admirable in relation to some of the other human possibilities on display in *Götterdämmerung*.

Siegfried's ultimate significance, we would suggest, is to make it palpable that his type of heroism is no panacea. Indeed, it carries within it the seeds of a good deal of destruction—its own included. The combination of the naïve and the heedless is an explosive mixture, that generally produces considerable damage. If there is an answer, either to Wotan's problem of order, or to some suitably revised version of that problem, or to the fundamental problem of the entire *Ring*—the problem of how life and death can be rendered meaningful in an indifferent and treacherous world—Siegfried is not it. He is far more a part of the problem than of any solution to it—and it is no small part of the problem precisely that there is such great appeal to the idea that such a hero *would be* the key to its solution. If this is merely hinted at in the opera that bears his name, it becomes painfully clear in its sequel. Only when he is felled and disabled with a mortal wound does his heroic persona give way to a more truly human countenance. The transformation is accompanied not merely by his return to his love of Brünnhilde but rather by the dawning of a higher and more valuable type of love than he had been capable of previously. At that point, and at last, he is no longer the center of his own universe, unable to see beyond his own whims, desires and needs—his desire and need to prove himself in particular.

When we first encounter Siegfried after the immensely moving climax with which *Walküre* ends (and his advent is announced), we are brought abruptly back down to earth. Our eagerly awaited hero-to-be turns out to be an impulsive, shallow adolescent. The whining Mime may be insufferable (although we think that this standard characterization is both exaggerated and misleading, since Mime's evil is genuine and insidious, and therefore no mere laughing matter); but so is Siegfried, even if in rather different ways. From their surface behavior in Act I, the wheedling, evasive dwarf and the crude bully seem a mismatched pair, who thoroughly deserve one another. Acts II and III provide little evidence of emotional or intellectual development on Siegfried's part. Indeed, it is hard to conceive of a youth more ridiculously obtuse than the one who goes charging off on a quest for a beautiful woman—at the merest suggestion by a Woodbird, seconded by a Wanderer who is a complete stranger to him—and who then reacts with such laughably silly surprise when he cuts away the armor of the slumbering figure he discovers on the mountaintop. His shallow simplicity is rendered all the more evident in that momentous scene by the contrasting evident emotional complexity of Brünnhilde. Her contributions to the scene express the conflicts of her love; his are about hormones.

Although there are glimmerings in the second scene of the Prelude to *Götterdämmerung* that there might be or become something more than this to Siegfried, it is only in his final moments that he starts to become humanly interesting as a character. After the hunt, after he has drunk from the cup prepared by Hagen, after he sings of his youth and at last is able to recall his discovery of Brünnhilde and the beginning of their love, he seems to be on the verge of a self-awareness hitherto entirely lacking. Hagen seizes the moment he has been waiting for, having been given some semblance of justification, and thrusts his spear into Siegfried's back. Siegfried falls—and then, dying, he begins to grow up, and, for the first time, to understand what life and love are all about. As a hero, he has consistently outdone his father; but in emotional terms he never approaches Siegmund's depth—until now, perhaps, when his dying words and music convey echoes of Siegmund's mature and noble understanding of the possibilities of human love. His death is entirely fitting; it marks the end of the heroism he has represented as a viable solution to Wotan's problem of order (or to ours, as we try to find our way into a future beyond the *Dämmerung* of all gods). When he ceases to be the embodiment of heroism and is transformed into a human being capable of the kind of love worth living and dying for, he has already ceased to exist as the Siegfried he was born to be.

The dream of The Hero as The Answer is a dream that dies hard; and its death is hard to take. Yet die it must, along with the gods. Siegfried's death is not only the death of a hero; it is also the death of that dream. The Funeral Music pays tribute to the passing, doing justice to the loss it represents, even as it leaves no doubt about the finality of that loss. The fourth opera is more than *Götterdämmerung*; it is also *Heldendämmerung*. Indeed, there seems to us to be an interesting connection between the two; for it may be no accident that Siegfried echoes the words of Christ on the Cross ("*Mich dürstet* [I thirst]"), or that his drinking-horn spills over, to "bring refreshment" to "Mother Earth." Moreover, Siegfried does not merely die. He is a sacrificial victim, whose own ending makes possible the many-sided act in which Brünnhilde expresses her ultimate love. His death is not only the demise of the dream of The Hero, but also an offering to love, in the service of love, gaining its meaning from the coming transfiguration and epiphany of love. Brünnhilde makes good on the promise she and Siegfried shared at the close of *Siegfried*, of joyful death. But in the end it is Siegfried her heroic true love, not Siegfried the beloved hero, whom she joyfully joins in death.

Many commentators have suggested that the task Wagner set for himself in the *Ring*—that of integrating medieval conceptions of the heroic with a post-Enlightenment perspective on human motivation—was difficult, if not insuperable. To make his characters dramatically persuasive, he would have had to equip them with a rich psychology; and, one might suppose, it is of the essence of the heroes of the old epics and myths that there are at least some psychological dimensions along which no such filling-in is possible. We are not convinced that there is a generic problem here; Odysseus (to cite just one obvious example) combines the characteristics of the hero with great psychological breadth and depth, and Wagner introduced into the *Ring* one version of the hero—Siegmund—who is, we believe, a clear dramatic success. Heroes of his sort, on Siegmund's scale and with his limitations, may well be not only real but admirable human possibilities. But as his fate makes clear, such heroes cannot be expected to prevail for long, let alone set the world aright.

The problem with Siegfried arises not simply because he is a hero, nor even simply because no one could possibly measure up to his billing as superhero capable of surpassing all mere Siegmunds. The problem with him is also a more specific one, related to the ways in which his character had to conform to the devices of Wagner's plot in its final form. He is to be brought up in profound ignorance, and his naïve recklessness is to enable him to overcome obstacles that would have blocked the path of anyone who knew fear. Nor could Wagner have allowed him a more extensive education on the rock, for his unpreparedness is critical to his undoing and to the corruption of his love. Hence it is essential to most of his time on stage that he remain naïve and shallow—less a paradigm of the heroic than a parody of the stereotypical hero as witless marvel.

If we are right about this, it might seem that Wagner's problems result from his initial choice of plot. He formed his conception of this music drama before writing the libretto, and constructed the text in advance of conceiving the music. Moreover, the drama originally evolved from back to front. Setting out to write an opera on Siegfried's death (*Siegfrieds Tod*), Wagner worked back into his early life; and as he did so, the scope of his canvas and project expanded enormously. He came to wrestle with issues of human meaning, and was impelled to construct a mythology suited to their exploration on a grand scale. In the course of this wonderful efflorescence, the youthful hero who had once been at the center of things could no longer be drawn with the depth and richness invested in other characters. The Siegfried we see on stage is, in a sense, a fossil, remaining from an earlier version of Wagner's project in a final version to which he and his life and death are no longer central.

Yet there is a deeper source of Siegfried's character and its shortcomings. Great and creative dramatist that he was, Wagner would have been eminently capable of modifying the plot had it failed to accord with his broader purposes. In fact, as we have suggested earlier, if heroism is to offer any promise of resolving Wotan's thinking, then it must be heroism of a very specific sort. As we reconstructed Wotan's judgments in Chapter 12, the ideal of Siegfried was that of a free being, unshackled by commitment to any system of laws and contracts. A Nordic counterpart of Odysseus would be useless—and moreover would surely prove too much like Wotan himself. Hence the particular package of qualities that Wagner assigns to his hero is beautifully adapted to one aspect of Wotan's problem—and it is that aspect on which the god, quite understandably, is most focused: the transcendence of his order by a bold, unfettered, reckless, and unknowing hero. Siegfried must have a heedless capacity for defying everything; he must be the ignorant boy who knows no fear. The plot, then, is no accident, and reflects no mere failure on Wagner's part to modify his original design as its evolution should have led him to do. Both it and the type of hero embedded in it proceed from the logic of the drama in the development and elaboration of which Wagner was engaged.

The obvious way of achieving a more sympathetic evaluation of Siegfried is to celebrate the heroic, to suggest that dismissal of the qualities he manifests is the expression of bourgeois prejudice, and to emphasize Wagner's desire to *épater les bourgeois*. There surely is a contrast between the free heroic spirits of the *Ring* and conventional moral standards, a contrast made easy by Fricka's myopic judgments. Yet just as it would be ludicrous to approach the work as a vindication of her moral perspective, so too it is nonsensical to assimilate the complex evolution of the thoughts and feelings of Wotan and Brünnhilde—or even Siegmund and Sieglinde—to the kind of rash and ignorant heroism of which Siegfried is the exemplar.

Siegfried thus pales not because he is at odds with bourgeois values or with post-Enlightenment liberal sympathies, but rather because he is so clearly a far less interesting human possibility than others whom Wagner brings before us. To view him as the centerpiece of the drama in its final form is to distort it, and risks mistaking it for an anticipation of a vulgar version of what is sometimes (wrongly) taken to be a Nietzschean perspective, featuring the glorification of the type Nietzsche refers to as the "blond beast of prey," brutal, rapacious, unthinking, and unfeeling. The upshot then would be to repel us, and so perhaps to return us to the basic options apparently on offer in *Don Giovanni*—the sheepish adoption of conventional pieties, on the one hand, and on the other the hedonistic alternative exemplified by the Don. On the approach we have taken, Wagner can be understood as attempting to go much further in the exploration of problems and possibilities relating to human meaning—and it is the burden of our discussion that his explorations are of very great interest indeed.

While celebrating the richness and significance of the *Ring* as a music drama revolving around Wotan and Brünnhilde, however, we certainly do not want to claim that it is flawless. Wagner's handling of Siegfried is a case in point; and it must be admitted that a good deal of the first two acts of *Siegfried* could be condensed (if not simply dispensed with) without great loss. There also are places, to our way of thinking, at which his attempt to convey grandeur degenerates into bombast. The exclamations of the Valkyries are tedious (when not comical); and their celebrated "ride" is a gratingly raucous but shallow introduction to a splendidly dramatic act, better suited to its many popular-cultural uses than to its original setting. Similarly, as we have noted, the plot mechanics of *Götterdämmerung* are creaky and cumbersome. The treatment of the Gibichungs, and of Gunther in particular, fails to animate medieval trappings with any psychology of dramatic power. We have tried to make some sense of the world of this final installment of the *Ring*; but it would be possible to combine our general perspective with a more impressionistic treatment, simply giving up on the details of the action and characterizing the work solely in the abstract terms of Siegfried's betrayal of love and the transformations that it produces in Brünnhilde.

Partly for such reasons, we have given dramatic precedence to the earlier parts of the tetralogy, spending considerable time on *Rheingold* and *Walküre*. Yet we and our ears are well aware that Wagner's compositional powers underwent an enormous advance subsequent to them, and that Act III of *Siegfried* and the whole of *Götterdämmerung* benefited greatly from the famous interval in which he shelved the *Ring* project to write *Tristan* and *Meistersinger*. We recognize that our approach might seem to give insufficient attention and weight to what transpires in much of its last two parts. But here too, we have had our reasons.

Once again we shall draw some distinctions. In Wagner's mature works, although not by any means in all operas, one can distinguish those parts of the drama that are rich in psychological or philosophical content from those whose purpose is to bring about situations in which psychological or philosophical issues can be explored. Further, one can obviously separate the musical complexity of a work from its dramatic complexity (despite Wagner's suggestion that mismatch in these respects is the hallmark of failure). We do not dispute the intensification of musical complexity in the parts of the *Ring* that postdate the *Tristan-Meistersinger* interval. But we do suppose that whatever *dramatic* complexity these parts possess is *largely* a matter of working out issues and mining philosophical and psychological riches that have been put before us earlier. So, for example, we have already been given a clear sense of all the main protagonists in the parts predating the interval. Indeed, apart from the closing of *Götterdämmerung*, there is nothing in the later parts of the *Ring* to match Wagner's treatment of Wotan's extended reflections in Act II, scene 2 of *Walküre*, or of the exchange between Wotan and Brünnhilde in the final scene of that work.

We believe that Wagner himself may have sensed the difference between the parts of his libretto. His decision to set the *Ring* aside after finishing the second act of *Siegfried* can be understood in several different ways. One prominent reason may have been that a version of Wotan's problem was also Wagner's: he too yearned for an ending he could not see how to achieve.

There are several extant versions of drafts of text for the end of the *Ring*. At early stages, when he was writing *Siegfrieds Tod*, Wagner began with a triumphant final scene. The gods continue to hold sway, and Brünnhilde brings the great hero to Valhalla; the funeral pyre consumes the lovers and simultaneously cleanses the Ring of its curse (so that it can be returned, purified, to the Rhinemaidens), while Valhalla itself survives. When Wagner came to conceive of the possibility that the conflagration would end the rule of the gods, he composed an ending in which Siegfried seems to ascend to a new position of power, as his—human and heroic—order is to replace that of Wotan, his creator. But neither of these endings offered a satisfactory resolution of the dramatic exploration of the themes his increasingly complex drama was introducing. The major candidates for his conclusion were apparently written with the whole four-part work clearly in mind.

First among these is the so-called "Feuerbach ending," in which the blaze consumes Valhalla as well as the lovers, but in which a note of triumph is preserved. Brünnhilde was to sing of the replacement of the divine order by a "world without rulers," one in which pomp and treaties give way to the sway of love. If Wagner had been content to stop at this point, then the familiar idea that the *Ring* is "all about" the tragedy of denying love in the search for power would be far more adequate than we have supposed. Love would be conceived as triumphing in the end, and to the extent that the resultant work made room for Wotan's complex concerns about the creation of significance, love (presumably the erotic love exemplified by the relationship between Brünnhilde and Siegfried) would be seen as the answer. From our perspective, if Wagner had decided on this ending, Wotan's predicament would be less moving, and Brünnhilde's dilemma about reconciling the forms of her love would disappear. The drama, we believe, would have been far shallower, reduced almost to cliché (and a very dubious cliché at that).

In any event, Wagner was dissatisfied. His famous "turn to Schopenhauer" led him to reconceive the ending, recognizing that the idea of "love triumphant" belies what has actually occurred. So, around 1856, he began to compose the "Schopenhauer ending," in which Brünnhilde declares herself to have passed beyond "desire and delusion." Through "grieving love's profoundest suffering"—as the lines, probably penned considerably later, put it—she attains a condition of enlightenment in which she can "see the world end." But this too did not solve Wagner's problem, for it cannot be reconciled with the *actions* that her words are meant to accompany. Moreover, the resolution that would be displayed here was one that was almost available two operas earlier: Wotan himself might have willed the ending, willed it without bitterness, and reconciled himself to whatever comes, whether it should be the triumph of Alberich and Hagen, or something else entirely. His punishment of Brünnhilde, his valediction, his hopes for Siegfried, his actions as the Wanderer, and his final anxiety that the Ring be returned to the Rhinemaidens—all these are consequences of a failure to achieve the state of abnegation to which he comes so close. Nor would there have been any need for Brünnhilde, in her new enlightenment, to celebrate the hero, or to bring about the end of the gods, or to cast the Ring into the Rhine. Seeing through the delusion would have been enough.

Wagner appreciated this. The words he set and the extraordinary orchestral music he composed negate both the "Feuerbach" and "Schopenhauer" endings, while drawing on elements from them in a new synthesis. As we suggested earlier (in Chapter 6), Wagner embodied in artistic form a philosophical conception that goes beyond anything to be found in the two philosophers who most influenced him. Love cannot overcome, but love must be given its due; there is no solution to the problem Wotan posed, but there is a way of acting that can profoundly affect the significance of the agent's life, and the lives of others with whose strivings the agent's life is bound up. We have repeatedly observed that Brünnhilde *acts*; and her action does not express abnegation of will but the transformation of her will into a new form of love. Wotan's failure, the passing of the gods, and Siegfried's and her own death all notwithstanding, it affirms and manifests that life can—as it here does—attain profoundly vindicating meaning.

Deciding on the text was not the whole of Wagner's problem of finding an ending for his drama. Quite apart from the close of *Götterdämmerung*, he faced a serious difficulty in matching his musical inclinations to the libretto he had crafted. With the resources of the motifs already introduced, and with an increasing facility in combining, condensing and varying an amazing array of thematic material, his musical language was developing in density and complexity even as the psychological and philosophical drama was becoming ever more diluted. One might have expected the theorist of *Opera and Drama* to have adjusted the music to the simple requirements of the action and to the replacement of the profoundly thoughtful Wotan with the terminally naïve Siegfried. But he quite evidently did not.

We suggest that Wagner eventually resolved the difficulty by sacrificing the theory, and by using the rich musical language of the latter part of the drama to give philosophical and psychological weight first to relatively straightforward actions, and ultimately to a whole that is greater than the sum of its parts. The musical language goes far beyond matching the protagonists' thoughts and feelings, serving rather to express the background of emotion and idea against which their doings could take on new meaning—and then to transcend them, with an authority higher than any of them have and that only Brünnhilde even approaches. Authority shifts from the various characters to the *Gesamtkunstwerk* itself; and it is used in the final minutes to express the essence of what is offered as its final, definitive judgment. We shall close with a brief look at the way in which this glorious resolution is achieved.

21

Ending and Renewal

Die liebe Erde allüberall blüht auf im Lenz und grünt
Aufs neu! Allüberall und ewig blauen licht die Fernen!
Ewig . . . ewig . . .

(The beloved earth everywhere blossoms and grows green in springtime
Anew. Everywhere and forever the distances brighten blue!
Forever . . . forever . . .)

Words added by Mahler to his setting of Hans Bethge's
free translation of a poem by Meng Kao-yen and Wang Wei,
as the closing vocal lines of *Das Lied von der Erde*

The four parts of Wagner's *Ring* provide us with five endings. Two of these—the closing moments of *Rheingold* and *Siegfried*—are apparently triumphant. After the Rhinemaidens have sung their beautiful lament, the orchestra seems to ignore them, swelling with great pomp as the gods enter Valhalla. Two operas later, the brief orchestral coda that succeeds the exultant heights to which Brünnhilde and Siegfried leap with their final "*Lachender Tod!* [Laughing death!]" seems to continue their ecstatic mood; the climbing trills of the violins and frenzied figurations in the rest of the orchestra swirl upward to the closing chord. In both instances, the affirmative mode is easily, and rightly, heard as deceptive: there is empty pomposity in the one case, and the overheated jubilation of unstable emotions in the other. (The lovers seem to protest their delight too much; their love is real, but they do not yet know themselves, or what they are doing, or what to make of what they are feeling, or what its limits and vulnerabilities might be.)

Each of the other three endings occurs at a much darker moment in the drama. Each responds to a defeat and a loss, and yet each is more genuinely affirmative. *Walküre* closes by setting evocations of fire in violins and harps against repetitions of themes we have heard throughout Wotan's poignant farewell—the lovely five-note phrase that occurs frequently in the high winds (and later in low strings), and the tender, slow-moving melody played by violas and cellos. The trumpets and trombones recall the promise of the free hero; and, toward the end, together with horns and winds, they sound a three-note phrase of bittersweet resignation. There is great sadness in this, but also a kind of peace—as if the orchestra were kissing away the tears that a grieving god might shed.

In Siegfried's *Trauermusik* (Funeral Music) there is, at first hearing, only mourning. Preceded by the unnatural quiet that follows Siegfried's simple last phrase (an expression of love that is far deeper than the strained ecstasy with which he sang on Brünnhilde's rock), the initial hammer blows of trombones and drums are shatteringly final, as though the coffin of the world were being firmly shut. The lament of the brass chorale (at the moment when, according to Wagner's stage directions, the moon breaks through the clouds), and the grieving phrases in cellos, English horns, clarinets, and lastly oboes to which it gives rise, reinforce an atmosphere of total desolation and despair. Yet out of this comes a kind of affirmation—a tribute, perhaps to what Siegfried has been and might have been (particularly, we think, in view of the growth we have just witnessed in the moments preceding his death), registered not only in the motif associated with the hero but even more in the fortissimo climaxes, with the marcato syncopations in winds and brass.

But then that momentary recollection of something noble passes, and the musical mood becomes bleaker yet. The detached phrases and sparer textures into which the *Trauermusik* dissolves present us with fragments of the world. In these residues, we hear Gutrune's anxieties and then the ugly triumph of Hagen's entry. The orchestra is all menace and confusion, forcing on us a full appreciation of the legacy of Siegfried's death—until Hagen reaches to pluck the Ring from the dead hero's hand, and the tempo slows.

We hear, quietly, the motif of the sword, and then, with a new radiance, the descending motif associated with the passing of the gods, as Brünnhilde comes forward. Her first words command that the agitated grieving should cease, for the clamor is unworthy of the great hero — but a new musical atmosphere has already been created, presaging the resolution her actions will bring.

We shall say no more about what Brünnhilde says and does in this final scene, but focus instead on the last ending — the orchestral epilogue that evokes the meaning of her presence and of her departure. After she gives the joyous greeting for which the dying Siegfried had yearned, the orchestra conjures the destruction of the world in fire, giving way to the themes of the primordial state as the Rhine rises and the maidens regain the Ring. Above this scene of destruction, borne by flutes and violins, there soars the theme that Sieglinde had sung in response to the news of her unborn child. And from this point on, what we hear are radiantly beautiful versions of three major motifs: the pure beauty of the natural world of the Rhinemaidens, the splendors of Valhalla set in genuine grandeur rather than false pomp, and the resolute firmness of the free hero.

How can this be? What are these motifs, with their resonances and reminders, doing here? Siegfried is dead; the hero and his love have failed. Valhalla has been consumed, and we have long known that it was not the answer. Beautiful though the Rhinemaidens and their primordial world may be, the drama began from a sense of their insufficiencies. Yet these themes are preceded by the soaring melody of Sieglinde's expression of wonder, and they lead back to it, as in the very last measures of the orchestral score that melody is extended to a new resolution, a final triumph and a final peace. To hear the three themes with a new beauty is to hear them in the context of that great melody, and to hear how, in response to them, the melody unfolds into even greater loveliness.

These five endings provide a revealing structure for the whole drama. The first offers a deceptive triumph, a closure that is pregnant with instability and with the reverses to come. The second retrieves from apparently devastating failure and irreplaceable loss, a sweetness in resignation—and a new hope. That hope will sweep to another false victory, a contrived and illusory celebration. Inevitably new defeat follows, defeat that can easily be seen as total. And yet, even here, one might find something to praise in the death of the hero. The *Trauermusik* is not the bitterest moment. What follows is worse, as we confront the remnants of the world, after it seems that everything has failed. Those elements, however, are transformed by Brünnhilde; and the orchestral ending of *Götterdämmerung* sings out her making new of everything that has gone before, as it infuses the themes of nature, gods, and heroes with a different and greater light.

The judgment of this closing is at once tragic and affirmative. All the *Ring*'s great figures are tragic, doomed by the very qualities that elevate them above the rest. The order of nature can indeed be disrupted; but its disruption more readily tends toward its corruption than it is amenable to a reordering perfection, even by the greatest of powers and lofty intentions to transcend and transfigure it. Even a divinity that makes bold to improve on it suffers hubris, and must fail and fall. And if the wisdom and power of Wotan cannot succeed in imposing and securing a new and more glorious order on the world, it should come as no surprise that neither the heroism of Siegfried nor the love of Brünnhilde fares any better in this respect. Neither proves a match for the world that Wotan's configuration of qualities enabled him to master in his prime, insufficient and self-subverting as his mastery turned out to be. But of the two alternatives, Brünnhilde's receives a final musical endorsement that stands in the most radical of contrasts to Siegfried's. It is only when touched and transformed by Brünnhilde's love that Siegfried even begins to become bearable, let alone capable and worthy of such a love, and estimable as a human being.

As we have repeatedly observed, Brünnhilde's love, even at its radiant best, is no more The Answer to Wotan's problem of how to achieve and secure an admirable world-order than is Siegfried's brand of heroism. Both are ill-suited to it, disruptive of order, and all too easily taken advantage of by those with ulterior purposes and superior cunning. But while that is one of the judgments delivered by *Götterdämmerung*, another—hammered home by the Funeral Music and then soaringly celebrated by the music of the immolation scene—is that only Brünnhilde's way holds the promise of an answer to the more fundamental problem that originally drove Wotan to the World-Ash: the problem of endowing life (and death) with meaning.

Wotan left the World-Ash, spear in hand, committed to the idea that a solution to this problem involved making the world a better place, which in turn required the imposition upon it of a stable order; and so he embarked on an enterprise that was doomed to fail. Neither the best of strategy nor the greatest of heroism would suffice to make that more specific enterprise succeed. Further, love does not and cannot conquer all, any more than can the best laid plans of gods and men, or the greatest feats of the best of heroes. None will bring more than temporary victory at most, as victory is commonly reckoned. Yet the possibility of a love like that expressed in Brünnhilde's final act changes everything, in a way that heroism does not, even in the face of death and the ending of the world as we know it.

And though the world ends, the earth remains, still capable of renewal, still charged with this promise that we have come to know. We also know that everything that comes to be in it must end, including all order and the very best of lives and loves. But in their mere presence, however ephemeral, they have the power to illumine the world in a manner that vindicates all.

A Synopsis of the *Ring*

Das Rheingold (Rhinegold)

Scene 1

In the Rhine, the three Rhinemaidens (Woglinde, Wellgunde, and Flosshilde) are at play, graceful and carefree. Their game is interrupted by the Nibelung (dwarf) Alberich, who makes sexual advances to them. In turn, each of the maidens leads him on, only to tease him for his ugliness, to taunt and reject him. Alberich's frustration mounts. As the sun shines into the water, illuminating a rock in which the Rhinegold is embedded, the maidens exclaim at its loveliness, prompting Alberich to speak dismissively of the gold. They reply that it is no mere bauble, but gold of extraordinary properties, with the potential to be fashioned into a Ring of enormous power by anyone who would be prepared to repudiate love for its sake. They suppose that the lustful dwarf will be unwilling to abandon the delights of love; but Alberich mounts the rock and seizes the gold, cursing and renouncing love. Horrified and dismayed, the maidens flee into the depths.

Scene 2

On a high mountaintop, Wotan, who reigns as chief among the gods, lies asleep with his wife, Fricka, beside him. Behind them, across a broad valley, stands the gleaming new stronghold of Valhalla. On waking, Wotan sings in celebration of this great fortress. Fricka expresses her concern, for Wotan has promised the giants Fasolt and Fafner that he will give them Freia, Fricka's sister, in return for their building of Valhalla. Wotan reassures her that he has never seriously considered trading Freia for the giants' labor.

Freia enters, fearful that the giants are coming to claim her, and Wotan explains that he is relying on the demigod Loge to find a substitute with which Fasolt and Fafner will be satisfied. Freia remains deeply perturbed, calling on her brothers, Donner and Froh, to save her from Wotan's betrayal. The giants arrive, demanding Freia, but to their surprise, Wotan refuses, announcing that Freia is not for sale. Fasolt responds that the god's power rests on his commitment to guarantee laws and contracts, and that he cannot be forsworn. His brother Fafner suggests that they may resort to force. Wotan expresses his impatience at Loge's delay; but when Donner and Froh propose answering violence with violence, Wotan acknowledges Fasolt's point: he and his spear must uphold the rule of law. Loge at last enters, and the gods turn to him in expectation that he will provide a way out of the contretemps with the giants.

Loge's first replies are evasive, prompting the anger of Fricka, Donner, and Froh. Wotan intervenes, protecting him and expressing confidence in his wisdom. As the giants reiterate their demands, Loge enters into a long account of his searches for an acceptable substitute for Freia. He has roamed the world, he explains, finding nothing that anyone would deem a worthy surrogate for the delights of love—with one exception: Alberich, the Nibelung, has renounced love to obtain the Rhinegold. And, Loge adds, he brings the appeal of the Rhinemaidens to Wotan for assistance in regaining it. Wotan's impulse is to chide Loge, but the curiosity of the giants has been piqued. They ask what special quality the gold has. Loge replies that the gold, forged into a ring, enables its possessor to rule the world—and that Alberich has already made such a ring of it for himself. Gods and giants alike are now captivated by the idea of gaining the Ring—and, as Loge points out, what the thief stole can be stolen from the thief (adding, to no one's interest, that it could then be returned to the Rhinemaidens). Fafner, who has always been less besotted with Freia than Fasolt, advises his brother that the gold would be a much better reward for their labors than Freia would be. The giants seize Freia as hostage, announcing that unless the Rhinegold is turned over to them by evening, they will keep her (as they are entitled to do by the terms of their contract); in the meanwhile, they take her off with them.

Loge comments on Freia's plight. Then, turning to the gods, he observes their lethargy. They retain their youth through eating Freia's golden apples, and have become so dependent on the fruit that without her, they will age and wither. His scathing diagnosis rouses Wotan, who summons him to an expedition to Nibelheim, Alberich's home. The god has determined to try to gain the gold himself so that Freia may be ransomed.

Scene 3

In Nibelheim, Alberich has exploited the power of the Ring to gain command of his fellow dwarves. Many of them labor to extract gold from seams that the Ring makes apparent to its owner; others work up the supplies of gold. As the scene opens, Mime, Alberich's brother and a master smith, is tormented by Alberich who charges that he has delayed in forging a magic helm. Mime turns over his work (the Tarnhelm), and Alberich displays its power by showing that donning it can make the wearer invisible. (We shall later learn that the wearer of the helm can assume whatever shape he pleases, and that the helm enables one to move instantly from place to place.) After making Mime painfully aware of his presence, Alberich departs, leaving his brother groveling and whimpering.

At this point, Wotan and Loge arrive and restore Mime to his feet. Mime tells them how Alberich's power has enabled him to dominate the dwarves. He confesses that he had tried to keep the helm for himself but had not understood the full nature of the magic, and so is now condemned to servitude. Alberich enters, driving a group of Nibelungs who are piling up a hoard of his treasure. He dismisses Mime and demonstrates the power of the Ring by holding it out toward the dwarves, who are immediately cowed and scatter howling before it.

Wotan explains that he has heard rumors of Alberich's new powers and has come to see for himself. Alberich is suspicious and rebuffs Loge's attempt to claim prior friendship. He boasts of his growing hoard; in response to Wotan's suggestion that the gold he is amassing is worthless, he proclaims that it will ultimately serve him as the source of extraordinary power, enabling him to challenge and overcome the rule of the gods. Wotan reacts angrily, but Loge quickly intervenes, smoothly expressing his admiration of Alberich's achievements and asking, with deceptive naïvete, whether the dwarf's situation is entirely secure or might be vulnerable to a thief who could take the Ring while its owner slept. Alberich answers that he has been clever enough to see the potential problem; he has required Mime to fashion the magic helm so that he can remain hidden when he chooses.

Loge expresses exaggerated awe at the idea of such a device, the like of which he has never seen, and his hint of skepticism provokes Alberich to demonstrate the power of the Tarnhelm. He does so first by transforming himself into a giant dragon, at which Loge feigns terror and Wotan offers applause. Still seeming to be frightened, Loge suggests that the ability to make oneself very small might be the cleverest way to escape danger, inquiring whether the Tarnhelm also allows for that strategy. Alberich, enjoying what he takes to be the astonishment and admiration of the clever gods, announces that this is easy, and uses the helm to transform himself into a toad. Loge immediately urges Wotan to step on the toad, and once the animal is trapped, Loge removes the Tarnhelm. Caught beneath Wotan's foot, Alberich is bound. He is dragged, a prisoner, out of Nibelheim.

Scene 4

Back on the mountaintop, the captive Alberich is taunted by Loge, and Wotan informs him that he must pay a ransom for his freedom, naming the hoard of gold as the fee. Alberich quietly hopes that he can retain the Ring, so that the treasure to be abandoned can swiftly be regained or replaced. He summons the Nibelungs, who pile up the gold and depart at his angry bidding. Alleging that he has now paid, the dwarf requests the Tarnhelm, but Loge tells him that it, too, is part of the ransom—a disappointment for Alberich but not a fatal blow to his plans and power, as long as he can keep the Ring. But Wotan insists on that as well, to Alberich's desperate protests; and when the Nibelung refuses to give it up, Wotan seizes him and tears it from his finger. Alberich is released and bitterly mourns his loss, declaring that the Ring shall bring only gloom and misery to its owner and that the lord of the Ring shall be the slave of the Ring. After issuing his grim curse, he slinks away.

Fasolt and Fafner approach, bearing Freia. Wotan tells them that the gold is ready; but Fasolt, grieving at the thought of parting with the goddess, demands that the gold must be heaped up into a wall that will hide her from sight. Fafner supervises the work, insisting that all the chinks in the wall that is to conceal her must be filled. After Loge announces that all the gold has been used, Fafner complains that he can still glimpse Freia's hair, and the Tarnhelm, which has been held back, has to be added. Fasolt, still in doubt as to whether the gold is worth the goddess, laments that he can no longer see Freia, but then spies a gap through which she is still barely visible. Fafner demands that it be filled, and observes that Wotan is wearing a Ring made of gold from the treasure. Loge protests that this is gold that must be returned to the Rhinemaidens. Wotan then goes further, angrily declaring that he intends to keep the Ring for himself and refuses to give it up. Fasolt therefore reclaims Freia. The other gods urge Wotan to relent; but he remains obdurate.

The impasse is broken by the appearance of Erda, the primal earth mother, who has come to warn Wotan. She declares that she knows all that was, is, and will be; that a dark day is dawning for the gods; and that Wotan should abandon the Ring. He demands to know more, but evading his requests, she vanishes. Impetuously, Wotan starts to pursue her, but is restrained by Fricka and Froh. After some moments of thought, Wotan decides to heed Erda's warning and to yield the Ring, completing Freia's ransom. Freia is released, and the giants start to divide up the treasure. Disagreements quickly erupt, flaring into anger when, at Loge's suggestion, Fasolt claims the Ring. The giants fight, and Fafner kills his brother. He departs with the Ring and the rest of the treasure.

Wotan is shaken by this sudden demonstration of the power of Alberich's curse. He declares that he must learn from Erda what he needs to know. Donner conjures a storm to dissolve the sultry haze, and with Froh, he constructs a rainbow bridge over which the gods will be able to make their entrance into Valhalla. Wotan continues to meditate, beset by gloomy thoughts, until, struck with a grand idea, he salutes the stronghold and invites Fricka to accompany him into it. Loge comments, aside, that the gods are hurrying toward their end. From the depths the Rhinemaidens are heard, pleading for the return of the gold. Loge asks Wotan what answer they should be given, prompting Wotan brusquely to dismiss their plea. As Loge invites the maidens to rejoice in the gods' splendor, they sing that the rejoicing on the heights is false. The gods enter Valhalla.

Between *Das Rheingold* and *Die Walküre* (The Valkyrie)

After the end of *Rheingold*, Wotan follows his impulse to go to Erda, by whom he has nine daughters, the Valkyries. Among them is one, Brünnhilde, the Valkyrie of this opera's title, who becomes especially dear to him. As he will later testify, Wotan also learns from Erda's great store of wisdom.

In the hopes of securing his reign, Wotan periodically sends out the Valkyries to bring heroes slain in battle to Valhalla, where they may serve post-mortem as defenders against any onslaught. The greatest threat to Wotan and the gods stems from the existence and possible use of the Ring, should it fall into the wrong hands—in particular, if used along the lines elaborated by Alberich when he boasted of his powers to Wotan and Loge. The Ring itself is currently in the possession of Fafner, who has used the Tarnhelm to change himself into a dragon and who sits in a cave (*Neidhöhle*) in a deserted forest, guarding his treasure.

Wotan has also sired two children by a mortal woman, the twins Siegmund and Sieglinde. Under the name of *Wälse*, the god lived as a mortal with his consort and their children, pursuing adventures that have inspired the hatred of other human beings. One day, while Wälse and the boy Siegmund were out on the hunt, a band of vengeful enemies burned down the family home, killing the woman and abducting Sieglinde. Thereafter Wälse (now sometimes called *Wolfe*) and his son roamed the forest, engaging in numerous conflicts and adventures. During one such episode, the young Siegmund was separated from his father, whom he never saw again. After that, the youth lived by his strength and his wits, often encountering trouble and danger, and faring poorly more often than not.

His sister, meanwhile, was forcibly married to a brutish man named Hunding, for whom she feels no love. On the day of their wedding, a stranger appeared at Hunding's hut—a man no longer young, one of whose eyes was hidden by his hat, who thrust a sword deep into the ash tree at the center of the hut, announcing that this sword would belong to the man who could withdraw it. Sieglinde has guessed that the mysterious stranger was her father, Wälse. (The audience of *Walküre* will know him to have been Wotan, both because of the characteristic way in which the god's blind eye is hidden and because of the musical motif that sounds when these events are described.) None of the guests was able to remove the sword, and it remains in the tree, buried to the hilt.

The course of the action between *Rheingold* and *Walküre* is reported, in fragments and from different perspectives, in the course of the latter opera.

Die Walküre (The Valkyrie)

Act I

Scene 1

The drama begins in Hunding's hut, where Siegmund, wounded and weaponless, has been driven in flight through a storm to take refuge. He collapses at the hearth. Sieglinde enters, and sees the stranger. Feeling compassion for him, she gives him water and tends to him. Their mutual attraction is almost immediate.

Sieglinde tells the stranger that she is Hunding's wife and that the hut belongs to Hunding. Siegmund revives and announces his resolve to be on his way, declaring that he is a luckless man who does not wish to bring ill fortune to the woman who has aided him. Sieglinde replies that he can hardly bring her ill fortune, since it already dwells in Hunding's house. Siegmund agrees to await Hunding's return.

Scene 2

Almost immediately, Hunding arrives. He is suspicious, and questions his wife, who explains that she has simply fulfilled the obligation of hospitality in caring for the weary and wounded stranger. Hunding orders her to prepare a meal and asks Siegmund to identify himself. After reluctantly giving his name as *Wehwalt* (the woeful one), Siegmund offers some fragments of his life's story. He begins by describing his early years with Wolfe, the sack of the family home and the death of his mother and loss of his sister, and his and his father's subsequent life as outlaws. He then tells of his separation from his father and of the later difficulties he had when his own views of what was right failed to coincide with those of the people with whom he had to deal. Finally, he recounts his efforts to aid a young woman whose kin were forcing her to marry a man she did not love; Siegmund fought her oppressive relatives, killing her brothers, but more members of the family came to the skirmish. The girl herself bewailed the slaughter; and, he recalls, refusing to stir, she seems eventually to have been killed herself. Siegmund lost his shield and weapons in the melee and was compelled to flee; and his escape has brought him to Hunding's hut. So, he declares, it should be clear why his name connotes sorrow.

Hunding replies that he knows of a clan of outlaws hated by all who love justice. He was summoned to seek revenge for the death of his kinsmen at their hands, but arrived too late, for the outlaws had already fled. Now he finds that one culprit has turned up on his own hearth. He has taken Siegmund in and will give him shelter for the night, as custom requires; but, he warns, in the morning he will come after him, and his guest should be prepared to defend himself with sturdy weapons. He commands Sieglinde to make his night drink, and she does so. Seeing her lingering glances toward the stranger, Hunding urges her into the bed chamber with a violent gesture, takes his weapons, and repeats his warning to Siegmund.

Scene 3

Left alone, Siegmund reflects on his predicament, recalling his father's promise that, in the hour of his most extreme need, he would find a sword. He expresses his tender feelings toward the woman who is enslaved by his enemy, and, looking up, he seems to see a light gleam in the ash tree. But the fire dies away, and the room becomes dark.

Sieglinde softly enters the darkened room and approaches the hearth. After reporting that she has drugged her husband to ensure that he will not awaken, she tells Siegmund of the day on which she was compelled to marry Hunding and of the stranger who plunged a sword into the ash tree. She suspects that the sword was left for her deliverance, for a hero who would liberate her and bring her love, expressing the fervent wish that this should be the day and he the hero. Siegmund embraces her, confessing his own love for her; and, as if in response, the door of the hut swings opens upon a verdant landscape, and the light of a full spring moon shines into the room. They join in ecstatic celebration of mutual love. Responding to Sieglinde's questions about his identity, Siegmund reveals that his father, whom he has referred to as "Wolfe," was Wälse; and so they joyfully realize that they are each other's long-lost twins. Sieglinde then bestows a name befitting a hero upon her brother: Siegmund. Turning his attention to the sword, he dubs it "Nothung," and draws it triumphantly from the ash tree, to Sieglinde's great joy. Proclaiming themselves lover and bride, the brother and sister unite passionately.

Act II

Scene 1

In the mountains, Wotan and Brünnhilde are preparing for battle. Wotan gives the Valkyrie her orders: Siegmund is to be victorious, and Hunding is of no interest as a potential recruit for Valhalla. Brünnhilde departs, observing that Fricka is on her way to confront Wotan and is apparently furious. Wotan resolves to stand firm against the coming emotional storm.

Fricka arrives, describing herself as the guardian of marriage who has come in response to Hunding's legitimate complaints. Wotan dismisses her arguments, which provoke her to detail his own unfaithfulness and apparent lack of concern for marriage vows. Wotan explains that his perspective is much more encompassing than hers and that it is necessary that there should be a hero unencumbered by the law of the gods. (As we shall learn later in this Act, the necessity arises from the threat posed by the power of the Ring, which Wotan cannot himself lawfully repossess from its present owner, Fafner. Wotan therefore needs an independent agent to do the deed for him.) Fricka replies that Wotan is trying to dupe her, and that the supposed free agent Wotan has been grooming for the task—Siegmund—is, in reality, simply an extension of the god himself. Wotan must therefore withdraw the power of the sword and may not order or even permit Brünnhilde to protect Siegmund. Recognizing the force of Fricka's arguments, Wotan can offer no reply; and, shattered and dejected, he accedes to her demands. She asks for his oath that Siegmund will fall, and the god is compelled to give it. As Brünnhilde returns, Fricka directs the Valkyrie to her father and then exits triumphantly.

Scene 2

Brünnhilde readily discerns Wotan's profound grief and attempts to elicit its causes. At first he can only lament his predicament; but her repeated entreaties move him to offer a detailed account of the matter, in the course of which he provides us with more details about his life and career than we have yet been given.

Wotan tells Brünnhilde that he long ago sought and gained supreme power and proceeded to establish a system of laws and treaties, but in the course of doing so he resorted to underhanded strategies. He recounts the events of *Rheingold*—Alberich's theft of the gold made possible by his renunciation of love, the contract with the giants, his own seizure of the Ring, the use of it to compensate Fasolt and Fafner for the construction of Valhalla, and Erda's warning. He recalls how he pursued Erda, how he gained wisdom from her, and how Brünnhilde herself, together with her eight-sister Valkyries, were the product of his union with Erda. The Valkyries were to bring slain heroes to the stronghold to defend it; but this, Wotan knows, would not be enough to counteract the power of the Ring, especially if it were to fall into the hands of Alberich, its original owner. Hence, Wotan explains, it is imperative that the Ring be regained from Fafner—but he himself, having given the Ring in payment, cannot simply take it back by force, for that would irretrievably weaken the order of law on which his power rests.

So Wotan has come up with the idea (the "great idea," we can assume, that occurred to him at the end of *Rheingold*) of creating a free being who is not bound as he is and so can do what he cannot, but, he laments bitterly, that has proven to be impossible, for he can only make servants. To Brünnhilde's suggestion that Siegmund acts for himself, Wotan admits his own self-deception, easily uncovered by Fricka: he has scripted and directed Siegmund's entire life. He must thus comply with Fricka's demand that he abandon Siegmund to his fate, and give up his plan of using Siegmund to regain the Ring. In despair, he thinks he must even acquiesce in the triumph of Alberich. Erda prophesied that the Nibelung would sire a son, and that this event would presage the end of the gods. Wotan has recently heard that Alberich has bribed a woman to give herself to him and that a pregnancy has resulted. With great bitterness, the god says that he bequeaths the world to Alberich's (as yet unborn and unnamed) son.

Brünnhilde asks what she should do, and Wotan replies that she must fight on Fricka's behalf rather than Siegmund's, defending the rights of marriage and ensuring Siegmund's death. She answers that she cannot turn against a hero whom her father loves. This provokes Wotan to rebuke her vehemently for her insolence and to warn her of the fearful consequences that will befall her if she disobeys. He storms off, reiterating that Siegmund must die.

Brünnhilde laments both Wotan's plight and the order that she must carry out.

Scene 3

Siegmund and Sieglinde are fleeing from Hunding and his kin. Sieglinde rushes ahead, declaring that she is unworthy of her hero; feeling the dishonor of her forced marriage to Hunding, she does not wish to bring shame upon Siegmund, the brother-lover who has awakened love in her. Siegmund tries to calm her, but her anguish flares again in a wild vision, in which she seems to see Siegmund surrounded and killed. She faints, and he holds her cradled in his arms.

Scene 4

Brünnhilde enters, hailing Siegmund and informing him that he must follow her. She has come to announce his death as a hero who has been chosen by Wotan to join him in Valhalla. He asks if he will find Wälse in Valhalla, and she tells him that he will indeed find his father there. Siegmund inquires next whether he will be greeted by a woman in Valhalla, and Brünnhilde assures him that the "wish-maidens" will welcome him. Finally, he poses his most significant question: will Sieglinde be with him there? The Valkyrie answers that Siegmund will not see his sister-wife in Valhalla. Siegmund then declares that, in that event, he has no interest in the delights of Valhalla and he refuses to accompany Brünnhilde there; for he only wants to remain with Sieglinde, come what may.

Brünnhilde replies that his death is inevitable, that it must separate him from Sieglinde, and that she has come to announce this to him. Siegmund dismisses the idea that he is to fall to Hunding, asserting the power of his sword. Brünnhilde explains that the giver of the sword has withdrawn its power. Siegmund's immediate first thought is to protect the sleeping Sieglinde from this terrible news; then, in grief and anger, he denounces the treachery of the sword-giver and vows that if he must fall, he prefers Hell to Valhalla. Brünnhilde is incredulous that the tired woman who lies in his arms means so much to him. He replies that she is unfeeling and hard; and spurning her offer to protect Sieglinde after his death, he vows that if they cannot remain together in life, he will kill both Sieglinde and himself with a single stroke, and he prepares to do so. As Brünnhilde recognizes his determination and the force of the love that underlies it, she orders him to halt. She has changed her mind, and determines that Siegmund and Sieglinde shall live. She tells him to trust in the sword and promises to shield him. Bidding him farewell, she departs.

Scene 5

Left alone with Sieglinde, Siegmund commends her to rest until the battle is over. As Hunding's horn is heard, he draws his sword and hurries off to the fray. Sieglinde stirs from her troubled sleep and starts up anxiously. The challenges issued by Hunding and Siegmund are heard and both appear against the mountain ridge. As Sieglinde pleads for the combat to cease, Brünnhilde appears, protecting Siegmund. Siegmund is about to strike Hunding when Wotan himself arrives on the scene. The god shatters Siegmund's sword with his spear, leaving him defenseless against a mortal blow from Hunding. He dies, and Sieglinde collapses. Brünnhilde hastens to her, quickly lifting her onto her horse and taking flight. Hunding withdraws his spear from the dead Siegmund. Wotan looks with sorrow on his son, and turning to Hunding, orders him to kneel before Fricka. At a flick of his hand, Hunding falls, dead. Furious, Wotan expresses his resolve to punish Brünnhilde.

Act III

Scene 1

Brünnhilde's eight sisters, the other Valkyries, assemble on a rocky summit. They have brought slain heroes who are to swell the defenses of Valhalla. Looking out, they see Brünnhilde riding furiously toward them and discern that she is bringing a woman. Brünnhilde arrives and asks her sisters to shield her, explaining that she is being pursued by Wotan. With her is Sieglinde, whom she has rescued after Siegmund's death. She confesses that she has defied Wotan's commands in attempting, unsuccessfully, to save the hero. As some of her sisters chide Brünnhilde for her folly, Waltraute, the Valkyrie stationed as lookout, observes Wotan approaching in a storm-cloud. Despite Brünnhilde's pleas, the Valkyries refuse to disobey their father and lend her aid in conveying Sieglinde to safety.

Sieglinde herself has been still and silent, but she now expresses her repudiation of Brünnhilde's efforts to help her. With Siegmund dead, she wants only death for herself. Brünnhilde urges her to live for the sake of love, now embodied in the child whom Sieglinde (previously unbeknownst to herself) is carrying. At this news, Sieglinde's attitude immediately changes, and she exhorts the Valkyries to protect her child. Brünnhilde urges her to flee while she remains to face Wotan's anger. Sieglinde is to go to the east, to the forest where Fafner guards his hoard; for although this is a wild and dangerous place, it is one that Wotan avoids. Brünnhilde counsels Sieglinde to bear up under the difficulties ahead of her, since she has in her womb the most noble of heroes. She gives Sieglinde the fragments of the sword that Siegmund had made his own and that Wotan had shattered, prophesying that the child, whom she names "Siegfried," will forge that sword anew. Sieglinde, deeply stirred, sings in praise of this most wonderful outcome and of the glorious maiden who has saved her and her child. As she hurries away, Wotan's voice is heard, commanding Brünnhilde to stay. The god has arrived at the mountain, and the other Valkyries crowd around Brünnhilde in an attempt to conceal her.

Scene 2

Wotan storms onto the summit, demanding to know where Brünnhilde is hidden. The Valkyries plead on her behalf, but he dismisses their wailing, telling them that Brünnhilde has broken faith with him and must be punished. He calls on her to emerge from her hiding place, and she steps forward to receive her chastisement. Wotan tells her that she has determined her own sentence: by defying his will, she has ceased to be a Valkyrie. Nor is that all. Cast out from Valhalla and banished from his sight, she shall lie on the mountain, bound in sleep by a spell; and whatever man finds her and awakens her shall claim her as his prize. The eight other Valkyries protest; but Wotan is adamant, advising them that if they do not wish to share Brünnhilde's fate, they must leave the mountaintop at once. In dismay, they ride away.

Scene 3

Left alone together, Wotan and Brünnhilde remain silent for a time. Then Brünnhilde slowly begins to speak, asking if her wrongdoing was so shameful that she deserves the abasement that he has announced. Wotan responds that she has contravened his explicit order. She answers that that order was issued against his own will and that she knew of his enduring love for Siegmund. She also reports her own encounter with Siegmund, and the impression wrought upon her by his readiness to die for love. Wotan tells her that he has had to quench his own love for the sake of the world, and as she has chosen to follow love, it is fitting that she should be left as prey to a mortal lover.

Brünnhilde protests that it would be dishonorable for her to be won by some coward. She reminds her father that he has engendered a race of heroes—the Wälsungs—and informs him that Sieglinde carries a child of that line. Wotan interrupts her, warning that he will not protect either Sieglinde or her unborn child. Brünnhide persists, telling him that the fragments of the sword have been preserved. As he reiterates his sentence and prepares to carry it out, she pleads with him to shield her with terrors that will allow only a hero to penetrate to her resting place, and to wake her from her sleep and claim her. Throwing herself at his feet, she asks that he surround the mountaintop with fire. Deeply moved by her passionate desire to avoid dishonor, Wotan relents, granting her request and bidding her farewell. Sadly, he tells her that she will no longer be his delight, and he bequeaths her to the hero who will awaken her—one who is freer than he. He lays her to rest. Summoning Loge, in his guise as fire, he surrounds with flame the rock on which she lies. Declaring that one who fears his spear point will never pass through the fire, he looks back at the sleeping Brünnhilde one last time, and leaves.

Between *Die Walküre* and *Siegfried* (Siegfried)

Sieglinde makes her way to the forest, where she gives birth to Siegfried. Shortly after the birth, she dies and the baby is adopted by Mime, Alberich's brother, whom we have met in *Rheingold* and who dwells in the vicinity. Mime talks with Sieglinde before her death, and so he knows the name that the boy is to bear. He also has the fragments of the sword, and knows from her of the sword's identity. (There are suggestions that he may have had a hand in her death, but these are not resolved by the drama.) Mime raises the boy. He hopes to equip Siegfried with the sword so that Siegfried will be able to kill Fafner and gain the gold—which the dwarf then intends to take from him. At the time *Siegfried* opens, the boy has grown into a vigorous youth.

Meanwhile, Wotan has abandoned Valhalla and the defense of the order he had attempted to establish. Now, in the guise of a Wanderer, he roams the earth, observing and questioning, but no longer attempting to direct the course of events.

Siegfried (Siegfried)

Act I

Scene 1

The drama opens in Mime's cave, which serves as both home and smithy. Siegfried is away in the forest, and the dwarf is attempting to forge the fragments of Nothung. Frustrated, he admits his failure, and elaborates his plan that the strong young man should use the sword to kill Fafner and to bring Mime the Ring.

Siegfried arrives with a bear tethered to a rope, using the animal to torment Mime. The dwarf produces a sword that he has forged. The boy releases the bear into the woods and tests the sword, which breaks under the force of his blow, moving him to vent his contempt for the smith and his supposed skill. Mime chides him for ingratitude, and self-pityingly recalls all that he has done for him. Siegfried exclaims that Mime disgusts him and asks what has happened to his mother, Mime's wife. The dwarf answers evasively, but Siegfried pursues the interrogation persistently and forcefully. Eventually, Mime confesses that he is no relation to the boy, that he took him into his care as a baby after the death of the boy's mother, who had given him the name "Siegfried." In response to Siegfried's demands for proof, Mime shows him the fragments of the sword, provoking the boy to demand that the smith make them into a proper weapon for him so that he may take it and leave this false (and hated) home for good. As Siegfried runs into the forest, Mime is left in fear and dejection; for despite his skill and all his efforts, he does not understand how to join the fragments of Nothung together.

Scene 2

At this point, the Wanderer (Wotan) enters the cave. Mime tries to persuade the unwanted intruder to leave, but Wotan persists, sitting down at the hearth and promising to wager his head in a riddle duel with the dwarf. Mime accepts and poses three questions—questions concerned with the governance of the earth's various regions—which Wotan answers easily. At this point, Mime expects that his unwelcome guest will leave; but after pointing out that the dwarf has failed to ask what he needed to know, the Wanderer claims that it is now his turn to ask the questions. First, he asks Mime to name the race that Wotan holds dearest and has also treated badly. Mime replies, correctly, that it is the Wälsungs. Next, Wotan challenges him to name the sword that the hero Siegfried must use to defeat Fafner. Once again, the reply is correct—Siegfried must use Nothung. Finally, the Wanderer wants to know who will fashion the fragments of Nothung into a sword. Mime cannot reply. Wotan rises, repeating his judgment that the dwarf had failed to pose riddles that addressed what he needed to know and telling him that only one who has never known fear can reforge the sword. He advises the dwarf to guard his head well for it will be forfeit to the one who knows no fear. Wotan then departs.

Scene 3

Mime is left in terror, apparently possessed by a vision that Fafner will catch him. Siegfried reappears, demanding the sword. The dwarf's answers are confused, for he is now obsessed with the idea that the boy must somehow come to know what fear is. Pulling himself together, he ascertains that the youth is indeed quite ignorant of fear and offers to arrange for him to have a lesson: he will take Siegfried to Neidhöhle, where an encounter with Fafner will teach him the meaning of fear. Siegfried agrees to the plan and reiterates his demand for the sword. When Mime confesses that he does not know how to reforge Nothung, the boy impatiently seizes the fragments and declares that he will do it himself. He dismisses Mime's criticisms that he has never learned the smith's craft, and goes to work. After the dwarf has told him the sword's name, Siegfried sings in praise of Nothung as he works at the forge. Mime stands aside, muttering, and planning to prepare a poisoned drink; after the youth has killed Fafner, the dwarf will give it to the thirsty victor—and once it has done its work, he will step in and gain the Ring and the dragon's hoard. Both of them are caught up in their dreams: Siegfried as he celebrates the renewal of his father's weapon, and Mime as he envisions the power that will be his when his scheme comes to fruition.

Act II

Scene 1

Deep in the forest, before Neidhöhle, Mime's brother Alberich is keeping watch. He sees a light, which he initially takes to be the dawn. But it is the Wanderer, who has come to Neidhöhle. Alberich rails at him as a shameless thief, but the Wanderer replies that he has come merely to observe, not to play any active part. The Ring is to fall to the one who wins it; and, Wotan explains, Mime intends to bring Siegfried to obtain it for him. Alberich finds it hard to believe that Wotan himself is not a serious rival for the Ring, but the Wanderer volunteers to help the Nibelung alert Fafner, tell the dragon of the coming danger, and advise him to save himself by giving up the Ring. They do so; but Fafner, confident of his ability to dispatch the hero, refuses to concede the Ring to Alberich and returns to sleep. The Wanderer advises Alberich to try outwitting Mime and rides away, leaving the dwarf to express his grim determination to gain the Ring and defeat the gods. He goes into a hiding place to wait.

Scene 2

As dawn breaks, Siegfried and Mime arrive at Neidhöhle. Mime continues to elaborate his promise that the dragon will convey the meaning of fear. Siegfried responds by using Mime's descriptions of Fafner's powers to formulate his plan for killing the dragon. He dismisses Mime, who promises to bring the boy refreshment after he is victorious.

Siegfried waits, alone, expressing his delight that the dwarf is not his true father and wondering about his mother. He hears a woodbird and, recalling how Mime had once told him that the songs of birds could be understood, he cuts himself a reed pipe with which he tries to imitate the bird. His efforts fail, but they do arouse Fafner. The dragon emerges for a drink, and is delighted by the prospect that the boy will serve him as a meal. They exchange threats, challenges, and boasts. Siegfried attacks and, after a fight, plunges Nothung into the dragon's heart. As Fafner lies dying, he asks for the name of the child who has defeated him and warns that whoever has sent the boy to the fight is plotting his death. Siegfried confesses his identity and asks for further counsel, but Fafner dies before responding. As the boy withdraws his sword, his hand is smeared with the dragon's blood. The blood burns him and he instinctively raises his hand to his mouth, sucking the blood away. At once, he becomes able to understand the song of the woodbird. The bird advises him to take both the Tarnhelm and the Ring from the dragon's cave. Siegfried does so.

Scene 3

Mime creeps back to Neidhöhle just as Alberich emerges from his hiding place. The brothers berate one another, each asserting their claims to the Ring, the Tarnhelm, and the gold: Alberich because he originally acquired them, and Mime because he has conceived and executed the plot for their recovery. For a moment, Mime is prepared to allow Alberich the Ring if he in turn can possess the Tarnhelm, but Alberich refuses this division. As they exchange further threats, Siegfried emerges from the cave. To their surprise and chagrin, they see that instead of useless baubles he has selected the Tarnhelm and the Ring. Both dwarves retreat into hiding.

Siegfried confesses that he has no idea what the booty he has chosen is good for, but he is prepared to rely on the advice of the woodbird. The woodbird sings again, urging Siegfried not to trust Mime and to attend to the dwarf's treacherous thoughts. Mime reappears, inquiring if Siegfried has yet learned the meaning of fear. The youth replies that he has not yet found a teacher, having killed Fafner—and he adds that he hates the dwarf who set him to the task far more than he did the dragon. Although Mime attempts to talk to Siegfried with tenderness and solicitude, the taste of the dragon's blood enables the boy to hear the malign thoughts behind what the dwarf is saying. So he learns in this manner of Mime's hatred for him, his intention to do him harm, and his plan to offer Siegfried a drink that will make him senseless. When Siegfried hears Mime gleefully think of how he will hack off Siegfried's head while he lies in drugged sleep, the youth responds by striking the dwarf with his sword. Mime falls, dead. Alberich, who has watched from his hiding place, laughs.

Siegfried heaves the body of the dragon across the entrance to the cave. As he looks around him, he reflects on his loneliness and asks the woodbird to provide a friend for him. The bird responds by singing of a woman who lies asleep on a high rock, protected by fire, and suggesting that she would make a wonderful bride for Siegfried. The boy is excited by the prospect and asks if he can break through the fire. When the bird tells him that Brünnhilde can only be won by one who knows no fear, Siegfried's confidence swells, and he decides to let the woodbird show him the way.

Act III

Scene 1

At the foot of the mountain on which Brünnhilde lies, the Wanderer appears, calling on Erda to awaken. She arises, and he tells her that he has come to her in search of knowledge. She evades his questions, referring him first to the Norns and then to Brünnhilde. When the Wanderer replies by telling her of the Valkyrie's disobedience and punishment, Erda confesses her confusion and expresses her wish to return to sleep. Wotan persists in his questioning, and she recognizes him. He replies by telling her of his own intentions: he is reconciled to the end of the gods and commits her to eternal sleep. He prophesies that Siegfried and Brünnhilde will defeat the plans of the Nibelung and will perform a deed that redeems the world. She descends.

Scene 2

Wotan sees that Siegfried is approaching. The boy has lost his guide, the woodbird, and as he tries to find his path up the mountain, he finds his way blocked by the Wanderer. In response to the old man's questions, he tells the story of his recent adventures, until, becoming impatient, he advises his interlocutor to step aside or, if he can, to show him the way. Wotan counsels patience, but the youth becomes more truculent, threatening to force his way past if the Wanderer does not stand aside. Wotan calmly explains that he is well disposed to Siegfried and his kind, but the boy will not listen. His threats arouse Wotan's anger; pointing with his spear, Wotan tells Siegfried of the fire that will consume him if he attempts to climb the mountain. Siegfried tries to advance and Wotan blocks his path with the spear, announcing that it once shattered the very sword he carries. Inspired by the thought of avenging his father, Siegfried attacks, striking the spear and breaking it. Wotan picks up the fragments and resignedly admits that he cannot stop Siegfried. He disappears. Siegfried strides forward and plunges into the fire.

Scene 3

Siegfried emerges at the top of the rock. He sees first Brünnhilde's horse, Grane, and then the sleeping Valkyrie, whom he takes to be a man in armor. Concerned that the helmet may be uncomfortable for the sleeper, he removes it, and then cuts away the breastplate. He is surprised to discover that the sleeper is not a man, but a woman. He tries to awaken her, eventually doing so with a kiss.

Brünnhilde sits up. She sees Siegfried, and sings in celebration of her awakening. She confesses her longstanding love for him. Then her eyes fall on Grane and on the other reminders of her life as a Valkyrie, and a wave of sadness and regret passes over her. Siegfried responds with ardor, attempting to embrace her. But she repulses his advances. He reminds her that she had confessed her love for him. She replies that she was always concerned only for his good, and she urges him to leave her undisturbed. Now doubting her love, he pleads with her to be his. She is won over. They embrace passionately and sing in ecstatic celebration of their love.

Götterdämmerung (Twilight of the Gods)

Prologue

On the mountaintop, where Siegfried awoke Brünnhilde, the three Norns, daughters of Erda, weave the rope of fate. They sing of the world's past, of Wotan's original sacrifice of an eye, his breaking of a branch from the World-Ash from which he fashioned a spear, and the tree's decline and decay. Their story continues with Wotan's use of the spear to institute the rule of law; but a hero has now shattered the spear. Wotan has retired to Valhalla, where he has had the wood of the felled World-Ash piled high, and sits in silence. The Norns foretell that the order of the gods will be consumed in fire. As their weaving and narration unfold, the rope becomes tangled. It catches on the rock around which they have wound it, and breaks, spelling the end of their wisdom. They descend to their mother.

Brünnhilde and Siegfried emerge on the rock. She sends him out to new adventures, regretting only that she may not have given him sufficient wisdom. They sing of their love and exchange tokens. Siegfried gives her the Ring he took from Neidhöhle, and she gives him her horse. After a joyous reaffirmation of their love and union, Siegfried departs.

Act I

Scene 1

In the hall of the Gibichungs, beside the Rhine, Gunther, chief of the Gibichungs, and his sister Gutrune sit in state. Gunther asks Hagen, his half-brother (who, as we quickly learn, is the son of Alberich by Gunther's mother, Grimhilde), how the reputation of the clan stands. Hagen replies that their fame is dimmed because both Gunther and Gutrune remain unwed. He tells them of Brünnhilde, suggesting that she would make a worthy wife for Gunther, and Siegfried a worthy husband for Gutrune. Both brother and sister are intrigued; but when they learn of the circumstances of Brünnhilde's confinement, they rebuke Hagen for even raising the idea. Hagen explains, however, that if Gutrune were to prepare a magic potion for Siegfried, the hero might forget all women he had previously seen, Brünnhilde included, and so proceed to fall in love with her; and to gain Gutrune's hand, he might then be willing to undertake the task of delivering Brünnhilde to be Gunther's bride. They agree on the plan. Hagen is confident that Siegfried will shortly find his way to the Rhine and to the Gibichungs' lands. Almost immediately, the hero's horn sounds, and Hagen sees his boat approaching. He calls out to Siegfried, who responds that he is seeking the Gibichungs.

Scene 2

Siegfried comes ashore and is welcomed. He has heard Gunther praised and says that he comes either to fight or to make friends. They decide on friendship, and Hagen inquires about the tales he has heard of Siegfried's exploits. Siegfried admits that he has won the treasure of the Nibelung and that he has taken from it a piece of metal of whose power he is ignorant. Upon being shown it, Hagen tells him that it is the Tarnhelm, and that it allows its wearer to change shape at will or to move from one place to another instantaneously. He then asks if Siegfried has taken anything else of the treasure. Siegfried replies that he took a ring, and that a woman has it in her keeping.

Gutrune presents the guest with a drink, in accordance with the plan. Siegfried makes a quiet vow to Brünnhilde before drinking, but once he has done so, he ceases to have any recollection of her and is seized with a sudden passion for Gutrune. He asks Gunther if he can have her for his wife, promising in return to help Gunther in his own marital quest. Gunther quickly informs him of a woman in whom he is interested who lies on a rock protected by fire. Siegfried declares that he will penetrate the fire, win her for him, and bring her to him, disguising himself as Gunther by means of the Tarnhelm to do so. They swear an oath to blood brotherhood. Hagen does not join them, claiming that his cold blood would spoil the drink. Siegfried and Gunther hurry off on their quest, leaving Hagen to guard the hall. Gutrune retires.

Hagen takes up his place as watchman. He comments on the adventure on which Gunther and Siegfried are embarked: it will gain Gunther a wife — but for him, Hagen, it will bring the Ring, enabling the despised Nibelung's son to become master.

Scene 3

Brünnhilde sits on the mountaintop. She hears the familiar sound of a Valkyrie's horse, and her sister, Waltraute, arrives. Brünnhilde's first thought is that Wotan's anger toward her may have passed, but Waltraute quickly disabuses her. She has not come to celebrate Brünnhilde's foolish love but in response to the plight of the gods. Wotan has returned with the fragments of the broken spear; he has cut down the World-Ash and has had the logs piled around Valhalla; he has summoned the gods and heroes; and all sit in silent gloom. Waltraute, who has clung to the god and wept on his breast, has observed a slight softening of his grim countenance as he thought of Brünnhilde, and has heard him whisper that the world might be freed of Alberich's curse if Brünnhilde would return the Ring to the Rhinemaidens. Waltraute has come to urge her to do so.

Brünnhilde refuses. The Ring is the pledge of Siegfried's love for her, and she will not cast it away, even if the price of retaining it should be the end of Valhalla. Waltraute is shocked by her disloyalty. Brünnhilde bids her sister depart.

Shortly after Waltraute leaves, the fire surrounding the rock begins to burn more brightly. Brünnhilde starts up joyously, thinking that Siegfried is returning to her. To her dismay, the man who comes through the flames does not appear to be her beloved. In a different, rougher voice, he announces himself as a suitor, declaring that he will take her by force if she resists. She is horrified and demands to know who he is. The invader announces himself as Gunther. Extending her arm, Brünnhilde tries to use the Ring to ward off this assailant. He advances and they struggle. The disguised Siegfried pulls the Ring from her finger. As she collapses, she looks up, momentarily meeting his gaze. He announces his triumph, ordering her into the sleeping chamber. Before following her in for the bridal night that is to make her Gunther's wife, he pledges that he will keep faith with his blood brother by placing Nothung between them.

Act II

Scene 1

Night. Hagen is asleep outside the Hall of the Gibichungs. Alberich appears to him, urging his son to hate those who are fortunate and to dedicate himself to bringing about their fall. When the Ring falls to them, they will jointly rule the world. Hagen replies in cryptic phrases, assuring his father that he will obtain the Ring. Alberich departs, exhorting his son to be true.

Scene 2

The new day dawns, and Siegfried's voice is heard, hailing Hagen. Siegfried has used the Tarnhelm to come swiftly from the mountaintop, leaving Gunther (who had accompanied him on his voyage to the mountain) to bring Brünnhilde. The hero asks for Gutrune, and when she appears, he announces that he has won her as his wife. He recounts his successful mission. Hagen observes a sail in the distance, and they prepare to welcome Gunther and his bride.

Scene 3

Hagen calls the men of the clan to the wedding celebration, commanding them to bring their weapons. They are to make sacrifices to the gods, and then drink to the happy couples. The boat with Gunther and Brünnhilde arrives.

Scene 4

Gunther's vassals hail him as he steps ashore, followed by the pale and downcast Brünnhilde. Gunther greets Siegfried and his sister, announcing the two happy couples. Brünnhilde looks up to see Siegfried. Astounded, she begins to tremble violently. The vassals, and Siegfried too, ask the cause of her strange behavior.

Brünnhilde stammers out her amazement that Siegfried is present. He tells her that he is wedded to Gutrune, as she is to Gunther. This provokes a vehement response, and she accuses him of lying. As she starts to collapse, Siegfried supports her, and she notices the Ring on his finger. She declares that the Ring was obtained from her by Gunther; but Siegfried denies having received it from him. Gunther is plainly confused. Brünnhilde leaps to an explanation for what has occurred: it was Siegfried himself who took the Ring from her. The hero replies that he won it at Neidhöhle. Hagen, intent on fanning the flames, charges Siegfried with treachery, while Brünnhilde, anguished, cries out that she has been betrayed. Gunther's pleas to her to calm herself are ignored. She asserts that she is married not to Gunther but to Siegfried, who is the one by whom she was ravished.

Siegfried responds that he has kept his oath of blood brotherhood to Gunther and that his sword, Nothung, defended Gunther's honor. Brünnhilde retorts that Nothung rested in its scabbard while its master won her. The vassals, Gunther, and Gutrune, all express their horror at the charge, urging Siegfried to refute it if it is untrue. The hero proclaims his willingness to swear an oath. Hagen holds out the point of his spear, on which Siegfried swears that he has been true. Brünnhilde snatches his hand from the spear's point, and responds with her own heated avowal that Siegfried has forsworn himself. Confusion reigns. Siegfried urges Gunther to calm his wife: this storm of words will quickly dissipate. Heedless of Brünnhilde's distress, he cheerfully exhorts everyone to be festive for the double wedding. His exuberance persuades the men and women of the Gibichung clan, and they follow as he sweeps Gutrune into the Hall. Only Gunther, Hagen, and Brünnhilde remain behind.

Scene 5

Brünnhilde expresses her grief and laments the loss of her wisdom. Hagen steps forward, ostensibly to comfort her and offers his aid in exacting revenge on Siegfried. She responds with incredulity, knowing him to be no match for Siegfried. He persists, asking if the hero is indeed invulnerable. She replies that she has protected his body with spells, but since she knew that he would never present his back to a foe, that remains unprotected. Hagen declares that his spear shall strike Siegfried's back, and attempts to cheer the dejected Gunther. Taunted by Brünnhilde and egged on by Hagen, Gunther reluctantly comes to agree that Siegfried must die for his treachery. Hagen suggests that they arrange a hunt for the next day, during which Siegfried will be killed. Despite his doubts, Gunther joins the plot. He and Brünnhilde call on Wotan for vengeance while Hagen quietly invokes his father. Alberich, he predicts, will soon be once again the lord of the Ring.

Act III

Scene 1

The scene is set in a valley through which the Rhine flows. The Rhinemaidens are swimming, regretting the loss of the Rhinegold. Siegfried appears, having been unlucky in the hunt. The maidens greet him flirtatiously. They ask for the golden ring that they see on his finger, offering to give him success in the chase in return. He responds that he won the ring by killing a dragon and that it is worth more than a bearskin. The maidens chide him for his stinginess and disappear beneath the water. Siegfried reflects, and deciding to grant their request, calls them back. When they appear, they are more serious, telling him that he does not know the nature of the Ring. If he does not yield the Ring to them, he is doomed to death—and indeed, to die that day. Siegfried, undaunted and irritated by their words, changes his mind again, telling them that he would gladly give them the Ring to win the favors of love, but that threats will not extort it from him. The maidens denounce his ignorance and predict that a proud woman will inherit the Ring from him. They resolve to seek her, and swim away.

Left alone, Siegfried reflects on the encounter. Were he not so true to Gutrune, he muses, he would happily have made love to one of these beautiful women. His thoughts are interrupted by a distant call from Hagen.

Scene 2

Hagen, Gunther, and some of the vassals appear. Siegfried confesses that he has had no luck in the hunt but tells them that he has found some "water birds" who have predicted his death. Hagen provides a drink for Siegfried to quench his thirst, asking whether the rumor that the hero can understand birdsong is true. Siegfried replies that he has not listened to the birds since he has discovered the beauties of women's singing. He exhorts the gloomy Gunther to be cheerful, volunteering to sing of his boyhood to raise Gunther's spirits. First he recounts his early life with Mime and the forging of the sword. Then he explains how he killed Fafner, licked the blood of the dragon, and so became able to understand the woodbird, which advised him to take the Tarnhelm and the Ring from the dragon's hoard. Next, he tells of the bird's counsel to beware of Mime, of the dwarf's unintentional revelation of his plan to murder Siegfried, and of how he prevented it by killing Mime first.

At this point Hagen interjects, proffering another drink—one which, as quickly becomes apparent, restores Siegfried's memory. The hero goes on to sing of the bird's next suggestion, that a glorious wife awaits him on a mountaintop surrounded by fire. Hagen asks if he took the advice. Innocently, Siegfried tells of his ascent through the flames, of his awakening of Brünnhilde, and of the delight of their love. As Gunther leaps up in horror, Hagen points toward two ravens who have flown out of a bush and asks if the hero can also understand their language. Siegfried turns toward the ravens, presenting his back to Hagen, who thrusts his spear into it. The hero falls. Gunther and some of the vassals protest Hagen's action, but Hagen replies that he has avenged a false oath.

Siegfried, mortally wounded, manages to sit up. He recalls Brünnhilde, and sings tenderly of her and of their love. As he imagines that she gives him her greeting, he falls back and dies. Gunther orders the vassals to take up the dead hero's body. They form themselves into a procession and begin their solemn return.

Scene 3

In the Hall of the Gibichungs, an agitated Gutrune has been aroused by a sound she takes to be Siegfried's horn. She confesses her fear of Brünnhilde, whom she may have seen going down to the Rhine. Hagen's voice is heard. He announces the arrival of the hero, and to Gutrune's anxious question, brutally informs her that her husband is dead. Gunther attempts to comfort his sister, who pushes him away. Gunther protests that he is not to blame and that Siegfried's death was Hagen's doing. Hagen proudly admits that he has killed Siegfried and claims the Ring as rightfully his, since he exacted just vengeance upon Siegfried for having broken his sworn oath. Gunther attempts to keep the Ring from him, contending that it belongs to Gutrune by inheritance from her husband. Hagen and Gunther fight, and Gunther is killed. As Hagen reaches for the Ring, however, Siegfried's arm rises. Hagen falls back, and all are stunned.

Brünnhilde enters and commands silence. She announces that she is Siegfried's betrayed wife, overriding Gutrune's protests. Her explanations convince Gutrune, who cries out in despair against Hagen and bends in grief over her dead brother's body.

Brünnhilde orders the vassals to build a funeral pyre around the Hall. She bids them place Siegfried's body on the pyre, and draws the Ring from his finger. She announces that the Ring will be returned to the Rhinemaidens, that the curse will be purged as she joins Siegfried on the pyre and that Loge will ignite Valhalla. Mounting Grane, she rides into the flames, exultantly greeting Siegfried as his wife.

The flames leap up, consuming the Hall. As they diminish, the Rhine overflows its banks, and the Rhinemaidens appear. Catching sight of the Ring in the flooding river, Hagen plunges into the water and attempts to seize it. Woglinde and Wellgunde drag him down into the depths, while Flosshilde holds up the Ring. High above, the sky begins to glow. Valhalla becomes visible, with gods and heroes assembled, and is consumed by fire. The conflagration subsides, leaving the Rhine flowing on.

Selected Bibliography

Books

Cooke, Deryck, *I Saw the World End* (Oxford: Oxford University Press, 1979)

This unfinished study by a great musicologist provides detailed discussions of *Rheingold* and the first two acts of *Walküre*. It is particularly valuable in tracing Wagner's use of the sources on which he drew.

Dahlhaus, Carl, *Richard Wagner's Music Dramas* (Cambridge: Cambridge University Press, 1979)

A concise, but masterly, musicological study. The discussions of musical structure are particularly valuable.

Donington, Robert, *Wagner's Ring and Its Symbols: The Music and the Myth* (London: Faber and Faber, 1963)

An attempt to interpret the *Ring* by tracing its use of universal—Jungian—symbols.

Holman, J. K., *Wagner's Ring: A Listener's Companion and Concordance* (Portland, OR: 1996)

A useful summary of the classifications of musical motifs provided by Cooke, Donington, and Newman, and of the appearances of these motifs in the *Ring*. There is also information on other aspects of the cycle.

Magee, Bryan, *The Tristan Chord* (New York: Henry Holt and Company, 2000). (*Wagner and Philosophy*, in England; London: Allen Lane, 2000)

A thoughtful broad-stroke study of Wagner's music dramas and their relationship to nineteenth-century philosophy, with an emphasis upon Schopenhauer.

Millington, Barry, *Wagner* (Princeton: Princeton University Press, 1992)

An authoritative introduction to Wagner's life and his music. It is an excellent source of biographical information and offers valuable insights about musical relationships in the *Ring*. Millington also gives balanced assessments of rival interpretations of the tetralogy.

Millington, Barry, (ed), *The Wagner Compendium* (London: Thames and Hudson, 1992)

A valuable study of many aspects of Wagner's life and music. The contributors are generally excellent, and provide much useful background information.

Newman, Ernest, *The Wagner Operas* (Princeton: Princeton University Press, 1991 [reprint: originally published 1949])

Somewhat dated and old-fashioned, this study of all Wagner's mature operas remains an excellent introduction to the dramas and their musical richness. Newman devotes five chapters to the *Ring*: one to the work as a whole, and one to each part of the cycle.

Shaw, George Bernard, *The Perfect Wagnerite* (New York: Dover 1967 [reprint: originally published 1898])

A characteristically astute, entertaining, and polemical attempt to interpret the *Ring* as a piece of political commentary. Many of Shaw's judgments about the drama and the music are almost diametrically opposed to our own.

Spencer, Stewart and Millington, Barry, (eds), *Wagner's Ring of the Nibelung: A Companion* (London: Thames and Hudson, 1993)

Contains Stewart Spencer's excellent translation of the text that Wagner set, together with variations that were rejected in the final version. In addition, there are some valuable short essays on several aspects of the *Ring*.

Spencer, Stewart and Millington, Barry, (eds), *Selected Letters of Richard Wagner* (London: Dent, 1987)

Excellent translations (by Stewart Spencer) of Wagner's most important letters. We have found the letters to Franz Liszt and August Röckel particularly revealing for thinking about the *Ring*.

Tanner, Michael, *Wagner* (Princeton: Princeton University Press, 1996)

A concise, precise, and philosophically sophisticated treatment of Wagner's music dramas. Of all accounts of Wagner and the *Ring* known to us, Tanner's approach is the closest to our own.

Scores

Full orchestral scores for all four parts of the *Ring—Das Rheingold, Die Walküre, Siegfried,* and *Götterdämmerung*—are available separately and inexpensively from Dover Publications (New York, 1982–85). *Rheingold, Siegfried,* and *Götterdämmerung* are reproductions of scores originally published in the 1870s by Schott; *Walküre* reproduces a Peters score from 1910. There are a few minor discrepancies with contemporary recordings, but in general, the reproductions are accurate and useful.

Audio Recordings

There are many excellent audio recordings of the *Ring*. We have principally relied on that of Georg Solti and the Vienna Philharmonic (London/Decca) and that of Herbert von Karajan and the Berlin

Philharmonic (Deutsche Grammaphon). The Solti recording provides an excellent all-round performance, although some individual elements of other recordings are superior. (Gerhard Stolze's performance as Loge in the Karajan *Rheingold* seems to us one such instance.)

There are some remarkable performances of individual scenes from the *Ring* on *Les Introuvables du Ring* (EMI Records). In particular, we recommend the performance of Act I of *Walküre* (Helga Dernesch, William Cochran, and Hans Sotin, with Otto Klemperer and the New Philharmonia Orchestra), and Dietrich Fischer-Dieskau's interpretation of Wotan's farewell to Brünnhilde in Act III of *Walküre* (with Raphael Kubelik and the Symphonie-Orchester des Bayerischen Rundfunks).

For moments when one might be inclined to take the *Ring* too seriously, there is no better antidote than the first track of Anna Russell's *The Best of Anna Russell*, a witty spoof of a plot synopsis that is done with vocal skill, genuine insight, and genuine sympathy.

Video Recordings

James Levine's conducting of the New York Metropolitan Opera production of the *Ring* is readily available and offers a serious and straightforward interpretation of the work. The highlights are the rich and subtle orchestral performance, under Levine's direction, and the gripping dramatic presentation of Wotan by James Morris (not vocally as beautiful as Hans Hotter or Dietrich Fischer-Dieskau, but a splendid piece of musical acting).

CD-ROM

The *Ring Disc*, produced by London/Decca, provides an "interactive guide to the *Ring*." It features the Solti recording, together with a piano reduction of the score and some straightforward commentary. A useful compendium for exploring the cycle.

Index